Louisiana Rambles

LOUISIANA RAMBLES

Exploring America's Cajun and Creole Heartland

Ian McNulty

* * *

University Press of Mississippi / Jackson

www.upress.state.ms.us

The University Press of Mississippi is a member of
the Association of American University Presses.

All photographs are by Ian McNulty.

First printing 2011

∞

Library of Congress Cataloging-in-Publication Data

McNulty, Ian, 1973–
Louisiana rambles : exploring America's Cajun and
Creole heartland / Ian McNulty.
p. cm.
Includes bibliographical references and index.
ISBN 978-1-60473-945-9 (cloth : alk. paper) — ISBN 978-
1-60473-946-6 (pbk. : alk. paper) — ISBN 978-1-60473-
947-3 (ebook) 1. Louisiana—Description and travel.
2. Louisiana—Social life and customs. 3. Louisiana—
Guidebooks. 4. Gulf Coast (La.)—Description and
travel. 5. Gulf Coast (La.)—Social life and customs. 6.
Gulf Coast (La.)—Guidebooks. 7. Mississippi River Delta
(La.)—Description and travel. 8. Mississippi River Delta
(La.)—Social life and customs. 9. Mississippi River Delta
(La.)—Guidebooks. 10. Cajuns—Social life and customs.
I. Title.
F369.M44 2011
976.3—dc22   2010029867

British Library Cataloging-in-Publication Data available

For Antonia and
all our rambles ahead

Contents

x   Contents

Introduction

Rambles and Revelations

When I first moved to New Orleans in 1999 I fell into an instant, headlong crush with the city. It was an easy love, one that over time would prove its substance and resilience through adversity but nevertheless one that registered at first sight. My relationship with Louisiana was much slower to start. It was one that took years to burn in, one that revealed itself in stages, and one that opened doors to beauty and experience that, at least in the beginning, I didn't even realize were waiting right in front of me.

I was raised in Rhode Island, a place I adore with all my heart. But a few years after I finished college and returned home, the romantic travel bug attached itself to my imagination. The notion of New Orleans loomed large as a place apart from what I'd known, and I fantasized about it as a foreign city within my own country. From afar it seemed just that exotic and colorful, and the first impressions I gleaned during a few weekend visits as a tourist were no less enthralling. I found a city where people spoke English and watched the same television programs but where the local culture boomed out with unbridled Caribbean flair set amid a framework of distilled Old World otherness. I found a mysterious place, decadent but also drenched with traditions that I didn't know and that I couldn't take for granted. New Orleans seemed like the antidote for the normality of home, and I wanted to experience it while I was young and had no commitments tying me to one place or another.

So at age twenty-five I decided to embark on a brief dalliance in Dixieland, as I then envisioned it. I asked my friends, my family, and even my employer not to change too much in my absence, because I was sure I'd return home in a year or so with plenty of wild French

Heading out in south Louisiana.

Quarter tales to blow away my Providence friends when I resumed New England life.

Once I began exploring New Orleans, however, the clichéd expectations and stereotypes I'd held about the city began to fall away, replaced by the infinitely more interesting, complex, sometimes infuriating but ultimately rewarding realities. As I delved further, logged more time, met more people, and discovered more layers, my life here grew richer and the prospect of ever leaving grew increasingly remote.

Even as I got to know my new home, the whole place remained different and intriguing to me. I had never experienced a community as powerfully influenced by black culture and politics. Nor had I ever lived in a place with such specific vocabulary. I learned that counties in Louisiana are called parishes, so that I lived in Orleans Parish as well as the city of New Orleans. Restaurant menus were filled with words from the French culinary canon—courtbouillon, sauce bordelaise, remoulade—signifying Louisiana preparations no Frenchmen would recognize on his plate. And I soon began my first struggles to understand the word Creole, with its myriad and seemingly contradictory local applications. So much of what I experienced here came through a cultural filter that was new and fascinating, and one that was unique to this peculiar place.

As if there were any question about moving elsewhere someday, I would later meet and fall in love with my wife, Antonia Keller. She is a New Orleans girl with a huge New Orleans family. For a transplant to this city, marrying such a girl is generally viewed as the demographic equivalent of Cortez burning his boats on the New World coast. There is no turning back.

* * *

I now have friends who grew up in New Orleans hearing from their parents that they did not live in the South, but rather that they were citizens of the northernmost port of the Caribbean. Even during my nascent explorations I felt I could relate to this attitude. I began to look at New Orleans as an island city-state. The core of the city is surrounded on all sides by fortified floodwalls and ringed by river, lake, and canal, or by swamps that are passable only on causeways. With the exception of the tiny, old two-lane River Road hugging the Mississippi River levee, the city is accessed entirely by a series of bridges. There is a definite sense of departure and arrival when people here come and go by land, though I found that I myself rarely left. For years, I was content to sit within the city's walls and moats and explore its beguiling ways. In a sense that was a confirmation of my growing New Orleans identity, because one of the accurate stereotypes about people from New Orleans is how rarely they feel compelled to leave home.

I had a hazy awareness of south Louisiana outside of New Orleans, and periodically I would take a road trip down the interstate to some specific destination in Cajun country. But as much as New Orleans seemed to stand apart from the rest of America, it also felt distinct from the rest of Louisiana. I had only the sketchiest idea of what made up south Louisiana between the highways. It was as if I lived in Vatican City but couldn't find my way around Rome.

The turning point came on the eve of Hurricane Katrina in 2005. The storm would clearly be very bad for New Orleans, so with great dread I made the decision to leave the city about eighteen hours before Katrina's landfall. At that time, I drove a 1971 Cadillac, a rust-pocked relic which was in good enough shape for cruising around town but which would never endure the rigors of inching evacuation traffic as the entire panicked region poured onto the interstate. My answer was to try the River Road, that thin, paved trickle paralleling the levee and leading upriver toward Baton Rouge. So into the old heap I heaved a backpack of clothes and my stoic yellow Labrador, the Amazing Dr. Watson. We set off to wend a series of city side streets until we found the River Road and broke out to the alternating rural and industrial areas upstream from New Orleans.

While millions hit the highway, the dog and I had this nearly forgotten route practically to ourselves for long stretches. Though I was consumed with angst for the coming storm, I also took note of all that we passed on our journey. There were landmark antebellum plantation houses and tiny, tin-roof cottages, little roadside barrooms and restaurants, modern refinery complexes, and one small, old Louisiana town after the next—St. Rose and New Sarpy, Convent, Burnside, and Darrow, all of them situated by the river. Together it made a picture of Louisiana much different from the orderly gray and green vistas I knew from interstate travel between cities. Even as I drove through the parishes closest to metro New Orleans I felt that I was seeing a different side of the state, and I found it fascinating.

As the old Cadillac rumbled upriver, I vowed, with a Labrador as my witness, that if Katrina left anything standing in south Louisiana, I would get out and experience it. For all the recent hurricane damage, the BP oil disaster, and the ongoing, less dramatic but constant changes here, south Louisiana is still standing, and this book chronicles the fulfillment of my evacuation vow.

* * *

A few years after Katrina, as the New Orleans recovery hit its stride and my own once-devastated Mid-City neighborhood began to thrive, I charted an itinerary of daytrip exploration. I sold the Cadillac and bought a ten-year-old Toyota RAV4, a glorified station wagon with better ground clearance and much better fuel efficiency, and I set off on the weekends and whatever weekdays I could steal away from work.

I did not attempt to travel all of Louisiana but instead stuck to the southern end of the state. This made for manageable daytrip journeys from New Orleans, and none of the destinations in this book are more than three hours driving time from the city. But more to the point, south Louisiana is where the state's defining Cajun and Creole cultures developed and thrive still.

This travel itinerary took me up and down the Mississippi River from the rolling hills just north of Baton Rouge to its brown outlet at the Gulf of Mexico, and it led me along the bayous of southeast Louisiana and up through the Cajun prairie, stretching west toward Texas. The Atchafalaya Basin, with its diligently controlled river and enormous swamp, cuts this range roughly in half, and so it provides the framework for this book with the "East of the Atchafalaya" and "West of the Atchafalaya" sections each covering destinations and experiences on either side of this grand divide.

There are no mountain ranges or canyons in Louisiana, and sweeping vistas are hard to come by in this flat, most alluvial of states. Yet I soon grew enamored of and enthralled by the quiet geographic drama here. It's something that comes from the massive, mechanically constant dynamic of water moving through land, from rivers looping around cities and towns, and from rich plains kneeling at scarcely discernible gradients into protean marsh, where land and water, plant and animal seem part of one enmeshed whole rather than separate actors distinct from each other.

In some parts of this south Louisiana territory, roads and towns cling to narrow ridges of riverside land, the ancient linear deposits that rise above the terrain and give way to cane fields, then to swamp, then to open salty Gulf. In other parts, ranchland and endless acres of rice stretch on for golden miles until a water tower and dark green cluster of oak tops materializes around a bend to announce a town.

Even in its rural distances, though, south Louisiana always seems able to evade monotony and offer the curious traveler something rewarding if not downright extraordinary. It could be the restaurant or dancehall that sits quietly in country seclusion until opening time, when it becomes a pulsing showcase for the region's food, foot-driving folk music, and heart-on-its-sleeve hospitality. It could be the dead-end road that leads to a boat launch and the rambunctiously fecund Louisiana wetlands. It could be the sleepy-seeming, rundown farm towns where entire communities still gather for traditional celebrations that are more in step with medieval Europe than twenty-first-century America. It could be a relic from the dark history of slavery or a lingering cultural vestige of European colonial power plays, or it could be some incomprehensibly huge apparatus of America's unsightly and hazardous but essential petrochemical industry stuck against a river or buried in the swamp.

While richly diverse, these areas all share more in common with each other than with the rest of Louisiana and, while indisputably southern, they still stand uniquely apart from the South. This is why I call the area covered in this book America's Cajun and Creole heartland, and I hope what follows in these pages will encourage people to experience these cultures at work while that is still possible.

* * *

South Louisiana faces an existential crisis as the Gulf of Mexico consumes its land. The southern end of the state is being converted to open water at a rate that experts estimate is about equal to one football field each thirty-eight minutes, or twenty-four square miles each year. Erosion and land loss are global concerns, but local advocates say no landmass on earth is vanishing faster than south Louisiana.

There are a few reasons for this, but the biggest factor is the Mississippi River and its role in Louisiana as the spout draining about 40 percent of America. Without a serious change in the way the country manages the business end of this river and its monumental power to alter landscapes, south Louisiana is doomed. Creeks, streams, dams, mighty rivers, and irrigation and industrial discharge programs from thirty-one states and two Canadian provinces impact the Mississippi and fundamentally direct life in south Louisiana. Sediment carried along in the river builds and sustains Louisiana's land, and fresh water from the river recharges and balances its coastal wetlands.

Currently, most of that sediment and fresh water is sluiced straight out to the open Gulf.

Government policy and industrial lobbying dictate the way Louisiana as we know it will die or persevere. This has been well known for many years now. But the tipping point for land loss is near. If serious, obvious, and large-scale change does not materialize within the next few years, many of the areas covered in this book will be degraded beyond redemption. Some will disappear completely into open water while others will surely face radical change as their roles and identities in a rapidly dissolving state are reordered. I wouldn't wish this fate on anyone's home, but it seems especially cruel that it's happening in an area where the culture is so rich, so unique, and so expressly tied to place.

* * *

One of the clichés frequently trotted out about Louisiana is that people here "love to have a good time," as if there are other places where people just love to sulk. But there is something to the cliché. South Louisiana isn't just an interesting place; it also is a relentlessly, extraordinarily fun place. The difference, I believe, is how ideas of what constitutes a good time here more often spring from tangled history, family traditions, and specific Louisiana geography than they do from pop culture. People here don't just share a culture; they use it hard and they use it together. Everywhere I traveled, I found a mixing of the generations. I didn't visit nursing homes and I didn't visit frat houses. But in the places representative of south Louisiana culture—the dancehalls and parade routes, the horse tracks and marinas, the waterways and the festivals, the places I recommend for finding Louisiana culture in action rather than on display—people of different generations mingle deeply, and everyone seems to have a blast.

To me, nothing sums up a quintessential Louisiana good time quite like a scene combining young people and old people in a distinctively local setting. It adds up to something nontransferable, something that speaks to this area's originality, allure, and endangered value.

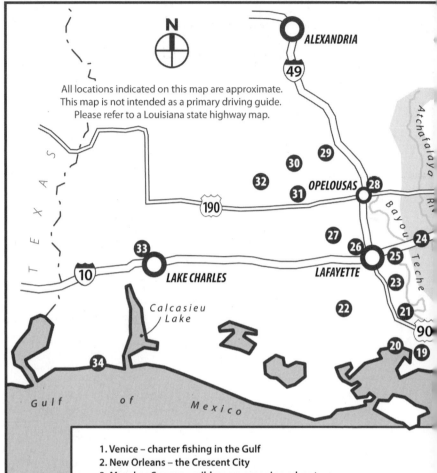

All locations indicated on this map are approximate.
This map is not intended as a primary driving guide.
Please refer to a Louisiana state highway map.

N

ALEXANDRIA

TEXAS

Atchafalaya River

Bayou Teche

OPELOUSAS

LAFAYETTE

LAKE CHARLES

Calcasieu Lake

Gulf   of   Mexico

1. Venice – charter fishing in the Gulf
2. New Orleans – the Crescent City
3. Manchac Swamp – wilderness canoeing adventures
4. LaPlace – andouille heaven on the German Coast
5. Port Vincent – "river rat" habitat on the Amite
6. Gramercy, Lutcher, Paulina – Christmas Eve bonfires
7. Vacherie – historic plantation museums
8. Donaldsonville – African American museum, Bayou Lafourche headwaters
9. Baton Rouge – state capitol and museums
10. Angola – prison rodeo and crafts market
11. Des Allemands – airboat tour departures
12. Kraemer – tours of the deep swamp
13. Thibodaux – bayou crossroads city
14. Port Fourchon – oil and gas hub
15. Grand Isle – beaches, fishing, and birding
16. Gibson – swamp tour departures
17. Morgan City – oil rig museum and shrimp fleet
18. Pierre Part – swamp pop hotbed on the bayou
19. Cypremort Point – sandy beach by the Gulf
20. Avery Island – Tabasco factory and botanical gardens

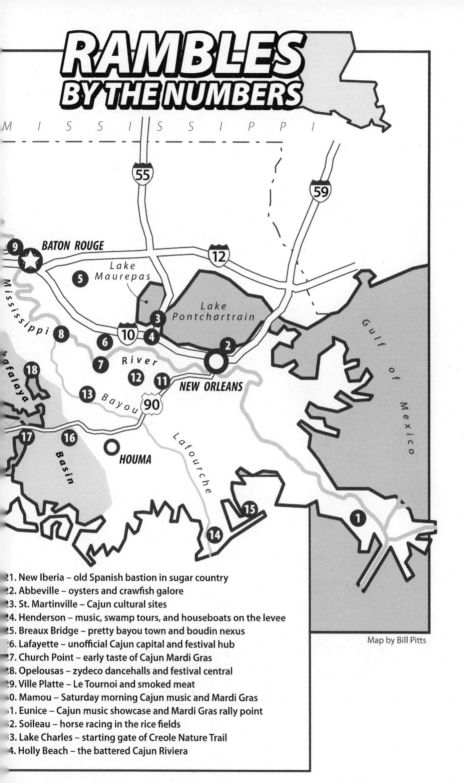

RAMBLES
BY THE NUMBERS

MISSISSIPPI

BATON ROUGE

Lake Maurepas

Lake Pontchartrain

Mississippi River

Atchafalaya

NEW ORLEANS

Bayou

HOUMA

Basin

Lafourche

Gulf of Mexico

21. New Iberia – old Spanish bastion in sugar country
22. Abbeville – oysters and crawfish galore
23. St. Martinville – Cajun cultural sites
24. Henderson – music, swamp tours, and houseboats on the levee
25. Breaux Bridge – pretty bayou town and boudin nexus
26. Lafayette – unofficial Cajun capital and festival hub
27. Church Point – early taste of Cajun Mardi Gras
28. Opelousas – zydeco dancehalls and festival central
29. Ville Platte – Le Tournoi and smoked meat
30. Mamou – Saturday morning Cajun music and Mardi Gras
31. Eunice – Cajun music showcase and Mardi Gras rally point
32. Soileau – horse racing in the rice fields
33. Lake Charles – starting gate of Creole Nature Trail
34. Holly Beach – the battered Cajun Riviera

Map by Bill Pitts

"Nothing in this state is done to spec," the Baton Rouge writer Alex V. Cook advised after I told him about my plans for this book. At that moment we were standing inside Teddy's Juke Joint, a tilting blues bar practically lashed together by strings of Christmas lights and sitting in a soggy field north of Baton Rouge.

"That's in good ways and bad ways," Alex said. "But you just have to know that going in. Everything will be a little off."

I nodded, thinking I knew what he meant. But I had no idea what was in store, nor could I imagine just how often his words would ring in my head during my rambles. Here is what I found.

PART I
EAST OF THE ATCHAFALAYA

Canoeing into the depths of the Manchac wetlands.

CHAPTER 1

MANCHAC BY MOONLIGHT
Paddling New Orleans's Wild Border by Day and Night

Two dozen canoes carrying at least fifty people might seem like a crowd, but as soon as this flotilla set off on a guided expedition into the Manchac wetlands we seemed swallowed by its immensity and secluded within its wilds.

We turned a bayou corner, breaking the sightline to our cars parked at the rustic, unmarked launching point behind us just off Highway 51 in St. John the Baptist Parish, and at once the extent of the dry, tidy world was reduced to the slim plastic hull of each canoe moving quietly through black water.

Over the next few hours, this trip took us though natural bayous, long-abandoned lumber canals, freshwater marsh, and labyrinthine cypress swamps. Then, after sunset, we would thread our return through the same route by the light of the moon and the sense of immersion would become complete. At night, another canoe could be just a few feet astern, but we felt quite on our own under the pearly moonlight and amid the ringing nocturnal cacophony of bugs and birds and beasts.

It was just the sort of plunge into Louisiana nature I needed after spending too much uninterrupted time tied up in urban New Orleans and sinking so deeply into the paths and patterns of my city life. One need only look at a regional map or through the window of a car departing the city over the highway to see how abruptly the ordered, developed realm of New Orleans and its suburbs ends. The defining south Louisiana terrain of swamp, marsh, river, and estuary lies immediately past the levees and floodwalls, presenting an easily accessible, occasionally menacing, reliably alluring territory just over the hedge of human maintenance.

To get a fresh view of this, Antonia and I booked a trip on what tour operator Canoe & Trail Adventures bills as its "moonlight paddle." We drove about thirty highway miles from our city home on a very hot, summer Saturday afternoon to meet our guides for this full, two-phase sensory soak, with its vibrant, lush scenes on the way in and its luminous, moonlit journey back.

The outing was led by Byron Almquist, a trim sixty-something with an easy manner and a calm voice. He originally formed Canoe & Trail Adventures in the 1970s as a New Orleans retail outlet for outdoors gear and started leading canoe and hiking trips to help promote his products. When the shop closed in 1988 the tours became his main line of business, and he's been taking people through these nearby wilds ever since.

"It's a hobby that turned into a living," said his son Chad Almquist, who helps guide many of the company's outings today, including this first one Antonia and I experienced.

Byron uses moon phase calendars to schedule his night paddles, choosing Saturdays closest to the monthly full moon. Our route too had been carefully calculated to take in a range of watery habitat around the edges of the Manchac wetlands, a tangled, trackless stretch covering some two hundred square miles between Lake Maurepas and the Mississippi River. It's just one of many huge swathes of named wilderness surrounding New Orleans, and this one proved a good choice both for its startling proximity to our home and its scenic diversity.

The settings, the sounds, and the water currents all changed as we moved in our canoes from relatively open bayous to tight swamp passages through dense forest. Everywhere, though, our canoes cut through a thin green growth of lentil-shaped platelets matting the water, and our path was lined by cypress trees draped with fleecy Spanish moss, waving like curtains in the light breeze. We occasionally spotted the snouts of alligators, which looked so much like floating branches that we assumed all future floating branches were alligators until they proved themselves otherwise. Overhead, enormous herons and egrets flapped from perch to perch, and other birds headed off purposefully in formation.

We paused at key forks in the route and clustered together so the senior Almquist could give some facts about the going so far and field questions we'd accumulated along the way. He would rise to stand in his canoe, a surefooted show of balance that made him look like a holy man addressing the attentive flock sitting by twos and threes in their own canoes under the sweep of his arms. But his approach was gentle and soft-spoken and he shared what was clearly a lifetime of observed and studied knowledge.

We learned that some of that vegetal mat over the water was native (the tiny duckweed), and some was invasive (the prodigious salvinia that chokes so many Louisiana waterways).

"What about the cypress knees?" asked one boater. "Why are some of the knees all red at the tops?"

I'd been wondering the same thing myself. Cypresses are the marquee trees of the Louisiana swamp. They grow tall, spreading their limbs out horizontally from their upper reaches like the arms of scarecrows strung with rags of moss. Sometimes they can look a bit ragged, but they are supremely well-suited to the wet south Louisiana environment and can grow stout and tall straight out of swamp water. Cypress knees are the trees' outcroppings, and they look like woody stalagmites or blunt, furry lances sprouting around their trunks to collect oxygen even as the roots sit submerged. Byron now explained that the ruddy, brass-colored knobs at the knees' tips indicated a healthy cypress tree pushing its projections skyward.

We also learned that the water around us looked black because of all the leaves and needles dropped from the trees, and that early loggers working these backwaters called the dark-seeming liquid "cypress tea." We learned that briny Gulf surges from disastrous storm seasons in 2005 (with hurricanes Katrina and Rita) and 2008 (with Gustav and Ike) made it all the way to this swamp, killing off wild irises and lilies as it did.

"It just shows you how sometimes the impact of these hurricanes isn't what you see, but what you don't, and sometimes that's months or years after the storm," Byron said.

* * *

The Almquists and their guides led us around trickles of swamp so thin our canoes bumped cypress knees on either side as we inexpertly oared our way through. The ambient feeling was dense, cloaking, feral, and I was briefly tempted to think of the area as virgin territory. But the stamp of man was still close at hand. The straight, broad canals we had paddled to get here were dug more than a century ago to extract billions of board feet of cypress, which eventually became the sort of lumber used to build most of the homes in my New Orleans neighborhood around that same time. It was part of a pattern of extraction from Louisiana's productive but delicate wetlands that would accelerate astronomically in the decades to follow as petrochemicals gained economic dominance.

Once we breached the thickest stand of cypress swamp, we emerged into a gentle, watery glade where the channel narrowed to a motionless corridor flanked by bottle-green rushes and the tall, flat leaves of arrowhead plants. We had packed our own suppers, and as the sun sank over the tall cypress tree line we dined in our canoes. Soon the soggy magentas and coral pinks of the western sky faded completely, and the promised moon shined down on the water, alternately beaming and shrouded as granite-shaded clouds cruised past.

The arrival of dark signaled a circadian shift change in the swamp, and on some deep, chromosomal cue the teeming insects, frogs, and birds were set to glorious shrieking, gurgling, singing, and ticking. They sounded like antsy children or cooped-up puppies finally unleashed to play. The authors of all this nightlife were invisible, but they were so close we could follow their individual sounds moving just behind a thick veil of reeds. It was like tracking unseen Muppets on a romp, and at times it sounded like they were giggling and chortling from offstage. The baritone bullfrogs were particularly impressive, letting loose their deep booms, like thuds against metal.

Never in my life had I heard an owl sound so completely and convincingly like an owl as one that then let out a manly, layered, multinote hoot as we paddled slowly along. It was a hoot that seemed to silence the chattering swamp, as if all those countless little green or furry items of potential owl prey out in the thick intuitively held their breaths for a moment, flinching for talons. The hush lasted just a few seconds, however, and then the creaking, croaking, skittering, burping sounds of the swamp resumed. The canoes slid on, adding the thin slithering sounds of their prows through the still water.

We had been in the dark for about forty-five minutes when the guides broke out powerful flashlights and began illuminating random stretches of the bayou banks. The rays were as bright and jarring as a state trooper's spotlight at a dead-of-night traffic stop, and the guides moved them around constantly, searching for something.

"There's one," said Byron. "Right there, everyone. Can you see his eyes?"

There, hugging the dark bank, about sixty feet distant, were two red dots, like dim LCDs. They could only be alligator eyes. Alligators were hard to spot by the light of day, but their eyes sparkled like red rubies when hit by a light at night.

"There's another one," Byron said calmly. "Any over there, Chad?"

"Yup, two over here," called his son, who was positioning his canoe while his friend, Paula, kept a light trained on the opposite bank.

"Actually three!" she said brightly.

The moving spotlights identified a few more, so the count rose to seven alligators sitting motionless in the water with their illuminated red dot eyes spaced as regularly as the taillights of distant cars. Suddenly, the bayou felt very narrow and hemmed within such parallel silent gazing.

It was a bit unnerving to realize so many toothy reptiles had been silently watching us from the banks all this time, but it was clear they wanted no business with us. If they moved at all under the spotlights, it was merely to submerge or silently propel themselves out of the ray. Anyway, our attention was soon commanded by more immediate company. In addition to showing the gators' eyes, our guides' lights revealed just how laughable our efforts had been to fight off the swarming mosquitoes. We'd been beating them with rising frequency ever since sunset, and within a half hour the rhythm of our swats had grown from random slaps to something worthy of a John Bonham drum solo.

Bug spray is as necessary on a nighttime canoe trip as oars, and we had been applying it regularly. But what is sufficient for an evening spell on the porch at home is good for only a few minutes in the swamp. The spotlights showed holding patterns of mosquitoes above the canoes.

Soon enough we would be back at the darkened launch site, where our cars would fairly glow where we had left them by the roadside and where the nearby interstate would boom above us with semis and the loud tailpipes of passing bikes driving in the night. But for the next little while, on this last leg of the trip, the alligator spotlights were dimmed and silence took hold again within the canoes. The nearest sound was the dipping paddle, and the reflected moon bounced and swirled on the little waves of each stroke.

Chapter 2

ALIGHT CHRISTMAS
River Levee Bonfires and Papa Noel

I barely knew a soul in Louisiana when I moved to the state in the fall of 1999. So when the holidays rolled around a few months later, and I discovered I wouldn't be able to make the trip home, I started looking for distractions to stave off the impending, predictable orphan Christmas blues. Somehow, when my desk neighbor at the office suggested I book a riverboat trip up the Mississippi on Christmas Eve to watch people light huge conflagrations on the levee, it seemed like just the thing.

"There are heaps of bonfires that burn all night and it's a big party on the levee," she said. "They say they do it to light the way for Papa Noel. You know, the Cajun Santa Claus."

And so on the afternoon of Christmas Eve I reported to a rudimentary river landing and waited to board a vessel called the Cajun Queen for a journey upriver to watch the spectacle. This landing stretched over a swath of batture, that periodically flooding no-man's-land of mud, driftwood, and spindly trees between the levee and the river current, and it was situated under the flight path of the exquisitely named Louis Armstrong New Orleans International Airport, which was busy that day with peak holiday travel. The Cajun Queen was essentially a steel barge built up with layered decks styled after the old gothic paddlewheel steamboats. It had room for hundreds. I filed into line with families and couples bound for their holiday trip and once aboard settled in for a very long cruise upriver.

Bonfires blaze on the levee top in St. James Parish.

The nexus for Christmas Eve bonfires in south Louisiana is the riverfront in St. James Parish, which sits about halfway between New Orleans and Baton Rouge. The trip takes only about forty-five minutes on the highway. But chugging around all the river's many twists on the Cajun Queen took more than four hours each way, and it was a dreary ride. For all the majesty and romance the Mississippi River conjures in the literary imagination, this particular stretch offered muddy miles of banks lined with dun-colored trees in winter drab, interrupted at regular intervals by the loading ports for huge refineries that towered up on the other side of the levees. The package deal for this holiday cruise included an open bar, however, and that made the entire roundtrip go more easily. As all the family groups began constricting together at their tables and the boat's orthodox party DJ plowed deeper into the sentimental Christmas songbook, I wandered the decks and tried to find new ways to engage the bartenders in conversation on each refill visit.

In time, the ship captain's voice came over the intercom to tell passengers the boat was approaching Gramercy, the first of three successive St. James Parish riverfront towns famous for their levee bonfires. Everyone bundled up against the cold river wind and headed to the top deck. Families clustered together and clutched their drinks, shivering and laughing. I wedged my way snugly between the coats and elbows of two groups to claim a little gap at the rail. I'd been confined to the boat for hours now on this lonely Christmas Eve, surrounded by tight-knit clans of happy strangers, and I was feeling the first low stirrings of self-pity. I was eager to get to the main event and see if this trip had been worth it.

The answer, in blazing affirmative, came courtesy of a scene I hadn't even properly imagined. Up ahead, just past the next dark bend of the nighttime river, the sky was glowing all warm pumpkin orange over the tree line, and I could hear indistinct sounds of popping and grumbling. After a few minutes more the full panorama was revealed. The girders of the Gramercy Bridge passed above us, and suddenly the east bank of the river was lit by so many bonfires the scene looked like a painted wall of rising flame, one broken only by the black superstructures of ships cruising past and circling around before us. A cannonade of heavy-duty fireworks ripped out from the shadowy levee ridge, and their payloads fell in the water nearby or exploded in huge bursts overhead. The air smelled like smoke and fuel, and it echoed loudly with the rumble of maritime engines. The deep call of ship horns boomed like excited truckers between the crack and zoom of fireworks.

Our boat maneuvered nearer to the banks, and by looking closely I could see darkened outlines of people clustered in tribes around individual bonfires or trotting the levee top, pausing to toss more fireworks at the bonfires or to kneel by launchers to aim rockets toward the river and, it appeared, toward us. It all looked so chaotic and wonderful.

The families around me on deck toasted and hugged and snapped pictures, and the captain's voice sounded over the intercom again urging us to join in Christmas carols. The people around me started singing "Silent Night," but I just leaned into the riverboat's railing, mesmerized, gripping a plastic cup of cold bourbon and imagining that the scene before me was a swirling naval battle or the fiery sacking of a waterfront village. I hope the other passengers on the Cajun

Queen that Christmas Eve came away with warm holiday memories, but I was glad to have these little historical fantasies to occupy my mind on the long cruise home. I couldn't wait to go back and join the melee on land, and up close.

* * *

Christmas Eve bonfires are a big deal in St. James Parish, which is made up of small towns, sprawling sugarcane fields, historic plantation houses, and the immense outposts of global industrial concerns. The center of the bonfire action on Christmas Eve is the narrow stretch of levee fronting the contiguous towns of Gramercy, Lutcher, and Paulina, and tens of thousands of people from all over the region stream down to the towns' shared riverfront each December 24 to check it out.

But evidence of the bonfire traditions turns up all over the parish and beyond. Many families build their own solitary bonfires at hunting camps and country homes, where they burn only for the eyes of their Christmas Eve guests. Anyone can visit the full-size model of a bonfire on display year-round at Gramercy's highway welcome center, and photos of the Christmas Eve blazes adorn the town's promotional brochures. Visiting Laura Plantation across the river in Vacherie one year, just after Thanksgiving, I saw that a neat bonfire pyre was already waiting by the front of the property. Later that day, during lunch at the nearby restaurant Spuddy's, I inspected a Christmas tree in the corner of the dining room and noticed it was decorated with numerous ornaments shaped unmistakably like the bonfire pyres. During the long cruise back from Gramercy on my first Louisiana Christmas Eve I even spied the occasional bonfire burning quite on its own amid miles of riverfront darkness.

The pop explanation of the tradition holds that the bonfires light the river journey of Papa Noel, just like my old coworker first explained. Another explanation suggests the fires were originally intended as welcoming markers for riverboats headed home on Christmas Eve. But the late local historian Emily Chenet Guidry did some digging and traced a much longer and deeper heritage behind the tradition. She linked the bonfires to pre-Christian druid rituals marking the winter solstice in Europe, as well as seasonal bonfire traditions that persist in parts of France and Germany. Through interviews with elderly residents of St. James Parish, she tracked the Louisiana rendition at least to the late nineteenth century, when they seemed to take the form of individual family gatherings.

She recorded how children were dispatched during the weeks between Thanksgiving and Christmas to forage for willow logs and other combustibles for the family pyres in the swampy backwoods or in the batture over the levee. All manner of flotsam wound up in the piles, and as automobiles became commonplace their discarded tires became especially prized as bonfire fuel. Thankfully, such noxious additions are no longer typical, and now fathers and sons are usually responsible for collecting the willows together to build their bonfires, starting the harvest and construction just after Thanksgiving.

Those familiar with rural Louisiana manliness should find it no surprise that in more recent times a competitive fever gripped the tradition, with families vying to build the most creative and richly detailed bonfire structures. Some were fantastical, built as faithfully wrought models of local plantation homes complete with smoke channels engineered into the structure so that when lit the first wafts would flow up willow-log chimneys. Others were based on familiar totems of the local oil industry, like rigs and helicopters and workboats, all of it fated to go up in raging flames on Christmas Eve.

These elaborately balanced structures had a tendency to collapse in unpredictable ways once set ablaze, however, and as the tradition morphed into today's massive public party, the bonfire pyres have been codified for safety. Now, most pyres are built in a uniform pyramid shape, standing eighteen feet tall and looking like sturdy log tepees. Each of the three big bonfire towns builds one special theme structure each year, however, just to keep the good creative challenge going. So amid the standardized ranks of tepee shapes, there can be the occasional fleur-de-lis shape or model Cajun cabin rendered in willow logs atop the levee, waiting for the torch.

There's no doubt the bonfire tradition is in full revival now, and it's really no mystery why. If any cultural group is primed to embrace a custom that sends the boys into the woods with tools and trucks, requires them to build something big, public, and possibly dangerous and then calls for a ritualistic party with lots of eating and drinking outdoors while the whole creation burns to the ground, it is the people of south Louisiana. The skills required to put on a good Christmas Eve bonfire have been honed at hunting camps and football stadium parking lots for generations.

Years after my first riverboat trip, Antonia and I embarked on a Christmas Eve drive up to St. James Parish to see the bonfires up close. We arrived shortly before sunset to find the riverfront teeming with activity. Cars poured along the narrow River Road and people toed the ditches on either side of it. There was a big party in progress at just about every home facing the levee, with rental tents set up in front yards and delicious, pork-scented grill smoke cutting through the chilly December air. Four-wheelers zipped up the levee, delivering more ice chests or steaming cast-iron tureens of hot food to the groups of people sitting around each of the unlit log tepees.

I could not believe the number of pyres. As we walked the levee top we came upon a new one every fifty yards or so. The municipal boundaries of the three big bonfire towns follow the old plantation land divisions, the French arpent system that gave each planter a narrow but extremely valuable frontage on the river from which to ship crops from the long property stretching on behind it. So although we parked upriver in Paulina, after less than three miles of walking the levee top we had crossed through Lutcher entirely and reached Gramercy and its overarching river bridge while passing perhaps a hundred pyres along the way.

As the sun sank completely, the vibe among the people walking the levee and encamped around the pyres turned from anticipation to rippling excitement. Men paced around the perimeters of their structures and kids tugged at their sleeves, asking when, when, when. People sitting in camp chairs around ice chests and barbecue grills kept glancing down the line, craning for any flicker on a distant pyre.

The signal to light the first bonfire comes from a council of the parish sheriff and the towns' fire departments, which traditionally issues the order at 7 p.m. Nobody wants to miss the first spark. Finally, word came down from the authorities convened by idling fire engines at a riverfront firehouse in Gramercy. Directly opposite the firehouse, a young man atop the levee lit a flare and chucked it into his awaiting tinderbox pyramid. The fire took just a second to catch, and the blaze spread as quickly as spilled water. Then the family at the next site lit their own fire, followed by the next and so on. People were patient and generally waited until the link in the chain ahead of them was lit before setting theirs ablaze. The effect was incredible. It looked like flames jumping up on the arm of a gigantic gas grill or a fiery wave cheer making its way along burning stadium stands.

While most bonfires now conform to a uniform size and shape, families have other ways to set their own apart. Following an old custom, some of the pyres are stuffed and layered with sugarcane, which smokes up fantastically, pops loudly, and shoots orange sparks into the air like nature's own pyrotechnic dream when set ablaze. Some also load their pyres with reams and reams of red firecrackers, which drape the log structures like belts of ammo. Further, the innards of the pyre may be jammed with wood scraps and kindling and then often liberally soaked in kerosene. These are structures of cartoon-like combustibility, like some explosive death trap Wile E. Coyote plants for Roadrunner but falls victim to himself.

No wonder, then, that as each party put a flare to its pyre, the thing went up so fiercely. Soon, the long, long string of fires looked like an ancient row of violent volcanoes spewing flames and launching showers of sparks. All the smoke made a low ceiling on the night sky, while the flames and the machine gun flashes from countless thousands of firecrackers heaped on the blazes kept the billows weirdly illuminated. Into this Götterdämmerung of fire and snapping noise, people from all quarters quickly introduced the heavy artillery, the really big fireworks they had kept all this time so precariously close to their pyres. Shells zoomed, rockets hissed, and the sky just above the flaming bonfires was filled with bright exploding constellations and falling spider webs of sparkle bursts.

Below, the levee scene was a huge, intermingling party. There were thousands of people gathering on the levee slope, and the people right beneath the fires occasionally had to scatter as chunks of the pyres came loose and rolled, burning, down the slope toward them. Others had staked out relatively peaceful ground between the big blazes. They sat on blankets or camp chairs, people-watching, drinking wine from plastic cups and eating Christmas Eve picnics by the wild, primordial light of a hundred raging levee-top fires.

* * *

The crowd was beginning to thin out as Antonia and I walked the three-town distance back to our car. The pyres began to crumble in succession, releasing more burning logs to roll down the levee. Guys on four-wheelers kept trucking up the slope, bearing more beer and fireworks to the hardcore crews in leaguer around the dwindling fires. We waved hello as we passed and they invariably bellowed "Merry Christmas!" in reply.

Driving out of town, I took a wrong turn at the highway, and we found ourselves on the Gramercy Bridge, heading over the river with nowhere to turn around until we made the other side. It was a mistake that proved to be an early Christmas gift.

I could steal only glances out the passenger-side window as I drove, but I'll never forget how the scene looked from way up on the bridge span. The hundred or so fires seemed meticulously spaced, like a string of orange pearls along the black river. The bursts of fireworks were now low and tiny, and each collapsed pyre looked like a steady burning wick. It could have been the culmination of some massive, ancient rite orchestrated by the druids themselves. I always want to make that wrong turn over the bridge whenever I come back to bonfire night. And if ever some gullible children are along for the ride, this detour is where I'll tell them about the time when I saw Papa Noel riding up the river late one Christmas Eve, and where they just might see him too if they look hard enough.

Chapter 3

AIRBOATS AND ALLIGATORS
Swamp Tours and Louisiana's Favorite Dinosaur

Thirteen-year-old Zamariah "ZZ" Loupe led me on the official back-yard tour of his family's home in Kraemer, a thread of a town running through deep Lafourche Parish swamp country. Built like a future college football lineman, his straight blond hair sweeping past his shoulders, he walked over the lawn with a heavy, early-adolescent plod and he carried an air rifle. But once we made it behind the white brick ranch house—once we'd passed the carport crammed with the family's half-dozen white Corvettes of varying vintage and passed the garage decorated with bleached-white alligator skulls—once we'd reached the fenced pen at the rear of the property, ZZ started looking more like a seasoned bushman than an eighth grader.

"Now do you want the whole tour, or do you just want to see the alligator?" he asked me.

"Let's do the whole tour," I said. "I mean, we're already out here."

Plus, I refrained from mentioning, I had already ponied up four dollars for this walkabout. The backyard tour is an add-on to Zam's Swamp Tours, a family business run by ZZ's mom, Dianalynn Tregle. I had dropped by the Zam's compound on a summer afternoon to get lunch at Edwina's Cooking Cajun, a restaurant attached to the tour office where alligator burgers and stuffed shrimp are served in a long, low dining hall with a bayou view. I didn't have time that day for the conventional, pontoon-boat swamp tour that Zam's offers, but Dianalynn easily talked me into the backyard edition.

Tastes like chicken: an alligator responds to a swamp tour handout.

"You should go in back and see the big alligator," she said. "It's four bucks, and the kids get three of it for taking you around."

I couldn't very well deny the kids their cut, so there I was following ZZ into the pen. There were rabbits in cages, a pair of goats roaming freely, a beak-jawed snapping turtle the size of a coffee table, and foot-long baby alligators sitting in a plastic paint bucket. There were probably more creatures too, but once the adult alligator appeared all else faded to the periphery.

ZZ led me to a short chain-link fence staked out just a few feet from the edge of a pond not much larger than a backyard swimming pool. We both peered ahead.

"You see him?" ZZ asked.

I scanned but didn't see a thing. The water was olive drab and still except for the impact of a few bugs lighting off the surface here and there.

"Hold on," ZZ sighed with the weariness of a put-upon bureaucrat. He found a stone and tossed it into the pond.

It hit the water with a dunking sound, and then, a beat later and without a noise, the biggest reptile I have ever seen rose to the surface from complete concealment. Its head appeared first, bobbing up like a submerged buoy. It was the size of a footlocker and looked flattened, with just the bulbs of its eyes and bump of its snout jutting up. The rest of the animal followed in stages, so that a second later its midsection showed up, studded with pyramidal bumps, followed by a long tail as thick as a telephone pole at its base and flared with fin-like spines toward the end.

"Holy shit, he's big!" I blurted, forgetting that I was talking to a thirteen-year-old.

"Yeah, twelve feet," the boy said calmly.

It was also very near, even before it started paddling closer to the wire fence, which suddenly looked more symbolic than protective. The creature stopped about five feet away from my sneakers and began making loud hissing and clicking noises, like a mechanical, unblinking version of itself. It seemed ancient, mythical, and a little unreal. It was as if a fantastical dragon had materialized in the green water beneath my eyes.

To ZZ though, and to lots of other kids growing up on the bayou, alligators like this are just part of the family business. Some children earn spending money by running lemonade stands or mowing the neighbor's lawn. ZZ shows off the modern day dinosaur that lives in his backyard for camera-toting strangers from the city.

* * *

Familiarity must breed such ease, because south Louisiana today is teeming with alligators. Even bayou families that don't happen to keep a twelve-footer penned next to the garage are literally surrounded by them.

The state's coastal marshes and swamps make ideal habitat for alligator mississippiensis, a.k.a. the American alligator, though not long ago the future of the species here seemed bleak. They had long been hunted for their hides, and by the nineteenth century their oil was even used to grease cotton gins and steam engines. But once an improved tanning process was developed to soften their famously tough skins for belts and boots and purses, commercial demand skyrocketed and their numbers dwindled. The combination of habitat loss and overhunting reduced the Louisiana alligator population to an estimated one hundred thousand by the 1970s.

A management program enacted since that nadir has done wonders for the species, however. Hunting is now heavily regulated and limited to a short season in September. Commercial alligator ranchers are required to return a portion of their stock to the wild once the animals grow big enough to fend for themselves. One of these operations, Insta-Gator Ranch and Hatchery in the town of Abita Springs, even offers tours, which end with the chance to pet and fondle tiny, helpless hatchlings.

Thanks to these efforts, the Louisiana Department of Wildlife and Fisheries now estimates the wild alligator population stands at 1.5 million. That equals about one alligator in the wild for every three people living in Louisiana, and there are many more alligators on ranches. In 2008 alone, Louisiana ranchers hatched more than 460,000 baby alligators. In that same year they returned some 48,578 mature gators to the wild, or enough to fill every seat at Chicago's Wrigley Field with an alligator and keep a few thousand more waiting in line outside for tickets.

You certainly don't need to venture to the swamp to spot them, at least not during the hot months when the animals are most active. Driving up to Baton Rouge one afternoon on Highway 61—the old, interesting, preinterstate route known as Airline Highway—I spotted a pair of them on the roadside pavement. They stood there with their toothy mouths agape, looking like irritated old ladies stranded at a crosswalk, glowering at discourteous motorists. On another trip, driving down to Morgan City, I passed the enormous carcass of an alligator that hadn't made it across a country highway. It must have been creamed by an eighteen-wheeler, because the dead creature looked big enough to flip my little Toyota truck had I hit it.

There are occasional news reports of alligators turning up in backyards or under cars in suburban driveways, though cases of attacks against people are very rare, which is another credit to the management program. The state takes about four thousand nuisance alligator calls a year. Regulators reward the licensed trappers dispatched to handle the problem with the valuable alligator carcass itself. They work like wildlife bounty hunters paid in hides, and the profit motive assures that alligators turning up in developed areas get quick attention.

* * *

For most visitors, though, alligator encounters come during swamp tours, like those offered by Zam's in Kraemer and many others across south Louisiana. Some are based very close to New Orleans, including the excellent Honey Island Swamp Tour in Slidell, and some even offer pickup service from city hotels. A twenty-minute drive from French Quarter courtyards and business district office towers is about all it takes to reach Louisiana wilderness and prime gator country.

These tours feature much more than alligators. For most of the outing, visitors simply get to experience the raw tranquility of the swamp with abundant flora and birdlife all around. Especially in the years since hurricanes Katrina and Rita, many tours also have begun emphasizing the ecological destruction that makes some of these tour areas see-them-while-you-can propositions unless the coastal crisis gets priority attention very soon.

But the star attraction on any of these tours is the alligator. Promotional brochures all but guarantee up-close alligator sightings, and many tour operators entice gators to play along with the show by feeding them chunks of raw chicken and other goodies from the side of the boats.

It's common for alligator bulls to grow to more than eight hundred pounds, while the brain controlling all that carnivorous, armored mass remains about the size of a golf ball. But that golf ball still is capable of putting one and one together, and thanks to consistent food conditioning some alligators clearly associate tour boats with free meals. State wildlife officials condemn the boatside feeding practice for the simple reason that when big alligators correlate humans with dinner, trouble can't be far behind. But there's no doubt most people who book Louisiana swamp tours want to see alligators, and the chicken bait goes a long way toward satisfying their expectations.

Ron "Black" Guidry, operator of A Cajun Man's Swamp Tour based in the town of Gibson, brings chicken for the gators. But he also lures the gators along with "Jambalaya," as in the Hank Williams song about big fun on the bayou.

I met up with Black at the busy recreational fishing launch of Bayou Black Marina, about a half hour's drive outside of Houma. Black, a one-time state trooper, is a lean, soft-spoken Cajun with a white mustache and the gentle bearing of a favorite uncle or young-at-heart grandfather. He got into the swamp tour business about twenty years ago and built his own boat, which is a small metal barge with an awning, an outboard engine, and a red, white, and blue paint job. It looks a bit like a float from a small-town Mardi Gras parade. I arrived for the tour by myself, but I had plenty of company amid a group of Mennonites taking a day off from a Katrina recovery volunteer mission. Together we chugged away from the dock under an overcast sky that threatened rain and started off along oilfield service canals busy with barges, tugs, and small aluminum-hulled maintenance boats shuttling here and there.

Periodically, Black pulled us off the main course to inspect swampy cul-de-sacs where the canal merged with bayous and gave way to dense forest. This was as close to the actual swamp as the barge could get us, but it still afforded a sense of otherworldliness. Ahead, the dark woods rattled with invisible insect masses, and the trees themselves seemed to slink out of the forest with their exploratory cypress knees jutting up all around the water's edge. Purple and white flowers formed wild grottos framed by palmetto fans. Zigzagging dragonflies buzzed the water's surface, and birds seemed to hop and leap from one tree to the next above us.

In time we came to one cove where Black showed us huge, wicker-like eagles' nests high up in the shoulders of bald cypress trees. While we scanned the skies for eagles, our guide brought out his small, boxy, Cajun accordion and his acoustic guitar. In addition to his other pursuits, Black is a musician with a number of original songs to his credit. These include the "Ballad of Poo-Poo Boudreaux" and "Walkin' in the Woods with My Parrain," a holiday number set to the tune of "Winter Wonderland" with lyrics all about the joys of hunting with your godfather. On the tour, however, he always plays a few classics to give tourists a quick tutorial in Cajun music. Hoisting his accordion, he introduced "Jolie Blond," a very old-timey tune.

"Now the song is in Cajun French," he said. "For those of you who don't understand French, I'll briefly interpret it for you. The song says, 'Pretty blonde, why did you run away and leave me for that Yankee from Baton Rouge you rascal you, and ain't you never coming back again or what?'"

Everyone laughed, but his creative interpretation of the lyrics still mined the essence of the song, which he delivered in French with a jolting, hollering singing style. Next he picked up the guitar, slung with an alligator hide strap, and started into "Jambalaya." It was a fine rendition, though again sung at startling volume, especially for the small captive audience on his boat. But it soon became clear he wasn't singing to us alone.

"Well, that didn't take long," he said, putting down the guitar. "These alligators know when I start singing, it's time to eat."

"Oh my God, here it comes!" gasped one of the Mennonites, pointing off the bow of the barge.

Sure enough, there at the head of the channel I could make out an expanding and approaching delta-shaped ripple, and soon I recognized the flatiron of an alligator head moving on the surface. I could see nothing behind it but the dark, swampy tree line under gathering storm clouds, and as the head drew closer bunches of floating hyacinths bobbed on its wake. Even from up on the boat, I felt very much inside the alligator's realm and outside of my own.

Meanwhile, Black had stowed his instruments and hooked a raw chicken thigh to an aluminum pole. Soon the alligator was right below our eyes and our cameras. It looked like a six-footer, and it maneuvered with slick ease through the dark water, paddling in circles so quickly by the side of the barge it seemed to almost catch its own tail. All the while it kept its reptile eyes on the meat hook that Black dangled over the side. As he lowered the chicken pole, the alligator rose from the water—possibly leaping, possibly using its powerful tail as support, but in any case looking like a dog up on its hind legs begging treats.

Black took care of a few more alligators in similar fashion as we made our way back to the marina, but for most of the return trip we just cruised through the beautiful and remote channel scenes. The gathering clouds finally let loose a shower that turned the water into gray slate jumping with tiny splashes. The rain clattered overhead on the barge's awning and, I couldn't help thinking, on the armored backs of countless alligators out there in the woods and water.

* * *

A canoe trip, like the one Byron Almquist led me along in Manchac, is the gentlest, most intimate method of accessing the Louisiana swamp. Tours on craft like Black Guidry's barge and Zam's pontoon boat are the most comfortable, with padded seating and room to stretch out. The most thrilling, though, is the often-derided but oh-so-fun-to-ride airboat.

Airboats are simple, loud and fast. They have flat-bottomed metal hulls and sport rows of bench seating that are raised up so high from the deck they look like lifeguard stands. Behind the pilot rises a huge, open motor, which is usually either custom built for the craft or salvaged from an old Cadillac. This motor turns a caged propeller that looks big enough to power a cargo aircraft. With all of its weight positioned so high, the craft can skim across the very top of the water, and occasionally the land. It's a rudimentary machine fitted with a control stick to direct the prop's airflow and steer the boat and an accelerator foot pedal to raise the speed—and that's it. There is no speedometer and there are no brakes.

My first airboat outing was with an operator called, plainly enough, Airboat Tours, which is run by Arthur and Cathy Matherne. I found the family compound/tour office just off Highway 90 near the fishing village of Des Allemands and met my guide, the Mathernes' adult son Craig, a stout, ruddy guy with an enveloping handshake and a thick, powerful build.

Yet again I joined a random group of tour companions, and this time I lucked out with the fun-loving, big-laughing Burnett-Chapman family visiting from Arkansas. It was good that we all got along, since the six-passenger airboat made for close quarters. Craig sized us up as we boarded the airboat and assigned our seats based on apparent weight in order keep the top-heavy craft in trim. Soon all of us were crammed together on the benches like one too many parties squeezing onto a love seat.

We puttered along a narrow bayou, waving to families headed out on whalers with fishing rods and to guys fishing from the docks behind Highway 90 gas stations. Craig used our slow time in this no-wake zone to go through his pretour safety instructions. This rigmarole was pretty brief.

"Just don't stand up while we're moving, okay? And if you need something, remember I can't hear you yelling once the engine gets going so just wave your hands. That's about it. Now, is this anyone's first time on an airboat?" he called.

All six of us raised our hands.

"That's cool, mine too," Craig said, giggling, just before he opened the throttle and gunned the airboat into the open blue water of Dufrene Pond.

The sudden acceleration knocked me back into the padded bench and we were off, buzzing over the tiny wave ripples on the pond as Craig showed us the boat's dynamics. We raced toward a clump of trees and veered left at the last moment, sending up reefs of water from the sharp edge of the boat. He weaved us through channel markers like a slalom course. Then, without any advance clue, he hit a sharp turn at the edge of the pond, and we were in a narrow channel just as suddenly as the Batmobile shooting into the Batcave. The swamp part of this swamp tour was about to start.

Airboats sometimes get a bad rap in this age of hands-off ecotourism. Their exposed engines are painfully loud, and indeed we were given ear protection to clamp on our heads before Craig's machine got roaring. They move very fast in an environment where everything else at least superficially seems still and peaceful, and they cut through it all like crude, gas-guzzling, homemade swamp hot rods. If paddling through the swamp in a canoe is like pedaling down a bicycle path, riding an airboat is like blasting through the park on a chopper bike.

Even some other tour operators criticize airboats as being so loud and so fast that they scare away the wildlife the tourists came to see in the first place. That certainly proved true on my trip with Airboat Tours, but it was one of my favorite parts of the outing. After all, it's not as though the wildlife turned invisible as it fled the onrushing noise and splatter of our craft. Quite to the contrary, in fact, we had a panorama of the fight or flight instinct in action as the roaring airboat effectively flushed all these creatures from the bush.

Craig gunned us down the marshy passes, and at every turn great flocks of egrets burst toward the sky like white, flapping explosions. Greasy-looking nutria and muskrats scrambled up swampy banks. Deer dashed high-stepping over marsh to the tree line and, in the water, the occasional alligator would do a startled barrel roll in front of us, splashing with its tail as it sought cover in a hurry. Maybe we would have had a longer look at some of these animals had we floated past in a pirogue, but I doubt we'd have seen so many.

Craig had calmer scenes in store for us too. One big advantage of the airboat, in addition to the exhilarating speed, is that it goes where most other craft can't. The constant shift of the marsh from land to water and back again is a major challenge to even the most shallow-draft watercraft, and it's impassible for any land vehicle short of an amphibious crawler. But the airboat splits the difference and can skip over water and wetland alike. We even cruised up and over a short levee to move from a canal to a mass of marsh, and later we skimmed the top of thickly weeded groves before hitting recognizable water again.

The payoff came when Craig cut the engine altogether so we could coast through cypress cloisters secluded in the swamp interior. The tree trunks rose all around us, and they were as bare as columns all the way up for a few stories until their first limbs cropped out to buttress a leafy green ceiling, vaulted here and there by gaps of penetrating sunlight. These swamp spaces were so still and thickly hemmed by growth they seemed like chambers, and Craig navigated us gently from one to the next.

"All right, y'all, now we going to see something different," he said, motoring slowly out from the cypress canopy and into a wider channel again. "But this is important, okay? You got to hold on real tight here and you'll see why in a second."

I gripped the rail by my seat just a moment before Craig floored it. Once again my hair was blown back, the boat ripped over the water, and quickly we were out in an open patch that looked like a broad, watery meadow.

"Hold on!" Craig yelled over the engine roar and then jerked the control stick back, sending the boat into a skidding, donut maneuver over the water. He stopped the engine, the boat corkscrewed to a halt, and as I regained my whirling senses and forced my eyes to focus, I saw, spread out all around us, a teeming stretch of American lotus. These water plants have a wonderland look, with their circular, fairy tale–big green leaves, and buttery-yellow blossoms held up on stiff stalks three feet above the water. One is captivating enough, and here we were surrounded by thousands upon thousands of them.

"Seventeen hundred acres of this, that's what you're looking at," said Craig, sounding earnestly awed himself. "After a little storm, you can come out here and drink the rainwater right out of these big leaves, see? Like cups waiting out here for you with pure rainwater."

He leapt down from the pilot's chair and plucked one of the lotus flowers for us to inspect up close. At its base, under the soft petals, we found a seedpod, which looked just like a green showerhead. Craig cracked it open and started digging out its acorn-sized seeds, which he handed around for us to eat.

"We call them Cajun peanuts," he said. "You can fry them, boil them with crab boil, or you stick them in a stew to thicken it up."

We sat there a while in the silence of this enormous, floating lotus field. I was pressed thigh to thigh against good-natured travel companions under a clear sky with the guidance of a jovial host, chewing over the mild but unfamiliar flavor of "Cajun peanuts." This outing had been filled with unexpected delights and seemed like a big success, but one ingredient still felt missing. The only alligators we'd seen were the ones diving in panic before our bouncing airboat. But Craig had a plan. On the way back to the dock, he pointed us along another narrow canal and throttled down. I looked back over my shoulder to see him pivoting his head from side to side, scanning the banks like a turret.

"There's one!" he hooted, cutting the engine and scrambling down again from the pilot chair. In a moment, he was scooping his hands through the water, and, as though grabbing a rubber ducky from the bathwater, he came up with a tiny baby alligator. Its head was no larger than my thumb.

"Aw! Look at its little teeth," squealed Lisa, one of the Arkansas girls.

We all took turns gently cupping the alligator in our palms, cooing at it and posing for photos with it held near our faces. It was undeniably very cute. Its infantile eyes were hugely out of proportion with its body, like a reptilian kewpie doll. But every other feature looked just like a scaled-down alligator. Eight hundred pounds later, I thought, this creature might still be on the tour.

Chapter 4

RIVER ROAD REVISITED

Plantation Tours and the Slavery Legacy

I cannot remember a time in my Rhode Island upbringing when I wasn't aware of the Newport mansions, those fantastically opulent seaside minicastles built by heirs and industrialists in the glory days before the federal income tax. I toured them on school field trips with my classmates, and when visitors came to stay with us in the summer I sometimes toured them again with my family. Glamour shots of their imposing facades and glittering interiors turn up in tourism campaigns and anything else attempting to posit the Biggest Little State in the Union as an elegant destination.

The River Road plantation homes of south Louisiana are drafted into the same role, and that's one reason why I had lived here for years before I finally got around to exploring them. In my mental catalogue of Louisiana travel destinations, I relegated them to tour bus fodder, sites for people interested in admiring formal gardens and antique furniture and oohing and ahhing over the displays of lost wealth like some antebellum episode of *Lifestyles of the Rich and Famous*. I was interested in Louisiana history and I have an abiding love for historic buildings. But I felt I could handily take care of all of that with a spin through the house museums in the French Quarter, which were much closer to home and were conveniently surrounded by other historic buildings now operated as bars and restaurants. This way, I knew, I could go to one historic building for the guided tour and then immediately visit another for drinks and a good meal.

Late summer sugarcane waves high in Vacherie, the heart of plantation country.

What turned things around for me, however, was Laura Plantation. This historic home is certainly on the motor coach circuit, but
it changed my uniform image of plantation visits as *Gone With the
Wind* fantasy tours. I had assumed a tour would be all about southern belles, social pomp, and architectural backdrops appropriate
for bridal portraits. But Laura is different and, after repeated visits
and some time spent exploring its River Road peers, I found that
the experience helped me appreciate a different perspective on the
whole region.

* * *

Laura Plantation sits in sugarcane country on the west bank of the
Mississippi River in a town called Vacherie, about fifty miles upstream
from New Orleans. When I started looking for plantations to visit,
I noticed that a number of them were clustered close together in
this area. Within a span of less than ten miles, there was Evergreen
Plantation, Laura, St. Joseph Plantation, and the most famous of all

the River Road manors, Oak Alley, the property used most often in Hollywood movies when a script calls for antebellum majesty.

Laura, however, bills itself as a "Creole plantation," and I was intrigued by how that would play out in a tour. Creole is one of the most important but variegated words in the Louisiana cultural lexicon, and it's also perhaps the most difficult, thanks to its pervasive racial connotations. Depending on who you ask, and in what company, people in Louisiana today will tell you that Creoles are whites descended from the aristocratic families of Louisiana's French colonial period or, alternately, that they are people descended from les gens de couleur libre, the free blacks from the slavery era. Some people will tell you Creoles have bloodlines mixing black with white and/or Indian and/or Hispanic. Some will claim it refers to black people who could passé blanc, or pass for white, and by doing so access social and economic advantage. Meanwhile, across the state, most people in southwest Louisiana seem to agree that Creole refers to blacks from traditionally French-speaking communities. In the subtitle of this book, I use Creole in the broadest sense, since the chapters cover areas where people apply the term in such different ways.

Trying to be precise when defining Creole gets touchy because it tends to broach uncomfortable implications of race-based social standing and the pecking orders of skin tone. I wondered how Laura Plantation would parse this minefield of identity politics to tour bus crowds.

Right from the start of the tour, my guide, Meze Folse, dived in with a discussion of color, though in this case she was talking about the Caribbean-bright palette scheme of sunny-yellow weatherboards, lavender porch spindles, crimson doors, and slate-blue carpentry trim that sets Laura Plantation apart from its white-painted River Road peers even at a glance.

"You may have noticed, our house here looks pretty different from the other plantations," Meze told our tour group as we stood under the oak limbs outside the house's picket fence gate. "This is a Creole house and Laura was a Creole plantation. Now you're thinking, okay, what does that mean? Well, Creole refers to someone born in the colonies, someone who was born here in Louisiana and was part of this culture here instead of someone coming from Europe."

I was standing with a group of eight other people, and I could see them either nodding or looking to each other with "ah-hah" expressions as her simple explanation of the Creole condition clicked. The term has evolved to cover a lot of ground in Louisiana, but she delivered the baseline definition from which the others grew here. When European-born settlers had children in Louisiana, their sons and daughters were Creole. Slaves born in Louisiana became "Creole slaves," as opposed to those freshly arrived from Africa, and later the Creole tag was used to differentiate both black and white locals from the newly arrived Americans after the Louisiana Purchase.

"Along River Road it was easy to tell which families lived in which house by the colors they chose," Meze continued. "The Creoles saw themselves as passionate, proud people. They were French-speaking Catholic people connected to the Caribbean world. When the Anglo-Saxon Protestants started moving in and taking things over, they built big white manor houses. The Creoles decided, 'If you can't beat them, paint them!' So they had colorful houses like this one you see here."

* * *

The house was built in 1805 by Guillaume Duparc, a French military man who fought for the American side during the Revolutionary War and battled the British elsewhere in the New World. After the Louisiana Purchase, he received the riverfront property that would become his sugar plantation from President Thomas Jefferson's administration. The manor is lovely, though it is strikingly different from Greek Revival archetypes of the Deep South big house, and it is different even from many of the other surviving River Road plantation homes nearby. It is raised high on brick piers, which is never a bad idea in flood-prone south Louisiana, and it is fronted by a high, deep porch lined by turned posts and touched with gingerbread woodwork. It would look at home in some parts of New Orleans and on the former French colonial Caribbean islands, but it is definitely no stand-in for Tara. And it isn't even that large. There are entire subdivisions around affluent modern America packed with Sheetrock chateaus big enough to dwarf the Laura house. Visitors expecting to be awed by antebellum grandeur may not be so impressed with Laura.

But what Laura has going for it is a rich and well-told story, thanks largely to the plantation's namesake, Laura Locoul Gore, the great-granddaughter of Guillaume Duparc. Her memoirs gave the property's current owners the narrative building blocks for their Creole-centric tour.

Laura was born on the plantation in 1861, on the eve of the Civil War when Lincoln was president. She died in St. Louis in 1963, in the midst of the civil rights movement when Kennedy was president. She began recording her recollections of postbellum plantation life and family stories in 1936 when she was in her seventies. The manuscript was written freehand in a spiral notebook, and in its pages she recorded a Creole family legacy of strong women.

Louisiana retained its colonial French legal code during its Americanization process, and this "civil law" system, known as the Napoleonic Code, survives today. In 1808, when Guillaume Duparc died, that law code allowed his widow, Nanette Prud'Homme Duparc, to take over control of the fledging, three-year-old plantation. Thanks to business deals and internecine alliances, the ownership and daily management of the sugar company would flow through the women in this family for three more generations.

"These Americans, when they started showing up in Louisiana to check out their new territory, they must have been a little surprised to find out they had purchased a foreign country," Meze told our group. "This was a place where women were presidents of companies, where if they wanted to do business with the Creoles they often had to do business with the woman of the house. This was new for them."

It wasn't the only culture shock waiting for the new Americans in Louisiana. By the time of the Louisiana Purchase the culture of plantation slave labor and free black residents here stood apart from anything else on the continent.

* * *

On some tours, in New Orleans itself and in plantation country, guides will recite the story of how slavery was a different experience in Louisiana because of the liberal provisions of the French colonial *Code Noir*, or "Black Code." This document, signed by King Louis XIV in 1685, did indeed set up some cultural distinctions for slave life in Louisiana, especially when compared to the norm in Britain's New World colonies. For instance, slave owners were legally required to provide support for slaves as they grew old or became ill, and two slaves who had married in the Catholic Church could not be sold off to separate owners. But this document was not quite as friendly as it is sometimes portrayed on today's tourist paths.

Its first order of business was to expel all Jews from French colonies. With that matter addressed, it went on to stipulate that slave owners were forbidden to practice torture, but slaves could still be chained and beaten. Fugitive slaves surely faced torture, and the *Code Noir* specified that those absent for a month could expect to be branded and have their ears cut off, while those missing for two months would have their hamstrings cut. Should such a repeat offender manage to hobble off for a third time, the *Code Noir* determined he should be killed.

The real change for slaves in Louisiana came after Spain gained control of the territory as part of a treaty ending the Seven Years' War in 1764. The accomplished scientist Antonio de Ulloa arrived two years later as the first Spanish governor, but he was driven from New Orleans in 1768 by irate locals who refused to recognize the shift in nationality. The next year, Alejandro O'Reilly, the Dublin-born inspector general of the Spanish army, arrived with twenty-six hundred solders on twelve ships and orders to assert Spanish rule over the errant Creoles. One of his first acts of power was to round up and kill the ringleaders of Ulloa's ouster, who are memorialized in New Orleans in the name of Frenchmen Street, which begins near the spot where these French colonial patriots faced the Spanish firing squad.

"Bloody O'Reilly," as the Creoles began calling him, soon announced that Spain's own laws governing colonial slaves would replace the French *Code Noir*. This meant that for the first time in Louisiana slaves could own property, enter into contracts, and receive inheritances, all of which were expressly forbidden by the *Code Noir*. They also had a right to "self-purchase," meaning that, at least in theory, they could demand a contract from their owners to purchase their own freedom.

The much harsher American regulations did away with all this when they came into force after the Louisiana Purchase in 1804. But the impact of the preceding thirty-six years of Spanish slave law would live on in Louisiana. At the start of Americanization, while the Laura Plantation was being built upriver, free people of color comprised close to 20 percent of the total population of New Orleans, while about one-third of the city's black population was free, according to Kimberly Hanger's illuminating study of free black society in colonial Louisiana, *Bounded Lives, Bounded Places*. Many free blacks in Louisiana owned slaves, and some of them owned plantations. Newly arriving Americans must have found this a very unusual state of affairs, since around the same time some 98 percent of blacks living in all other areas of the American South were slaves.

* * *

Few people would visit the surviving River Road plantations if they did not boast beautiful homes and grounds. I think at some level most people like to fantasize about what it would be like to live in such grand style. I certainly dreamed of the Gatsby-like parties I could throw at those Newport mansions given half the chance and someone else's inheritance. And make no mistake, these Louisiana sugar palaces are gorgeous.

The San Francisco Plantation, on the east bank of the river in Garyville, has enough fine millwork and architectural details all on its own to fit out an entire historic district in gingerbread, while Houmas House Plantation, located in Darrow, is as magnificent an example of Greek Revival grandeur as they come. Massive white columns stake its perimeter, distinctive, turret-like garçonnières (or quarters for young men) stand on either side, and a belvedere crowning the roof gives views over the levee to the river. The place gleams from a fresh restoration and is surrounded by twelve parklike acres of gardens, ponds, fountains and footbridges, while its fine— though very expensive—restaurant is a rewarding exception to the rule that dining within tourist attractions should be avoided. Just a few miles downstream from Houmas House, the Bocage Plantation is a much smaller property that travelers along River Road have long gazed upon as a sort of ghost. For decades it stood in gray neglect, like an architectural fossil amid the lush green of its riverside lot. But after an extensive restoration by new owners, it was opened in 2009 for tours and as a bed-and-breakfast and now it looks like an elegant jewel box along the rural route.

Oak Alley was at the head of the plantation preservation movement when it was first restored in the 1920s, and the reason it is used as a movie location so often is because, quite simply, the property is stunning. My experience inside Oak Alley was rather dull, with a teenager in a period hoop dress herding us from one room to the next while mechanically delivering stories about the house, its owners, and their fine possessions. But redemption came when we finally got outside to admire the plantation's namesake, the quarter-mile-long tunnel of epic oaks extending from the river levee to the manor itself. Walking along the columned corridor formed by their massive, dark trunks and beneath their entwining limbs was like strolling through a living sculpture garden. The trees seemed to hold up the overcast sky on the chilly November day when I visited, and at the end of their path the manor fairly glowed with photogenic invitation.

But unlike the society showplaces of Newport, which were built for leisure, plantation manor houses were just one part of agro-industrial complexes powered by black slave labor. The best place to get a sense of what they might have looked like at full steam is Evergreen, in the small river town of Edgard, where the tour takes in an entire plantation complex rather than just a manor house and gardens. The property is still run as a modernized sugar plantation, while the public components open for tours reveal a remarkably intact campus of thirty-seven buildings. Some surviving plantations on the tourist circuit feature one or two slave cabins, but Evergreen has twenty-two of these humble, clapboard, weather-beaten structures. They are arrayed in rows facing their own oak alley of trees, each hung with Spanish moss, and the sight of so many of these dark, rudimentary, quietly ominous structures stretching back toward the fields finally relayed some sense of the scale these slavery operations once attained.

Still, it seemed inevitable that Evergreen's big house, with its sweeping, almost heart-shaped exterior staircase and its noble columns, would be the focal point of the tour, and that is indeed where visitors spend the most time and snap the most photos.

The one River Road destination where the slave story comes first isn't even on a plantation, and it has no manor to compete for visitor attention. It's the River Road African American Museum, housed in a Victorian cottage in Donaldsonville, the town where Bayou Lafourche branches off from the Mississippi.

The museum was founded by Kathe Hambrick, a native of Gonzales, a town just across the Mississippi. She left Louisiana for a career in California's computer industry, and when she moved back in the early 1990s she started exploring the area again, though it wasn't always a happy homecoming. She was particularly bothered by plantation tourism's focus on the wealth and lifestyle of slave owners, while the suffering and subjugation of her ancestors' slave experience got little mention.

"She had a revelation, standing on a levee where she imagined slaves had been unloaded all those years ago. She knew things happened here that needed to be told today, and that's what we're here to do," said Kenyota Coombs, the energetic and engaging curator who showed me around the museum.

"This museum is here to make you think," he told me. "It'll bring up things that aren't comfortable or easy to see."

It is a small museum, taking up four rooms in a cottage in Donaldsonville's downtown historic district. The museum includes a little from a lot of local black history, stretching from slave auction ads to much more recent headlines about civil rights achievements. There are displays showing African influences in Louisiana food customs and others on black artists and inventors, including Leonard Julien, the local man who devised an important sugarcane planting machine in 1964. Another room highlights the roles played by free people of color in Louisiana history. Other exhibits focus on local black people's accomplishments in medicine, the performing arts, and politics, including the story of Pierre Caliste Landry, who was born into slavery in 1841 and became America's first black mayor when Donaldsonville voters sent him to city hall in 1868.

But the slavery legacy is at the heart of the museum, with exhibits explaining the basics of the trade and the extent of the African diaspora. What I found most moving were the ways in which the museum conveyed individual stories of slaves, pulling their tales from the nullifying blank of the "peculiar institution," as slavery was once so politely termed by some in the South. A narrated recording told the story of runaway slave Tom Wilson, using the veracity of his own words to describe the abuse he received in the field and the chilling punishments doled out upon him after repeated attempts to escape. Another display featured a photo of Houmas House, a pretty shot worthy of a tourism brochure, and beneath this listed the names of 180 people documented as slaves there in 1858. The catalogue covered the breadth of shackled humanity, from the most elderly, like ninety-year-old Diana Cook, all the way to Septimus Hampton, age two months.

* * *

Only a handful of slave cabins remain at Laura, but a trove of historic documentation from the site, the details from Laura Locoul Gore's memoirs, and the guides' own comfort in shifting from the story of a wealthy family to the very different experience of their human property made my plantation tours here feel more complete.

In 1808, when Laura's widowed great-grandmother assumed ownership, the plantation was run with just eight slaves, according to the property's own historic account, *Memories of the Old Plantation Home*. But as demand for sugar skyrocketed and business growth seemed limitless, the family put all it had into expanding the operation. In 1829, the Duparc family sold off its Normandy estates back in France to free up more growth capital for the Louisiana plantation. A year later they began a shopping spree at the New Orleans slave marts. They bought a mix of men and women specifically to breed a future work force, and by 1840 the plantation "was awash in slave children," as the Laura history notes. More slave cabins were built, and eventually they would stretch in a row three miles long behind the manor house. By the start of the Civil War, the plantation company owned 183 slaves. Together, they were producing 460,000 pounds of granulated sugar a year, plus 30,000 gallons of molasses, while making their owners very rich.

Through repetition and broad overview, the textbook narrative of slavery can seem numbingly distant. But I found its inhumanity somewhat easier to grasp at Laura while standing on the same ground where enslaved people lived, while looking at the same sugar fields where they worked, and while peering out over the same River Road and river current that must have carried away their relatives to new owners. Most of all, though, the darkness of slavery was driven home by the transactional specifics and the money trail attached to the people who lived and worked at Laura, and the modern tour shows some of the brass-tacks bureaucracy that ushered this cruel industry along.

A few years ago, the Laura tour operators dusted off old plantation records listing purchase prices for the Duparc family's slaves in the early nineteenth century, and then updated those figures to reflect values in modern U.S. currency. So while our tour group stood around inside a ramshackle outbuilding situated about halfway between the manor house and the slave cabins, Meze introduced us to some of the people who worked the lands and she described what they likely would have been worth in today's dollars. We learned that a slave named Jean-Pierre, age twenty-five and described as a "Creole mulatto" and "highly skilled worker," was valued at one hundred thousand dollars, making him a considerable, long-term capital investment for the Duparc family. Roze, age thirteen, "a half black and half Indian Creole," rated not quite half as much at forty-five thousand. Marie, age twenty-six, cost eighty thousand dollars, but she was bought in a package deal that included her children, Tusso, an eight-year-old mulatto, and Liza, described as a five-year-old black house servant. Darince, an eight-year-old orphan, went for twenty-three thousand dollars with a full life of enslaved toil ahead of him.

* * *

Assuming Darince remained healthy and kept out of harm's way, he would have been sixty-three at the time of the Emancipation

Proclamation. Confederate forces had already been routed in south Louisiana by then, and when the Civil War ended two years later Darince would have found himself in a ravaged rural countryside where the social and economic order had been fractured, though hardly swept away. If he had stayed at Laura Plantation all his years, his lifestyle and prospects likely would not have seemed all that different after emancipation.

"Many of the former slaves stayed on the plantation, they didn't really have anywhere else to go," Meze said as we made our way into one of the slave cabins.

Our group of nine adults crammed into one chamber of a four-room cabin that would have housed two families.

"They were paid twelve dollars a year, and they were paid only once a year and that was on December 31. Now before they were paid the plantation company would deduct all the expenses they ran up buying food and tools and clothing from the plantation over the year on credit, and you know that didn't leave them with anything at the end at all but more debt," Meze said.

Naturally, this company store system ensured the laborers had very little mobility. Many stayed on the same plantations and worked the same fields for the same people, who shifted from owners to bosses. The cabin in which we stood at the edge of the cane fields, originally built for slave housing, was used as laborers' residences until 1977. Meze pointed out spots around the cabin where electrical fixtures had been added as the humble structures were minimally updated for new generations of field hands in modern times. The fixtures themselves were later removed to improve the cabin's historic feel, but we could clearly see the outlines where the plugs and conduits had run down the patched-up, timeworn walls.

Modern times did not come barreling along the River Road as some grand force of change. Rather, modern times grafted themselves onto the existing structure, which has always been fixed to the river in this part of Louisiana. The scores of plantation homes that once lined the Mississippi's banks have dwindled to a handful. The levees grew taller and broader, and behind them many huge chemical refineries have cropped up, stretching over square miles like volatile cities of distillation towers, tank farms, and endless silver, white, and brown piping. These are the economic giants of the region now, drawn to the river's edge for easy shipping access, just as the early planters had been.

Today a drive along River Road can be a disorienting tour of naked modern industry standing next to the most photogenic leavings of the slave industry, the old plantation homes. Between them, local farmers still plant fields of sugarcane from the levee to the swamp. The green cane waves high and bushy by the end of the summer, rumbles off to mills in tractor wagon trains during the fall, and crops up anew each spring as an agricultural reminder of Louisiana's slave legacy.

Chapter 5

ANGOLA'S INCARCERATED COWBOYS
A Culture That Persists Behind Bars

I've heard it said that after prolonged incarceration even prison can feel like home. But I'm always amazed when visiting Angola, the state penitentiary fifty miles upriver from Baton Rouge, how quickly this place can seem less like a maximum security prison and more like a peculiar but functional agrarian society.

Of course, this feeling didn't come about from touring Angola's various camps of barracks-style inmate housing, home to more than fifty-one hundred men, nor its death row, where at this writing more than eighty inmates sat awaiting possible execution. Those areas were off limits.

No, this strange sense of dropping in for the day on a self-contained colony came while joining some ten thousand other free citizens at the famous Angola Prison Rodeo, a spectacle pitting untrained but endlessly ballsy prisoners against two-thousand-pound bulls and kicking broncos, complete with an outdoor food court and a prisoner crafts fair that has assumed a life of its own.

I've attended the annual rodeo several times, but repeat visits haven't made the experience any less surreal. A day at the rodeo means walking freely among men who will never leave the prison gates. It means buying gumbo and boiled turkey necks from rapists and talking to a convicted kidnapper about his handiwork in the carpentry shop. It means waiting in line for a urinal behind prison guards and the children of prison inmates. It means seeing young kids clap and wave in arena grandstands as murderers wrestle

Inmates compete in the "guts 'n' glory" event during the Angola Prison Rodeo.

calves to the muddy ground and get tossed violently over the horns of irate bulls.

In the realm of rodeos, Angola stands awkwardly apart. There are a few events on the daily roster featuring rodeo pros. These are the free men and women who come to compete or perform as part of the rodeo production. Angola is even a stop on the Women's Professional Rodeo Association circuit for barrel racing, an event requiring skills, instinct, and practice. But most Angola rodeo contests involve inmates who have volunteered for challenges that any sane pro would dismiss as crazy hazardous.

There's "wild cow milking," which is exactly what it sounds like. For another event called "guts 'n' glory" a group of inmates is sent into the ring against a provoked bull, and each tries to be the man who retrieves the plastic chip glued between the animal's horns. This is like standing by the side of the road and trying to grab the hat off someone swerving past in a convertible. The most extreme event of the day requires zero dexterity but calls on the intangible currency of prison communities everywhere: hard nerves and luck.

This showstopper is called "inmate poker," a teeth-grinding display of intensity where four inmates in flak jackets sit around a folding table while a bull weighing more than a Honda Civic is released in their midst. The idea is for the inmates to keep poker faces while rodeo clowns taunt and lure the bull closer to their table. The result is always the same. The huge animal comes crashing through the assembled players, shattering the table like balsa wood and sending inmates flying. If there is a man left sitting in his plastic chair when the bull is through, he wins.

Most inmate rodeo contestants come from Louisiana's urban centers, especially New Orleans, Baton Rouge, and Shreveport. Visitors are reminded constantly—through mentions in the printed rodeo program and by announcers drawling over the rodeo arena's public address system—that few of them had ever encountered an animal larger than a dog before coming to Angola. Ambulances are always standing by, and they're needed. Inmates get thrown, stomped, and rammed. Broken bones are common.

I've made the Angola rodeo trip with different people, and some of them left vowing they would never return. Only volunteer inmates enter the ring, but the idea of prisoners putting their limbs and perhaps their lives on the line for small cash prizes and cell block glory brought to mind too much of the coliseum for them.

I have my own mixed feelings about the rodeo. I can't shake an underlying discomfort with the idea of day-tripping to a prison for a bit of weekend amusement. But I also can't deny a fascination with the access this extraordinary event affords to Angola's foreign realm, however partial and selective that access remains. My appreciation for the rodeo only deepened once I started talking with inmate participants and learned what some of them see when they look out from the ring.

I met Danny Fabre, a native of Albany, Louisiana, who is serving a life sentence for first-degree murder. He had signed up for the rodeo each of the past fifteen years and said he has suffered broken ribs and a stomped hand, among other rodeo injuries. I asked him why he keeps at it.

"To me, it's a responsibility thing," Fabre said. "I've done a lot of bad things in my life. This is my way to make it up. You're giving these people entertainment. They pay to see this and we give them something worthwhile. I know you got victims' families here who actually want to see us get hurt. But I don't think about that. I'm trying to look for people I haven't seen in twenty-six years, people from back home. They come up and shake my hand. And when they go back home later, they'll be saying, 'I saw Danny today, and he was doing good in the rodeo.'"

* * *

To understand the rodeo, it helps to know a bit about Angola. The prison is in West Feliciana Parish, in a part of the state known as "English Louisiana." With its historic Anglo-Saxon cultural influences and rolling, hilly geography, this area stands sharply apart from the Creole and Cajun communities that inspired this book. But if south Louisiana sometimes symbolizes the romanticized, good-timey notions of this state, Angola exists at least in part to deal with the broken ends of the story, the ugly but undeniable consequences of its economics, its racism, its educational failings, and its politics. When the peculiarities of south Louisiana shine they end up in tourism campaigns, and when they fester and go severely wrong they often end up at Angola. Prison isn't a happy extension of the state's culture, but it is an extension nonetheless.

Incarceration is serious business in Louisiana. Maybe some states do it better, but none do it so often, at least per capita. One in every fifty-five Louisianians sits in prison, according to a 2009 study from the Pew Research Center. The hardest cases go to Angola, where more than 70 percent of inmates are serving sentences so long they have no chance of leaving.

But the prison image of the walled blockhouse doesn't apply to Angola. This is a farm prison. Its roots and unusual name go back to a nineteenth-century cotton plantation that was called Angola, purportedly because that was the African homeland of the slaves who worked it during antebellum days. It became a prison not long after the Civil War. The modern facility is composed of a series of mini-prisons arrayed as individual campuses of bunkhouses and support buildings. These are separated by vast stretches of cultivated land and pasture within a great bend of the Mississippi River covering some eighteen thousand acres, an area large enough to swallow Manhattan. The Mississippi's swift, tangling current provides a formidable boundary to escape on three sides, and through its history of alluvial deposits the river has supplied the fantastically rich soil that made slave plantations so profitable here in the first place. Today, inmates work the prison's fields to produce some five million pounds of food a year, which the state uses to feed prisoners at Angola and at other corrections facilities.

Like many other farms, this huge penal operation has horses. According to the official prison history, the Angola rodeo tradition began in 1965 when guards backed their pickup trucks together to form a rudimentary ring and used their mounts for offhand rodeo contests. Prisoners got involved, and in 1967 the event was opened to the public, though these early spectators had only wood crates and truck tailgates as their seating. By 1969, the prison began to institutionalize the rodeo and built the first in a succession of official rodeo arenas. Things grew from there, and now Angola warden Burl Cain hires a professional rodeo producer to run what has become a huge event. The rodeo is held each weekend in October and during one April weekend, and each date draws enough people to sell out the modern, ten-thousand-seat prison arena, which, like so much else at Angola, was built with inmate labor.

This rodeo is the marquee event for a prison that, for a maximum-security facility, makes itself remarkably open to the public. Angola invites golfers to come within its fence line and play a nine-hole course, provided these visitors are willing to undergo background checks first. Anyone within a hundred-watt range of Angola can tune in to KLSP 91.7 FM—a.k.a. the "Incarceration Station" or "The Station that Kicks Behind the Bricks"—to hear inmate disc jockeys spin gospel, country, and rock tunes on the only prison radio station licensed by the Federal Communications Commission. Interested readers can subscribe to *The Angolite* and can get this fascinating, inmate-produced magazine mailed to their homes so they can read poetry, news, sports reporting, and history pieces from within the prison. One of *The Angolite*'s former editors, Wilbert Rideau, won numerous mainstream journalism awards for his documentary work in its pages before his 2005 release from Angola.

The public also can tour the Louisiana State Penitentiary Museum, located just outside the main prison entrance. On one visit I inspected Angola's original electric chair—darkly dubbed "Old Sparky"—and a queasy collection of improvised prisoner weapons. There were exhibits about the facility's long history, and a gift shop with such Angola-logo items as tote bags, pencils, beer koozies, boxer shorts, and shot glasses. This is a prison with a creative merchandise program.

But the Angola Prison Rodeo trumps all these other invitations to public participation within the penitentiary. It turns the prison rodeo arena into festival grounds, albeit one hemmed by coils of concertina and overseen by guards perched in watchtowers and sauntering past on horseback.

* * *

The inmates who participate in the rodeo—those allowed to walk among the men, women, and children of the visiting public, those allowed to put their bodies on the line against bulls and broncos, those who perform with inmate gospel and country bands before the big show, and even those who man the garbage patrols—have all qualified for inclusion based on good behavior. They may never leave, but these are the men who are getting along under the pressure of permanent prison life. In this way, the rodeo provides one huge incentive, coping mechanism, and release valve for the inmates who make it to the event. And, at least for me, it was a lesson in the humanity always present behind a label, even those as caustic as prison inmate or convicted killer.

A stroll through the grounds during the spring 2009 rodeo drove this home before the first chute opened in the rodeo ring. The event starts in the morning and lasts through the late afternoon, and the thousands of people visiting the prison need to eat during the long day. So dozens of inmate organizations run food booths, selling snacks and lunches to the public and raising money for their causes. A group called Vets Incarcerated offered coffee and donuts, and the Students of Islam sold candy apples. The Camp D Social Orientation Club prepared sausage on a stick and blooming onions, while the Angola Lifers Association filled paper cones with sno-balls, a frozen treat of shaved ice and syrup. The Angola Drama Club sold tacos and burritos. The Asian American Cultural Society had shrimp fried rice.

This food selection has expanded over the years at pace with greater rodeo attendance. But nothing has grown faster than the Angola crafts fair. Inmates have their mandatory prison jobs, and after these shifts are completed many of the men have time to work on their own craft projects in Angola's hobby shops. Those inmates cleared to participate in the rodeo are allowed to sell their wares to visitors. Their craft tables and displays now encompass a huge flea market spread of goods. Some inmates who have yet to earn full rodeo rights wait behind wire fences just beyond the craft tables, and they call out to passersby like barroom barkers, asking them to look more closely at the leather belts and carved roses that other inmates will sell for them by proxy. But most booths are manned directly by the inmate craftsmen themselves.

The inauguration of President Obama a few months prior to my most recent visit had clearly made an impact on prison craft themes. Inmates worked the Obama campaign slogan "Yes We Can" into leather wallets and cigarette cases, and the president's chin-up profile adorned bare wood bassinets and lionizing painted portraits. Other items involved magazine clippings of rap stars and images of cartoon characters shellacked onto basic jigsaw shapes. These were the entry-level crafts. But other booths showed the results of years of practice over the many long and permanent Angola sentences.

"Once I give the warden his time, I get mine," said Edward Jackson, a tall, lean New Orleans native who has been serving a life sentence for murder since 1969. "I done a lot of jobs here, but whenever my prison job's through I go work in the shop until I'm done with my day."

Thirty years ago Edward ordered a model ship kit through the mail and eventually learned to make his own miniature vessels using scraps of wood collected from the prison carpentry shop. At this rodeo he displayed a fleet of intricate model vessels, including galleons, fan-rigged jonques, and a modern river tug he said was based on a photo sent to him by a rodeo visitor who appreciated his earlier work. A group of uniformed guards stopped to silently admire the detailed rigging on Edward's rendition of a Napoleonic-era warship as he showed me how he split popsicle sticks to make its railings.

About two hundred booths away, lifer Greg Zumwalt explained how he used a rotary tool and automotive paint to make his etchings of hummingbirds appear to float in slabs of clear resin. Other visitors approached to ask questions about his technique, and Zumwalt stretched out his long, tattooed arm over the craft table to shake hands with repeat patrons from past rodeos. Here, even cons have fans and followers.

"Once I got out from under the drugs and alcohol, I found out there was something else under there," Greg said.

The biggest success story on the Angola arts front, though, is Marlowe Parker, who at age forty-five was about halfway through a twenty-five-year sentence for drug offenses when I met him among his towering displays of canvases. Parker is a self-taught artist who started painting in prison, following the example of his stepfather, Arthur Green, who was also incarcerated at Angola. The exposure that Parker's work gained at the rodeo has made him a jailhouse celebrity. He's been profiled in magazine pieces, and his work has appeared in a Washington, D.C., art show even as he continues his sentence. He paints graphic allegories of ghetto perils, celebrity portraits, and lighthearted rural idylls, and at the rodeo these paintings routinely sell for six hundred to eight hundred dollars each.

"I hate selling the originals," Marlowe said. "If I wasn't incarcerated, you'd get a print of these."

* * *

Many people visit the rodeo expressly for the crafts fair, and some drive home in pickups crammed with prisoner-made swings for their porches, barbecue pits and picnic tables for their backyards, and armoires for their bedrooms. Inmates push their purchases on carts through the razor-topped rodeo arena gates to the parking lot, where they load it all over visitors' tailgates for them.

But once the rodeo action starts up, the ring inside Angola's open-air arena becomes the center of attention. On my spring 2009 visit, the proceedings began with a Christian invocation and the national anthem. Fifty or so inmate rodeo participants convened in the mud-died ring and formed a circle of clasped hands. They wore black-and-white-striped jailbird shirts with their contestant numbers pinned to their backs. Men and women from the rodeo production team slogged out through the mud to join them and held their hands to complete the circle during the prayers and song. Visitors rose in the stands and cowboy hats were doffed all over the arena as a singer in the center of this circle began "The Star-Spangled Banner."

For the next two hours, the inmates did their best to ride bulls, and they went flying to the ground under a rain of hooves. They worked together in three-man teams to grab the loose reigns of excited broncos and tried to get one of their partners to mount it as the animal dragged all of them through wet sloughs in the ring. They waited at the mouths of rodeo chutes for five-hundred-pound calves to charge out, and they tried to muscle them to their backs without getting kicked in the teeth. Like the extreme events to follow—wild cow milking, guts 'n' glory, convict poker—these contests didn't showcase skill so much as bare determination.

The professional rodeo announcers gave the crowd updates on the action, and they reminded everyone yet again how little experience these incarcerated cowboys had around large animals. The crowd cheered for them. These were men who went bad and got caught. They were here in Angola and Angola is where most of them would stay until they died. And in the moment of competition they were outmatched underdogs, so the crowd roared when they overcame the odds, when they stayed on the heaving bull, rode across the ring on the snorting horse and grabbed the chip from between the surging horns. I knew for some men in the arena, that applause was all that mattered.

"You don't have a lot of chances for really good things to happen here," convicted kidnapper Adam Coffey told me before heading into the rodeo mud. "When someone cheers, you know if someone up there in the stands chooses me and is cheering for me, that makes us feel good."

CHAPTER 6

PETROLEUM PIPE DREAMS

Oil, Oil Everywhere and the Future of the Coast

There can't be too many places where a vintage, beached oil rig would seem right at home. But the Atchafalaya riverfront in Morgan City is one of those places.

The rig is called Mr. Charlie, and it's a training facility, a museum, an artifact of industrial history, and a unique attraction for visitors in a hardworking town that doesn't otherwise offer much in the way of mainstream tourism draws.

Morgan City is an oil industry town in an oil industry state. Its hotel rooms are more often filled with oil field workers in transit than with leisure travelers, and even the big annual event that does bring lots of visitors here doubles as a civic tribute to the oil industry: the Louisiana Shrimp & Petroleum Festival, held each Labor Day weekend. A particular festival highlight is a blessing of the fleet ceremony, which sees the big, ferrylike workboats that service offshore oil platforms parading past town alongside smaller shrimp boats. All of them are colorfully decorated for the day with buntings and streamers, and their crews receive the benediction of a Catholic priest who reviews this whole diesel-powered procession from shore. Festival emblems of oil derricks and cartoon shrimp wearing hardhats are emblazoned on posters, T-shirts, and collectible beer koozies. It's a telling illustration of how closely meshed fishing and oil patch work are in the economy and culture of south Louisiana. Morgan City is particularly attuned to this relationship. This is a

One among thousands of oil and gas platforms off the Louisiana coast.

town where kids grow up knowing where oil comes from in the way that ranchers' children know how hamburger starts out.

The early offshore oil industry was nurtured in Morgan City, beginning in 1947 when an experimental rig operated by Kerr-McGee Oil Industries began drilling in the Gulf of Mexico some forty-three miles south of the town's docks. Oil prospectors had been drilling wells over water for about half a century before then, usually in lakes, marshes, or tidal zones. But the Kerr-McGee strike is remembered as the first oil-producing well located out of sight of land. Morgan City was the home base for this innovation, and the offshore industry as we know it started wading deeper and deeper into the energy-rich Gulf.

Mr. Charlie, the prime attraction of the International Petroleum Museum & Exposition, helped it get farther out there. Designed by wartime naval engineer and Marksville, Louisiana, native A. J. "Doc" LaBorde, the floating facility became the world's first fully transportable drilling platform when it began hunting for oil in the Gulf in 1954. Previously, oil exploration companies like Kerr-McGee and its competitors hauled all their equipment out to a prospective well site on boats and barges, built up a stationary derrick from the Gulf floor, drilled a well, and then moved on to the next site to start over. Crewmen lived and worked on boats the whole time.

Doc LaBorde's innovation was to build an entire drilling operation and crew living quarters on a metal deck and mount this on high legs over a barge. It was towed to a drilling location, where the barge was filled with water and sunk to the Gulf floor to create a stable platform for drilling. The barge could later be pumped out and raised to the surface and Mr. Charlie would then be towed to the next job as a production rig took over to service the new well.

This rig was a game changer, allowing oil companies to drill wells faster, cheaper, and deeper in the Gulf. It was in service for more than thirty years, all through the oil boom of the 1970s, and it was finally retired when Gulf drilling moved to waters much deeper than it could handle. While open to the public as a museum now, it still serves as an active training center for the freshest recruits headed out to the larger and more complex rigs drilling far out in the Gulf.

On a tour one hot, quiet July day, I strolled Mr. Charlie's metal catwalks, took in the view of downtown Morgan City from the rig's rust-pocked helicopter landing pad, and poked through crew quarters of narrow, paneled passageways and barracks-style bunkrooms. No one else had turned up for the tour, so it was just me and my guide, a friendly, stout lady in a T-shirt and jeans with her hair pulled back in a ponytail. For the next hour and a half, the two of us wandered through every part of the rig as she explained offshore life in astoundingly intimate detail, from routines in the galley and the gym-like shower rooms to the basics of drilling operations on deck. All the while, young men in oil company uniforms shyly edged around us as they completed training tasks on deck and inside the rig's boxy superstructure.

People who like visiting historic warships or old factories should find this unique tour pretty appealing. What I found most fascinating, however, was the chance it offered to crawl around an authentic and instructive piece of an industrial culture I had encountered constantly on my own Louisiana travels—one that profoundly affects the state's economic and environmental prospects—but that I could previously observe only from afar.

While the oil and gas industry isn't tourist-oriented, you can't miss its massive and omnipresent infrastructure in south Louisiana once you begin exploring the towns, swamps, and waterways that are on the travel agenda.

Louisiana is the nation's top oil-producing state and it ranks second for natural gas production, counting the yield of the thousands of rigs drilling and pumping away off its coast. Altogether, the state supplies about one-fifth of America's domestic oil, while much of our imported oil first hits U.S. soil at the Louisiana coast.

To move all of this oil and gas, the state is laced with at least eighty-three thousand miles of pipeline, a pulsing industrial circulatory system that could ring the earth's equator three times over with plenty of metal mileage to spare. Most of these lines are sunk in the marsh or buried underground and remain out of sight, though they play a role in the daily lives of millions of Americans. Just one of these oil transit systems—picturesquely named the Plantation Pipeline and originating near Baton Rouge—supplies most of the South with its gasoline, home heating fuel, and jet fuel, to the tune of thirty million gallons each day.

"Because pipelines are effectively hidden from view, Louisianans are little aware of the massive amount of oil and gas products that move underground in this state," the LSU economist Dr. Loren Scott wrote in a 2007 industry report.

The BP oil disaster in 2010 brought a lot more attention to all this infrastructure. But even before that calamity, the industry had long made its presence felt to the south Louisiana traveler in many other ways. Some are as startling as the fireballs that shoot up periodically from the stacks of gigantic refineries, suddenly illuminating rural nighttime darkness with burning light. But other manifestations quietly weave themselves into the local way of life. All over the bayou country around Houma and Thibodaux, for instance, radio stations typically feature employment ads seeking oil field workboat captains, underwater welders, and rig crews, plus announcements from contractors ready to handle all your inland, coastal, and offshore oilfield construction needs. Driving the local roads, you pass heliports and shipyards, great metal buildings loaded with offshore equipment and tool yards lined with acres of drilling pipe, with all this gear laid out on the grass as though it were sunbathing. Even aboard Black Guidry's musical Cajun swamp tour in Gibson, we passed many wellhead gauge stations, which sprout from the water in the cypress-edged coves of the alligator wilderness like iron totem poles bristling with wheels and handles.

On the highways south of Interstate 10, it's common to see flatbeds piled with bright, boxy, exotic-looking machinery, all of it bound for the state's big oil field ports, where it will be conveyed over the horizon to the rigs. Sometimes, eighteen-wheelers will race down from cities and distribution points with just a single valve or some crane component strapped down to their trailers, making express, on-demand, and no doubt hugely expensive deliveries to waiting workboats bound for rigs with equipment problems. I always try to keep my Toyota out of the way when I see these trucks barreling along.

I shared the narrow lanes of Highway 1 with plenty of these truckers on my way to visit Grand Isle for the first time, a trip that turned into yet another inadvertent exploration of Louisiana's energy sector. Highway 1 becomes the last trickle of the state roadway system, a long, solitary extension of the grid descending all the way down the course of Bayou Lafourche to the Gulf. After about an hour of driving through the small towns along the highway and the bayou, the road carried me into the open, low, watery wetlands leading to the state's outermost edge at Grand Isle itself. It's a landscape that is more water than soil, with green, marshy clumps and clods forming a random patchwork around the raised strip of road.

Highway 1 crosses Bayou Lafourche down here at the tiny fishing village of Leeville, where the masts and booms of shrimp boats tower over any of the low buildings in town. Dominating everything in these surroundings, though, is a huge, modern, four-lane bridge that sweeps majestically high, like a gray, concrete rainbow arching over seven miles of marsh and open water, before regaining level ground again to continue the highway's final leg toward the Gulf. This bridge is just the first phase of a planned nineteen-mile span designed to carry traffic above the rapidly eroding land and ever-widening waters between Leeville and Grand Isle. I really didn't know my way around the area on this first trip, but the bridge sure seemed like an awfully grand gesture of civil engineering just to get motorists to their island vacation homes and marinas. It made much more sense, however, once I realized that the other destination sharing the far end of this bridge with the leisure town of Grand Isle is the oil center of Port Fourchon.

There are marinas, a few related businesses, a truck stop casino, and even new condo developments around Port Fourchon, which sits directly on the Gulf Coast at the mouth of Bayou Lafourche, a few miles west of Grand Isle. Technically it could be called a town. But that would be like calling Las Vegas a hippy enclave because it contains a few vegetarian restaurants.

Port Fourchon is a pipeline beachhead, a jumping-off point for the offshore drilling sector and one of the most important nodes in the entire American energy grid. Morgan City may have been the town to launch the offshore industry, but Port Fourchon is the modern hub for the thousands of metal citadels of men and equipment sitting near and far offshore. About one-third of the nation's domestic oil supply comes from platforms in the Gulf, and Port Fourchon is the base servicing more than 80 percent of these rigs. It's also the landing point for the Louisiana Offshore Oil Port, or LOOP, a platform situated about eighteen miles off the coast that takes oil from supertankers that are so large it's easier just to pump them dry while they moor in the Gulf than to bring them to a dock. This all happens out of sight of land, but there's plenty of work going on out there. All on its own, the pipeline connecting the LOOP with Port Fourchon accounts for anywhere between 10 and 15 percent of the nation's imported oil in a given year.

This place is an enormous, bustling, futuristic metropolis of work, a border town between mainland civilization and offshore rig life. Each day, an estimated one thousand heavy trucks travel the last slim stretch of Highway 1—grinding up and over that monumental new bridge—to service Port Fourchon. I took a detour on my way to Grand Isle to follow a few of them through. The orderly roads revealed a waterfront campus of improbably large metal buildings, standing like giant covered carports for oceangoing ships. There were tank farms of squat liquid storage cylinders, all manner of workshops and staging areas with acres and acres of palletized supplies, stenciled with such domestic-sounding labels as "kitchen" and "laundry," and all hemmed by wire fences. There was action everywhere, with crew boats arriving and departing like rush hour commuter ferries, helicopters lighting off for the rigs and elaborate-looking pieces of equipment painted in prime colors all being conveyed by cranes, trucks, and forklifts.

Eventually, the road came to a fork. To the right, the pavement continued to the closed, wire-topped gates of a secured pipeline facility. To the left, the path turned to sand, and I followed the wheel tracks through it to the top of a dune trail. With disorienting swiftness, the scene had changed from utilitarian base camp to a broad beach of light-colored sand and abundant marsh grass in varying stripes of green and heather. A few station wagons and pickups were parked on the sand, and groups of families had set up beach canopies. Some people splashed in the water while others just beside them were surf casting. A few men were swimming out to the near breakwaters with their fishing rods, hoping for better bites farther out. It was a pretty shoreline vista, though the horizon still looked very busy. The first line of rigs and platforms were close and densely clustered, and over them danced the specks of helicopters while workboats plowed along on shuttle runs between the rigs and the port now just behind me.

It was a calm, clear, hot day when I visited, and the light breeze rolling in from the Gulf felt good. I wondered, though, how this spot would look with a really large tropical storm lashing the shore. Surely the waves would breach higher than the dune bank on which I stood. Later I learned this was indeed the case. The entire industrial city of Port Fourchon is separated from the Gulf by a low rampart of dunes, bolstered here and there with sandbags and chunks of concrete debris. It looks pitiful, and it is not enough. Hurricane Gustav in 2008 sent a six-foot storm surge though Port Fourchon, and along with wind damage this knocked the port out of action for days. The situation grows worse as wave action batters the coastline on one side of Port Fourchon and the degraded wetlands behind it continue to slip away, leaving one of the nation's most important concentrations of energy infrastructure increasingly exposed on all sides.

* * *

It's like this all over coastal Louisiana, where so many of the refineries, pipelines, wellheads, and storage facilities for American energy are planted, areas that are increasingly vulnerable to storm damage thanks in part to this very infrastructure.

To extract Louisiana's oil and gas resources, companies have chewed thousands upon thousands of miles of canals through coastal wetlands. Most were dug during periods of lax or nonexistent environmental regulation, and they are used to access wellheads, move product around by barge, and sink that potent network of pipelines. Any map of Louisiana wetlands will show the straight runs, right angles and branching cul-de-sac paths of these canals, which look so similar to the canals logging companies sliced through Louisiana swamps generations earlier. They have plainly cut the coast to pieces, helping salty Gulf water creep ever deeper into the marsh, killing the vegetation that holds it all together and contributing massively to the existential crisis of America's largest wetlands.

Coastal land loss in Louisiana is estimated at twenty-four square miles per year. To make this loss more tangible, coastal advocates have recently begun describing it as the equivalent of one football field worth of American soil ceded to the Gulf every thirty-eight minutes. This process destroys habitat and degrades the nation's natural heritage. Some fishing communities see water lapping at their doorsteps, and metropolitan New Orleans faces greater exposure to hurricanes as the wetlands that have historically buffered storm surges are increasingly converted to water. The extent of damage caused by oil from BP's massive Gulf blowout washing into the wetlands remains unknown at this writing, though most of us watching from south Louisiana share a sense of dread and anger over the disaster.

Still, it's not as though the oil and gas business did this all on its own. The primary factor is the control of the Mississippi River behind levees. These flood barriers protect cities and towns and maintain the Mississippi as America's most important industrial river. But they also deprive the coast of its natural, land-building sediment, much of which now washes straight out to the Gulf. The forces of geological subsidence are dragging the coast down too, adding another dimension to the dilemma. And, to make things more exotic, large, bucktoothed, humpback water rodents known as nutria, originally imported to Louisiana from South America by fur ranchers, run amuck through the coastal area and are actively chewing apart the vegetation that holds marshland together. But those canals, dug to fill American gas tanks, keep doing their daily part to destroy Louisiana too.

Journalist Mike Tidwell tells the story better than anyone in his book *Bayou Farewell*, which began as a travel adventure and turned into an environmental exposé. Since *Bayou Farewell* was published in 2003 the land loss situation has only worsened, and Hurricane Katrina demonstrated, in catastrophic fashion, how south Louisiana's vulnerability to storms increases as its protecting wetlands continue to shear away.

* * *

The most infuriating part for me as I've watched the building crisis play out on my own Louisiana travels is the ample evidence that land loss can be stemmed and even rolled back, while still keeping the Mississippi as the levee-walled, reliable, industrial superhighway that serves the nation today. Coastal restoration projects are under way around Louisiana, including engineering maneuvers known as freshwater diversions, which remove portions of the Mississippi's flow from its levee-directed main path and send these tangents into damaged wetlands areas. The fresh river water helps push encroaching salt water back, giving marsh vegetation some breathing room, and the river sediment quickly gets back to its old job of building new land. Separate projects have been successful in sucking sediment-rich river water from other spots on the Mississippi and moving it by pipeline to vulnerably depleted wetlands areas farther off. This is called "sediment harvesting," and it has a vivid effect on targeted areas. The scale of these projects, however, remains puny compared with the voracious march of land loss along the coast.

So why isn't more of this happening faster? I believe it comes down to a lack of coordinated political will, which means a lack of political pressure, which means a lack of funding and a lack of urgency from the only entity big enough to do the job: the federal government.

The cause has received more political lip service since Hurricane Katrina, but the response has been limited, slow, and stymied by bureaucracy in a way that suggests a grave disconnect between government mission statements and government work orders. For instance, the U.S. Army Corps of Engineers annually dredges about sixty million cubic yards of sediment from Louisiana rivers to keep them clear for navigation. State coastal restoration authorities believe that if that volume of sediment were deposited in depleted wetlands it would be enough, all on its own, to build back more than eighteen square miles of land per year, or about three-quarters of the amount now vanishing annually into the Gulf. Instead, the Corps loads much of this dredged river sediment on barges and dumps it into the open Gulf. At this writing the state is still lobbying for a change in Corps policy.

Major wetlands and coastal restoration projects are just as expensive and complex as they sound, but we've seen how the government can snap to and make things happen when monumental tasks are presented as priorities. Gigantic, "too-big-to-fail" Wall Street banks can be bought and taken over very quickly, one after the next. Wars across the globe can be mounted very quickly. But Louisiana continues to dissolve because its recovery has not become a political priority, a point agonizingly illustrated again in 2010 by the disjointed and inept response to the nation's largest oil disaster just off this endangered coast.

* * *

For a hands-on lesson in just how much industrious Americans can accomplish, and the seemingly insurmountable challenges they can master, I look to that fifty-year-old relic on the Morgan City waterfront. I look to Mr. Charlie. While the BP disaster revealed how much can go wrong offshore when safety is marginalized, for me the story of this early rig still embodies the sort of ingenuity and determination we must apply to fixing the coast.

On my tour of Mr. Charlie, I learned that in the late 1940s Doc LaBorde first brought his idea for a moveable, submersible platform to his then-employer, the oil company Kerr-McGee. His supervisors there saw too many problems and question marks in the project, and declined to pursue it. So Doc LaBorde began shopping the idea around to other oil companies working along the coast, and each of these in turn gave him the brush-off too. Finally, he found interest from Murphy Oil Co., which then operated in landlocked Arkansas but saw the potential for deeper Gulf drilling. Murphy Oil became Doc LaBorde's first investor, and Charles Murphy, the father of company president Charles Murphy, Jr., was the rig's namesake.

The modern drilling and pumping platforms that followed in Mr. Charlie's path are far more technologically sophisticated. But they share enough fundamentals of rig life and basic drilling procedures that the vintage station continues to serve as a training facility for offshore companies' new hires. They handle functional machinery, and they also live on board to get a taste of the confined, military-like living conditions of a rig. GED classes are also big customers for the tours, with groups of students peering around a lifelike model of a potential future workplace.

What left the biggest impression with me on my tour, however, was the industrial improvisation and the very audacity of the engineering attempts that first led Mr. Charlie out to sea. The idea of floating a heavy, ungainly collection of towers, cranes, and metal boxes far into the Gulf, partially sinking it, driving a drill bit from its deck through the underwater mud, and eventually extracting oil from the unseen depths must have seemed farfetched before it became commonplace.

As I continued my tour, I learned about the employment opportunities available offshore, which still go by the disarmingly folksy job titles in use during Mr. Charlie's early days. There are entry-level positions such as "roustabouts" and "roughnecks" for the pipe-hitting guys near the bottom of the rig hierarchy. There are "tool pushers," who, naturally, are in charge of equipment. And there are "mud men," who oversee the rigs' mudlike drilling fluids. Clearly, this was an industry pioneered by men who didn't consider their work rocket science nor see themselves as rocket scientists.

Even the rig itself seems to embody this unaffected, can-do attitude. Its superstructure looks like it was made from storage containers welded together, and its big yellow crane looks like it was originally built on treads to roll around construction sites. It doesn't have some militaristic code name, like XR-33 or whatever, and it wasn't christened as the Murphy Submersible Offshore Drilling Unit, or any other such serious-sounding tag. It was called Mr. Charlie, a tribute to dad from the guy who believed the far-out project was worth the effort.

Investors backed the idea and men went to work, moving pipe, extracting product and opening a new frontier for the oil industry. In time, more specialized equipment was developed, and techniques and tools unforeseen at Mr. Charlie's launch came along to make extensive Gulf oil and gas production a profitable industry. If the same attitude, innovation, and urgency were applied to coastal restoration, maybe our nation's wetlands would soon be on the way to redemption, and we would have a potentially profitable new service and engineering industry to export to areas around the world also grappling with land loss.

My hope is that some powerful national politicians will make the restoration of the Louisiana coast their priority. Then, if the canals start getting stitched back together, if the wetlands begin rolling back toward the Gulf, if the habitat begins to rebound, if the natural hurricane barrier for New Orleans and our coastal communities is bolstered, and if America's energy infrastructure is a little better insulated from sea and storm, maybe we can name some big restoration projects after them, in the spirit of Mr. Charlie.

CHAPTER 7

ANDOUILLE EVER
Sausage Road Trips and a Kitchen Divided

Farmers turn to almanacs to judge harvest time. Hunters mark the start of game seasons on their calendars. And at his LaPlace smokehouse, David Rauch tracks weather forecasts to determine when to boost production of his primary product, the thick sticks of andouille that have made this town thirty miles up the Mississippi River from New Orleans one of my favorite destinations for sausage-gathering road trips.

"Whenever I see a cold front is coming in, I know there's going to be a run on andouille in a few days and I better start making a lot more," said David, a tall, dark-haired man of thirty with a broad smile and a trim goatee.

A few years back he took over ownership of the generations-old Wayne Jacob's Smokehouse, a place with its own production rhythm.

"I make andouille all year round as I need it," David said. "In the summer I might make it once a week but when it gets a little cold here I'm making it every day."

At its simplest, andouille is a smoked sausage made with coarse-ground chunks of pork shoulder. There's nothing at all seasonal about its ingredients, but the intangibles of tradition in Louisiana ensure that demand will skyrocket as the days shorten, temperatures dip, and local cooks head back to the stoves with their gumbo pots and stew pans.

Andouille from three different smokehouses in LaPlace.

"You get the first rush when football season starts, when people start tailgating and get that first whiff of fall," said E. J. Bailey, third-generation family owner of the smokehouse Bailey's World Famous Andouille, also in LaPlace. "Then there's another push when it actually gets a little chilly. But things really pick up as we get toward the holidays. Everyone's making gumbos, and people are traveling too, bringing this andouille with them when they go visit family."

Sausage is taken seriously in south Louisiana, where so many staple dishes call for smoked pork flavor, and andouille is by far the region's most famous style. To my palate, andouille reaches its most intense and complete form at the handful of deeply traditional smokehouses in LaPlace, a small town that manages to support three distinct andouille makers. Bailey's and its much older neighbor Jacob's World Famous Andouille sit practically beside each other on one block of Airline Highway in the center of the town's busiest suburban shopping strip. About two miles away, closer to the river, the air is again aromatically seasoned by andouille in progress at Wayne Jacob's Smokehouse (which, despite the shared name, is not affiliated with Jacob's on Airline Highway). Of the three, Jacob's has the heaviest smoke and Wayne Jacob's is the thickest and spiciest, while Bailey's holds down the middle ground.

These sticks—as the stiff, dense LaPlace links are called—are remarkably different from the packaged versions of andouille widely available in Louisiana grocery stores. Huge and potent, they are redolent with pecan wood smoke. They are brown as cigars, thick as a lady's wrist and neatly tapered at each end. The casings crackle delightfully when crisped on the grill or in the broiler, and a cross-section slice reveals different colors, from pink to brick red to burgundy, in the different pieces of pork pressed together in the casings. Sliced, coined, or diced, they suffuse their peppery, campfire flavor through the roux of gumbo, the grains of jambalaya, the very body of red beans, and countless other dishes on the Louisiana table. And, as we shall see below, while andouille is an intimate part of Cajun cooking, its traditional makers in LaPlace and elsewhere link it to the state's early German history.

The andouille tradition is by no means limited to LaPlace, but here the style is bigger, darker, brawnier, chunkier and, most of all, smokier than even the closest peers. Sausage makers here fret over the smallest details of production and put their own nuanced stamp on seasoning, mixing, and smoking. This means that finished andouille sticks at each smokehouse in this small town can differ as greatly from each other as wines produced in the same valley, and parsing their distinctions can be as pleasurable as chasing the same varietal from one vineyard to the next.

* * *

Once I discovered LaPlace andouille, I found myself responding with Pavlovian cravings for that deep smoke flavor whenever I heard the town's name or, eventually, even when I saw LaPlace marked on highway exit signs. For a few years I worked at a regional, New Orleans–based bank, and whenever I needed to visit our Baton Rouge offices I always tried to build a LaPlace sausage detour into the itinerary to elevate the mundane business trip up Interstate 10. It didn't take long before the pretense of other travel destinations fell away and LaPlace andouille became the entire goal behind thirty-mile highway runs.

It's not like I had to go roaming to sate my sausage cravings. I happen to live within easy bicycling distance of two great, traditional New Orleans producers—the Creole Country sausage plant, well hidden inside an old shotgun house down an obscure side street, and Terranova Supermarket, a classic corner grocery run by the same family since 1925. I insist their proximity to my home is a coincidence, but it certainly is convenient for someone who has more than a passing interest in butcher shop products. When I want to make a Monday pot of red beans, I can dash over to Terranova and get a pound of fresh hot sausage to spike things up. Meanwhile, a visit to Creole Country is like an audience with an unheralded oracle. This place does virtually all its business with commercial clients, but knock on their door and someone in a hairnet and clear plastic apron will let you in, sell you some links from the fridge, and maybe even cook up a few coins of sample sausage on the household range that sits in the office. The place turns out an amazing array of pork products, including hog headcheese that is so good even people who "don't like" headcheese make an exception when I put out a block of it at parties.

But once I had a taste of the different types of sausage and smoked meat specialties in towns afield I developed a sort of acquisitive fever. From Pavlovian responses near LaPlace, the fixation moved to hunter-gatherer themes. Anytime I found myself outside of metro New Orleans during normal business hours I was always scanning for signs of a butcher shop among the local businesses. This is what it must feel like to be a tabloid shooter in Los Angeles or a cheesemonger touring English shires. I wanted always to come back home with something in hand. I started bringing an ice chest along in the truck whenever I traveled in south Louisiana, expressly to collect meats. I stocked my freezer with links and set aside special finds for specific occasions. When I visited friends at home, I often brought them hand-selected links as little gifts, like clippings from the garden. I kept a special reserve just for my contractor, and soon we established that a few pounds of Cajun smoked meats would be the expected gratuity for small jobs. It seemed like whenever I cooked at home, I was looking for ways to include sausage or tasso, the intense Cajun ham, into the recipe, no matter the dish's original context.

The floodgates of full-blown sausage mania were groaning, and after a few formative trips to the porcine promised land of central Acadiana those gates would bend back on their hinges.

* * *

The Acadiana region across the Atchafalaya Basin, and especially the subregions around Lafayette and to the north on the Cajun prairie, are a shopper's dream for butcher shop meats. There are so many producers, in fact, that decisions about where to get which specific items can become obsessing, especially for someone visiting the area and not necessarily tied to one hometown shop. Most of these places offer more or less the same products, so innovation is not necessarily what I'm after. Instead, I'm just driven to try as full a range in the palette of pork products as possible. And it seems like no single item of the Cajun charcuterie gets quite so bound up in this hunt as boudin, which, if it had petals, could be the official flower of Acadiana. The stuff crops up everywhere.

If you've never been formally introduced, Louisiana boudin is a Cajun sausage made by cramming pig intestines with a lava flow mixture of rice, bits of pork, and abundant seasonings. It shares a name but not much else with classic French boudin, a more delicate, mousse-like sausage. In south Louisiana, boudin evolved as part of le boucherie, or communal events where several neighboring families would gather at one farm and share the labor and rewards of slaughtering a hog. The collective approach was a way to make the most of perishable meat in the days before adequate refrigeration, and the fastidious use of the entire animal led to delicious byproducts. Andouille also came out of this process, and in addition to hams and chops le boucherie would see pig skin fried for gratons, or cracklin's, and the pig's head boiled down to turn tiny bits of meat and gelatin into hog headcheese.

"It was part of the lagniappe of le boucherie. When all the work was done, everyone would go home with their bag of cracklin's, their boudin, and a pan of hog headcheese," says John Folse, a renowned

Louisiana chef and culinary entrepreneur who grew up attending these old-fashioned events at his family's sugar plantation in St. James Parish.

Once a frugal necessity, today le boucherie is carried on in the name of tradition by some families or hosted as a community event in some towns. For instance, the local Lions Club holds its Boucherie Festival each October in Sorrento, a town in the River Parishes area, and traditional boucheries are put on in St. Martinville on Bayou Teche and in Eunice on the Cajun prairie as part of celebrations on the Saturday before Mardi Gras.

But many of le boucherie products also live on at commercial butcher shops, and of all their offerings boudin proves the most versatile. Squeezed from its casing onto crackers or eaten whole by hand, it's an easy snack. It can be breakfast food eaten in the car with a cup of coffee, fishing trip food eaten on the way to the dock, Mardi Gras food, jam session food, festival food, comfort food or between-meal treat.

While I enjoy hunting down different boudin makers, some enthusiasts are as devoted to their personal favorite butcher shops as other people are to their hairdressers or therapists. Once fixated, they'll defend their beloved version over any other on the basis of texture, peppery spice intensity, the presence or absence of liver, casing consistency, meatiness, and grease levels.

But I like to try a range on any given road trip through the region, and I hit a trifecta of different boudin links during one circuit through Breaux Bridge, a pretty bayou town near Lafayette. At Poche's Market, a huge butcher shop and restaurant on the outskirts of town, the links were noticeably darker than most thanks to the smooth liver running through the rice and meat mix. Downtown at the squat, brick storefront of Charlie T's Specialty Meats, the air inside was scented by the vats of fresh boudin being prepared just behind the display counter, and I was able to loiter a bit and buy some of the first links from the batch.

Around the corner, perched on Bayou Teche, I found the rustic complex called Bayou Boudin & Cracklin's where proprietor Rocky Sonnier runs a small butcher shop and rents cute, vintage cabins for visitor lodging. Locals drop in for links and cans of beer, while overnight guests are treated to the establishment's complimentary "Cajun platter," a sampler of boudin, fried pork skins, hog head-cheese, and root beer, all made on premises.

"When you go to some hotels you get wine and cheese," explained Eli Breaux, the young, effusive Breaux Bridge native manning the combination check-in desk/butcher case. "Well, here it's like that but the cheese is hog headcheese and the wine is root beer."

* * *

I know my wife, Antonia, would love those Bayou Teche cabins, and I've thought of bringing her there for a weekend getaway sometime. But the sad part is that the root beer would be the only part of that whole welcome platter she'd find appealing. My life partner is a vege-tarian. To each his own, I believe, but when we were first dating I did seriously wonder how far I could take a relationship with a woman who recuses herself from one of my prime pursuits, and for no good reason besides personal health, environmental stewardship, and an awareness of unsettling factory farming practices. The saving grace for our early dating days, however, was the revelation that she is a "New Orleans vegetarian." This means she will eat most local seafood, which is simply too abundant to ignore, and occasionally she does succumb to the food triggers of her New Orleans upbring-ing. For instance, if I leave a wedge of muffuletta sandwich on the kitchen counter unattended and later discover a small bite removed from its olive-dripping, salami-stacked corner, I do not immediately suspect rodents.

This is the reason I hold out faith that she may one day see what I see in andouille, and I believe if I can convincingly present the stuff as a culturally distinctive, local, artisanal product we may never have to cook red beans in two separate pots in our household again. When it comes to LaPlace andouille, I even have an ethnic ace in the hole.

Both sides of Antonia's family came to Louisiana as part of a small wave of immigration to the nascent colony in the eighteenth century from the Alsace border region between France and Germany. They settled upriver from New Orleans in the River Parishes area, close to where we watched the Christmas Eve bonfires on the riverfront.

These early German-speaking immigrants set up riverside farms that would help feed colonial New Orleans, and soon both banks of the river in this area became known, collectively, as le Côte des Allemands, or the German Coast. As is the case for so many other ethnic groups in south Louisiana, French culture came to dominate, supplanting the German language and transforming many family names, with Foltz becoming Folse, for instance, and Troxler changing to Trosclair.

This is the area that would spawn the cultural hybrid that is Louisiana andouille, which, like boudin, is so different from the delicacy of the same name served in France. There, the sausage called andouille is made with tripe and chitterlings. But in Louisiana, ethnic Germans and their French neighbors developed a distinctively local andouille style that is lean, chunky, and peppery, and altogether more akin to thick German wurst. I started asking local sausage makers if they knew how this change came about, all the while building the dossier of evidence I hoped would convince Antonia to eat andouille.

"What you had up here were French-speaking Germans, and over the years a lot of French traditions and German traditions blended," said Wayne Schexnayder, Jr., who runs a Kenner-based sausage company, Schexnayder's Acadian Foods, and who traces his German family roots to the early German Coast settlements.

So, right there, we can see andouille as a symbol of Louisiana's often overshadowed German heritage, which by extension is part of Antonia's own family roots on le Côte des Allemands. But can I convince her this stuff is artisanal? Is LaPlace andouille a pure, handmade product?

"On my hand I can show all the ingredients we need for our andouille," said David Rauch, when I posed the question to him at Wayne Jacob's. He started counting down his ingredient list on his fingers and thumb.

"In this order, all we need is pork, salt, red pepper, black pepper, and fresh garlic, that's it," he said. "Well, and the beef middles, of course, so that's six."

"Beef middles" is the polite term for the cow intestines that andouille makers use as sausage casings. I know bringing up intestines isn't the best way to tempt a vegetarian, even a New Orleans vegetarian. But I must mention it here because these middles, let's call them, are an important part of the regional product, and I find the entire, quite-artisanal, production method fascinating. David walked me through the process at his small shop.

The beef middles are much larger than the casings used for so many other sausages, and this leads to a much thicker andouille. Once the sticks are stuffed, David rests them in the cooler for about a day to "set up," and give the salt a chance to draw off the pork's moisture. Then it's time for the smoker. This stage of the process can take up to twelve hours, depending on the temperature and humidity that particular day. The attentive andouille maker stays busy the whole time, checking the sticks, feeling their density, eyeing their color, regulating the slow-burning pecan wood fire beneath and perhaps adding a green log for an extra blast of smoke.

The smokehouses themselves resemble deeply singed tool sheds, measuring about four feet by eight feet, and they are darkly stained by years of meaty smoke. That's called the "cure," and andouille makers consider the smokehouse cure as essential to the end product as the black on well-seasoned cast-iron skillets.

Though effective, this hands-on, traditional smoking process doesn't meet the U.S. Department of Agriculture's certification requirements to ship product or even to distribute it through grocery stores. This means andouille makers who keep most strictly to the regional tradition can only sell their sticks at their own shops. To my mind, nothing says local artisanal food product like having the USDA tell you not to spread it around too far.

I thought my case to Antonia would be ironclad. I told her about the commingled German and French heritage of her people embodied in the andouille stick, which I described as an edible totem of their Louisiana journey. Then I described how the process was so tradition bound and old-fashioned that the government has effectively rendered LaPlace andouille a controlled substance. But she wasn't budging, and in fact she turned my own argument against me. She reminded me, with an air of neat finality, that she's just not into controlled substances.

Chapter 8

HAVE COOLER, WILL FLOAT

Tubing Your Time Away on the Amite River

We were halfway to Tiki Tubing on the Amite River in Denham Springs on a Sunday morning in July when a note of alarm went around the crew cab of the big, barreling pickup truck.

"No one brought a funnel?" cried Greg, one of three passengers crammed in the back. "Well, where are we going to get one now?"

Calls were placed to friends traveling behind us in two other trucks, and it was duly confirmed that no one in our morning caravan had remembered to pack that essential of auto shops and keg parties alike, the flexible plastic funnel. There was a moment of glum silence around the truck cab. Eventually though, Tommy, the driver, spoke up.

"Don't worry, guys," he said, nodding coolly behind the wheel. "Someone on the river will have one. We can just share."

It was reassuring counsel. After all, we were on our way to a summer day of river tubing in south Louisiana, and thousands of others were headed to the same river that morning. Like us, they would be lavishly supplied with beer and booze. Some would surely also have funnels, and no one sharing the river would begrudge a fellow tuber a quick loan in order to throttle down a few cans of beer. That's a cause practically everyone who embarks on a Louisiana tubing trip would endorse.

Tubing, Louisiana-style, means slumping in puffy, industrial-sized inner tubes to float over one of the region's shallow, trickling, brown creeks. It hasn't the faintest relation to white water, rapids,

Tubing, very slowly, down the Amite River.

or any other kind of sporty activity pursued in the name of tub-ing elsewhere. The terrain here is far too flat to allow the water on these small rivers to get that ambitious. Instead, tubing in Louisi-ana means saturating in utter lethargy. It calls on less energy than walking—barely more than sleeping—but it does require a tremen-dous amount of drinking. People go tubing in Louisiana with certain expectations, and those usually revolve around getting ripped while passing very slowly through hot, rural, riverine scenery.

That lazy allure is mixed with the pretense of outdoor adventure. Anyone can get loaded in a barroom. But in the summer, with many weeks to go until football season, there could be a measure of guilt in spending a bright day inside the same old smoky, neighborhood joint, especially if you're young and eager to do interesting things while drunk. So many people go tubing to spend the day floating and drinking.

Tube rental operations furnish the primitive necessary gear—a tube for yourself, another for your ice chest, and lengths of string to tether them—and they provide a ride upriver to some muddy drop-off point. The float distance might be just two or three miles as the crow flies, but no crow has ever flown as slowly as these rivers move. With the slumping pace and the many opportunities for full-stop distraction along the river route, the typical tubing trip can last four or six hours—time spent pruning in the brown water, pickling in alcohol, and basting in the sun. It's a binge-level undertaking that lasts longer than a consultant's typical workday.

These trips always begin so hopefully. People bring sun hats and sun block. The first will be lost, the second forgotten. Cell phones and digital cameras are thoughtfully stowed in watertight bags, which will prove fatally faulty for their expensive contents after a few inadvertent submersions. Substantial lunches are packed to buffer against all the booze, but after a few hours it seems the river has claimed these too. Water overtakes sandwich bags, swamps the fried chicken box, turns chips to slime and for the rest of the day fixings will float by constantly, a slice of Bunny Bread here, a slab of luncheon meat there.

I've been on separate tubing trips with lawyers and doctors, New Orleans cops, and college students. The outcome never changes much. Tubing is an endurance game that gets the better of so many who enter. By the end, there will have been crying girls, sunburned backs and bellies, broken hearts, misunderstandings, car keys lost to the current, possibly a fist fight, and probably grounds for a few misdemeanor charges. Sometimes, in the middle of such a float, it seems a wonder anyone makes it back home at all.

*　*　*

This particular trip to Tiki Tubing was conceived as a social outing for the rugby team I train with in New Orleans. It was organized by a few of my younger teammates, a couple of guys just one year out of LSU. But few other players actually showed on the designated morning. So I ended up as the senior representative, by far, among the twenty-two-year-old trip organizers and a dozen of their friends as we drove north to Denham Springs, fretting about beer funnels.

We arrived at Tiki Tubing's grounds to find a grassy meadow quickly filling with acre after acre of cars and pickups parked in roughly ordered rows. It looked like the scene outside a football stadium. Parties of friends formed up around tailgates as people made final ice chest inventories and slathered on sunscreen. Someone broke out a Frisbee, a guy transferred a handle of vodka into a series of emptied Sprite bottles, and a girl ducked between parked cars to slip out of her shorts and into a bikini.

We loaded into Tiki Tubing's fleet of wheezing, retired school buses for the short, jostling ride from the parking lot to the launching point upriver, arriving sweaty, coated in roadway dust, and eager to get in the water. The trip from the bus to the river itself was a scene of shuffling majesty worthy of the *March of the Penguins*. The guys slung tubes over their shoulders, hauled up coolers in both hands, and plodded in loose-fitting river shoes to the water's edge, while the girls hurried beside them rubbing more sunscreen onto each other's backs and shoulders on the way. Someone from our group had customized a cooler to carry a sound system, complete with iPod dock and car battery power supply. This was wedged into its own tube, and it supplied a classic rock soundtrack as we splashed down into the water to begin our float.

Few people on a tubing trip wait until they hit water to start drinking, but anyone who did this time out began catching up with gusto. Our group of sixteen people towed along a fleet train of no fewer than five ice chests and each one of these was kept fully employed. All around us, everyone was doing the same. There were all manner of different tubes and floating apparatus, some resembling buoyant futons with room for two or three people to recline abreast. We were surrounded by perhaps two hundred other tubers just disgorged onto the river. Hundreds more were well ahead of us, and hundreds more would follow as the buses kept shuttling the crowd.

Our group clustered together as one shifting mass of tubes and coolers. It was like a floating island with electric guitar riffs blaring from its center and the constant cricket sound of cracking beer can lids keeping a steady rhythm.

The river twisted in regular coils, lined by hot, sun-bleached trees. They threw almost no shade but some had earlier collapsed into the water, creating roadblocks of trunks and sharp, half-submerged branches. Pushing around these was about the extent of exertion for long stretches of the trip. The water level was rarely more than knee deep, but in patches it plunged to eight feet and alternately grew so shallow that only the thinnest of girls could keep floating without bottoming out. The rest of us had to rise with our tubes around our waists and slosh through to deeper water.

* * *

We had been at this for about an hour when someone in the group decided it was time to land the tubes for a while at a "beach," one of the sandy shoals built up along turns in the river. These make good stops at which to eat waterlogged lunches and reapply sunscreen, but they can also become stages for the regrettable decisions that so often plague tubing trips.

It was on such a beach during an earlier outing, on a different river, that I happened upon a pair of obese teenage boys slapping each other red while an apparently related girl sat sobbing on the edge of her tube. During another trip, our happy group of tubers found a disturbingly intense wrestling match in progress on one of these sandy bends, featuring one skinny dude in trunks atop another while the dozen or so people gathered around them shouted slogans from Ultimate Fighting matches.

"Choke him out!" someone had hollered.

"Finish him!" yelled another.

When you get out of your tube, it seems, anything can happen. So I was a bit anxious to see what my current companions had in mind as we duck-walked our tubes out of the water and onto the first beach.

"Physical challenge!" yelled Jason, one of my young rugby team-mates. "Come on, let's do it. Physical challenge!"

The "physical challenge" was a recurring motif for this group of friends, a legacy from previous tubing trips and keggers. They would crop up throughout the rest of this outing too. They were contests, made up on the spot, pitting guys against guys, or girls against girls, for some feat of strength, coordination, or tolerance. First up was the crowd-pleasing tube joust. Jason and another guy each squeezed tubes around their waists, squared off, and charged at each other to collide tube to tube. The other guy went flying, Jason remained standing in his tube, and the group cheered their winner.

A few more rounds went down like this; then it was time for a "boat race," a drinking contest into which I was drafted. We formed four-man teams and lined up facing each other. The idea was for one man from each team to chug a beer as fast as possible, followed by the next man, and so on, in a race to see which team could progress down the line and back again first. My turn came up, and I choked. The foamy beer went in my mouth but somehow most of it just exploded from my nose. There was some booing from the sidelines. I staggered off to recover, wondering why these people didn't just funnel beers like civilized drinkers.

I was bent over, still trying to drain Miller Lite foam from my sinuses, when one of the guys from the winning team sidled over.

"So what's your name, man?" he asked, in a tone implying more questions would follow.

"I'm Ian."

"Cool. So, uh, how old are you anyway?" he immediately continued.

"Thirty-five."

"Whoa!" he blurted. "That's awesome!"

"Thanks," I said.

"Hey, if you want a beer, man, anytime, just check my cooler, okay?" he said, and sloshed off to the beached tubes.

* * *

I was in a contemplative mood, and drunk, when we returned to the river, so I decided to float on my own for a bit and chill out. But you can't stay alone for long on one of these river outings. Large clusters of friends break apart, some float into other clusters, and social cross-pollination is achieved. Whirling around on my own, enjoying the sight of the twenty-somethings in my group floating down above me, my tube gently rolled into another. I looked up to offer my apologies and found a middle-aged couple and their preteen son smiling at me from their own family flotilla. The parents were the first people I'd seen on the river all day who looked even older than me.

"Great day out here," I said.

"Oh yeah, we love it," said the dad. "Where are you from?"

"New Orleans."

"That's great. We're from here. Come out almost every weekend. Live for it," he said.

"Live for it,'" echoed the mom behind her sunglasses, sounding sincere.

Their kid kept smiling at me from his tube a few strokes away. What a nice family picture they made on their own float together, I thought. They seemed so tolerant amid the tattooed, bikinied party animals come to invade this low-key oasis in their backyard.

"Want a shot?" the dad asked.

Did I hear him right?

"Here," said the mom, peeling open a red Tupperware rectangle. It was filled with paper cups of blue Jello shots. I took one, and the mom and dad did the same. The son kept floating and smiling on his own. We said "cheers" and then all crushed the paper cups into our mouths, squishing down the unnamed jellied liquor.

"Lemme take that trash," said the mom, helpfully stowing my emptied cup back in the Tupperware.

I thanked them and let the current float me back toward the young rowdy bunch.

* * *

On we went, like huddles of inebriated water blossoms, for hours more. There were increasingly dangerous physical challenges. Someone lost her tube in the water and had to float on the lap of the guy she had been flirting with the entire time anyway. More sandwich fillings cruised past on their own faster currents, along with a steady, spiraling flow of empty beer cans and the occasional T-shirt, hat, or untended tube.

We turned a final corner and the end loomed ahead. We were back at Tiki Tubing, where employees stood on a low launch helping people out of their rings. The slick clay banks of the river shone honey-gold in the fading light of the midsummer evening, and looking back I could see tubers walking against the current, trying to backtrack upstream a bit to eke the most from these last minutes of the trip.

I paddled myself faster to the launch, which looked to me like this marathon's finish line. I couldn't wait to get out of the water, pull on dry socks, and begin first aid procedures for my sun-scorched belly. I was more than ready for this trip to end. It's like this every time I go tubing, even when the company doesn't make me look quite so elderly. I'm always glad when the trip is over, and part of me always thinks, slogging back onto dry land, that it will be my last tubing trip. But that must just be the influence of sunburn and drunken fatigue, because every summer, when someone calls with a tubing invitation, I find myself packing an ice chest to tow along behind me. Maybe someday I'll even pack a tub of Jello shots to share with middle-aged strangers along the float.

CHAPTER 9

THE SEARCH FOR SAND
Casting Off from Grand Isle

The distance straight across Louisiana at its widest point is about 250 miles. But let's say someone was to travel the state hugging every nook and cranny of its coastline. It's hard to imagine the reason why—maybe for an archaic geological survey, maybe under a sadistic form of alternative sentencing. But if someone had to do it, he'd have to travel more than 7,700 miles of tidal shoreline.

"Tidal shoreline" is a measurement that includes all the sounds, bays, islands, and other waterfront niches honeycombing a coast. Endlessly undulating Louisiana has an awful lot of it—more than twice that of California and more than all the New England states combined. If all those little coastal curves and bends were ironed into a straight line, Louisiana's tidal shoreline could cover the distance from Seattle to New Zealand.

It's a massive though tightly wound frontage along the warm Gulf Coast. Even accounting for the delta of the Mississippi River clouding the eastern corner with its muddy outflow, one might assume that 7,700 miles of subtropical Gulf Coast would give Louisiana many opportunities for great beaches. And if one planned a little summer getaway around such an assumption, without much prior research, one would not be the most popular person in the car during the long drive home. It turns out there are a few beaches in Louisiana, but they aren't for everyone.

Anglers line a pier on Grand Isle.

"I'm not going to just run in there so calm down," Antonia advised coolly from the waterline at Cypremort Point State Park, perched on Vermilion Bay in St. Mary Parish.

"Come on!" I pleaded, yelling from the water. "This is great!"

I was trying to sound sincere, but I might not have made the most convincing picture. I was about forty feet out from the beach, and the water was still so shallow that the only way I could actually get it to cover most of my body was to fall down and roll around. I'm sure I looked like a tide-stranded sea mammal lolling about there, calling to his mate. But Antonia is a Louisiana native, and she knew the summer water would be blood warm and loaded with brown grit. She would come for a swim, but she wasn't exactly bounding in.

But I had ripped into the bay like I was auditioning for a suntan lotion commercial. I was excited to finally discover a beach in Louisiana, and I was diligently trying to look past all of the ways in which it fell short of postcard status. Sometimes, this is what it takes to have a good time on a Louisiana beach.

* * *

Antonia and I had spent a June afternoon driving around the sugar country between New Iberia and Morgan City. While plotting the trip, I saw that just one detour off Highway 90 would lead us to Cypremort Point State Park. Admittedly, it was a long detour, leading down twenty miles of country road lined by not much besides waving sugarcane fields and colorfully named petrochemical facilities, like the Ivanhoe Carbon Black Plant, which produces an ingredient for car tires. I felt the trip was worth the wear on my own tires, however, because the promotional literature about Cypremort Point described it as one of the only car-accessible spots where people can get into Gulf waters between Grand Isle and Cameron—or basically from one end of Louisiana to the other. Cypremort Point actually juts into Vermilion Bay, a brackish body that opens into the Gulf not far away. But with so few Louisiana beaches around, I wasn't about to split hairs. On a long drive through Cajun country on a very hot day, I was thrilled by the prospect of getting to swim in the sea and soak up some beach time.

There is a community at Cypremort Point, but it's one of those Louisiana leisure towns with no commercial attractions for tourists—no shops to browse, no restaurants to visit, and no hotels in which to stay. Instead, fishing fanatics keep camps here for the benefit of direct boat access to the water and the clustered seclusion of staying way, way down a rural road no one else has much reason to travel. The road dead-ends at a small commercial shrimping harbor surrounded by camps and vacation homes jacked high up on pilings.

We finally made it to the state park and encountered a scene that was not exactly breathtaking but still was strikingly rare along Louisiana's long, curled coast. There, in a manmade cove of rock jetties, a manmade strip of sandy beach sat in the shape of a gentle crescent, where small waves lapped up to break on the sand and over the shiny backs of children playing by its edge.

I could not get into the water fast enough, and I nearly tripped over my sneakers in the hurry to get them off. Antonia was taking her time, the smart girl. I skipped to the water expecting to dive headlong in after a few paces. But after slogging through for a while, the water hadn't even come up to my knees, while my feet were already invisible under the coffee-colored water. The blue sheen I saw as we pulled into the park must have been a mirage of the reflected sky. This was good old Louisiana Gulf water—muddy, shallow, and warm. I plopped down, determined to get my back and hair wet, and as I rolled there, hollering to Antonia to join me, I could practically feel the heavy water filling the pockets of my shorts with floating sand.

* * *

There's a reason why most New Orleanians in search of some beach time just drive east to Mississippi or on to Alabama and the Florida panhandle. Along that route the sands grow increasingly white, the water becomes azure blue, and the coastline is liberally supplied with civilized amenities like condos, casinos, and tourist attractions. Back home, most of the Louisiana coastline is composed of muck, disintegrating marsh, and stark, delicate barrier islands which parallel the shore. The Mississippi River, the Atchafalaya River, and the innumerable bayous veining the state's southern extremities contribute to that gritty, cloudy nature of the water near the shore. And being so flat and malleable, all of it is bare to the ravages of storms. Along the whole coastline, there are only a handful of developed notches at all, and most of these are heavily industrialized support points for the offshore oil industry.

There are some good swimming beaches in Louisiana, but most of them are on freshwater lakes. What makes Louisiana's Gulf beaches worth the gas to get there, though, isn't swimming. Rather, it's the rare access they afford to the Gulf and the spoils of this state's untidy but gargantuan fecundity, which translates to loads and loads of fish and birds. For fishermen, for bird watchers, and for anyone who likes to spend time in remote, unlikely places, the beach kingdom of Grand Isle is Louisiana's end-of-the-rainbow destination.

Sitting due south from New Orleans at the end of a two-hour drive, Grand Isle measures eight miles long and, at its thickest, about a mile wide. It's the state's only inhabited barrier island, and it's home to Louisiana's largest and most popular beach.

I'd heard varied opinions about the place before I ever ventured down myself. On the one hand, my young neighbor Zack Reynolds had told stories about staying up all night with his French Quarter friends and driving down to Grand Isle to drink bloody Marys on the beach at sunrise and surf the waves of minor Gulf storms rolling in. It sounded quite romantically bohemian. The counterpoint came from my friend Jim Bartkus, father of three (at last count) and an economics professor in New Orleans.

"As far as beaches go, basically an unmitigated hell," he warned. "You spend all this time in the car, you get there, and it's this rock-hard sand with no shade and the sun is just killing you. Bugs everywhere. The water is warm and brown, and all you can see are oil rigs out in the water and they're really not very far away."

I think Jim's background in the dismal science gave him an appreciation for the opportunity cost invested in the two-hour drive from New Orleans to Grand Isle, which he could have expended to reach the first stretch of pretty Alabama beaches. But all his points still ring true. The beach is packed hard and collects a great deal of jetsam from industrial and recreational boats plying the nearby waters. Early settlers of Grand Isle may have collected driftwood and washed-up timbers from wrecked schooners, but today the beach is more likely to be decorated with sand-caught fishing nets and discarded plastic bins. Oil rigs are so close you can make out details of their super-structures from shore. The water is tepid in summer and it's always brown. There is no real town to explore, but rather clusters of camps and homes on stilts interrupted by a few bars and restaurants.

The island had an early turn as a bona fide resort area, though this met a tragic fate. An antebellum plantation on Grand Isle had been converted into a hotel in the 1860s, and in 1892 developer P. F. Herwig opened the Ocean Club Hotel, complete with 160 rooms, tennis courts, and a bowling alley. The very next season, in 1893, a hurricane that would later be called the Great October Storm swept ashore with cataclysmic consequences for the barrier islands. The hurricane killed some two thousand people. About half of these casualties were counted on Grand Isle's neighbor to the immediate west, Cheniere Caminada, which was practically wiped off the map.

There was plenty of devastation to go around, and the disaster had a chilling effect on Louisiana's barrier island tourism.

Many more hurricanes and lesser storms would follow, and while none exacted such a huge human toll, the predictable pounding has defined Grand Isle. Practically every house is raised high off the ground. On the bay side of the island, where most of the year-round residents live, small homes and trailers are hoisted to the height of surrounding oaks, making them all look like grownup tree forts.

But no one visits Grand Isle for the architecture, and it didn't take long during my first visit to figure out why so many people do make the trip. Every other road here seems to end with a boat launch, from which countless fishing craft set off for the bays north of the island and to the Gulf to the south. The beauty of Grand Isle, however, is that you don't even need a boat to feel like you're fishing from one.

Rolling onto the island, I found people fishing from old piers and from the stumps of retired bridges. All along the shore, people were surf casting into the water, walking the beach and jerking their poles to make their bait dance in the currents. They filled buckets and coolers with impressive catches of redfish and sea trout. I had come for a swim, but it turned out I would have been better off packing fishing tackle than a beach blanket. People were fishing from every edge of the island and coming away winners. That's when it struck me that Grand Isle isn't so much a beach community as it is a giant fishing boat, anchored (if tenuously) over a prime fishing spot with anglers lining its edges like fishermen at the gunwales.

* * *

Fish aren't the only abundance around Grand Isle, and while most visitors come packing fishing rods plenty of others arrive with binoculars and birding lists, bound for gentle, hands-off safaris of the Louisiana coast's resplendent avian inventory.

Grand Isle is situated along the Mississippi flyway, one of the world's great aerial paths for migratory birds. These are the routes chosen by birds for their annual travels between wintering areas in the south and breeding areas in the north, and the Mississippi flyway stretches from Alaska's Arctic coast, down the length of the continent, over the Gulf, and all the way south to Patagonia.

Though the journey seems daunting on a human scale, imagined from a bird's eye this Mississippi flyway has a lot of advantages. There are no mountains to get in the way, and the flyway has reliable navigational aids and abundant food sources thanks to the two great rivers marking this north-to-south course—the Mackenzie from the Arctic through Canada and the Mississippi for the rest of the route to the Gulf. Millions upon millions of birds cruise over Louisiana, funneled along this instinctual path of least resistance. And when they get here, the watery, reedy, open, snow-free, food-rich ecosystems of the Louisiana coast present ideal places to rest and refuel or to spend the whole winter.

During the twice-yearly migratory season, birds from all over the Americas practically pour onto Grand Isle. Many of these small birds will continue on to complete an incredible five-hundred-mile airborne journey across the Caribbean in the fall, and on their way back north in the spring Grand Isle and Louisiana's other barrier islands are often the first spots they find to land, rest, and eat. When the birds have to fight through heavy weather during these globetrotting feats of stamina, they plunge out of the sky in utter exhaustion, like triathletes collapsing at the finish tape.

Birders call it the "fallout," because so many of these birds appear to drop from the clouds, and Grand Isle hosts a festival for birders each spring when the island is teeming with so many recuperating birds.

The Nature Conservancy says only a meager 10 percent of the forest cover that once greeted these intrepid birds remains on Grand Isle, and the environmental advocacy group is trying to add to that sum with tiny but vital parcels of wooded land. Small as they are, these forest remnants still harbor an incredible volume and diversity of feathered friends. They cluster in the small, resilient stands of wind-whipped trees and brush that still green the slim island's center, and in the spring you can watch great flocks of them erupt from oaks and chinaberry trees like blasts of confetti. During one birding event in 2008, bird watchers identified 170 different winged species on the island in two days.

I thought about all this while driving back home from Grand Isle at sunset after that first visit. The trip from New Orleans may seem like a long trek just to swim in brown water, drop some bait in the water, and watch the doings of oil rigs. But I'll never see the beach here again without thinking how it must look to a tiny, wind-blown bird falling out of the sky toward some blessed rest and relaxation.

Chapter 10

CAPITOL IDEAS

Stalking the Halls of Power in Baton Rouge

River Road plantation homes usually rank first on the must-see list for architectural tourism in Louisiana. But the modern state capitol in Baton Rouge blows them all away. It is literally towering, a limestone-clad, art deco skyscraper stretching to thirty-four stories. That would be small potatoes in high-rise cities, but it dwarfs anything else on the Baton Rouge skyline, and since completion in 1932 it has reigned as America's tallest state capitol.

Inside, the halls and chambers are packed with outrageous detail. It is a glorifying temple to Louisiana, from the Soviet-scale statues of early state leaders to renderings of mineral wealth and agricultural plenty done in marble, exotic woods, and detailed grillwork. Depression-era craftsmanship is everywhere, in all its echoing, solid, smooth-gliding glory, and boldface symbolism was worked into the very corners and crannies of the building. Silhouettes of sugarcane and cotton were carved into limestone, and the noble pelican, wings outstretched to envelop her brood, a state emblem, appears in every conceivable detail. She's perched in the woodwork above vestibules. She's revealed on elevator doors as they slide closed. Grab a doorknob in the state capitol, and a pelican is likely to be right there embedded in the brass. There is something interesting and meaningful in this building at every turn.

The capitol is like a public art exhibit, free and open for visits from its citizen-owners and anyone else interested in poking around. It's

A robotic statue of Huey P. Long tells his own tale at the Old State Capitol.

also the focal point of a campus of impressive state buildings, like the Louisiana State Museum, opened in 2006, and historic sites, like the Pentagon Barracks, a one-time military post that dates to 1819 and is now used as apartments for legislators and as state office space. The skyscraper capitol's retired predecessor, called the Old State Capitol, sits less than a mile away and it is no slouch either. Built in 1850, this older building has some unforgettable architectural moments and is now home to a museum of political history.

But what I think makes the current Louisiana capitol such an interesting place to visit isn't its architecture or history so much as its ongoing role as stage for contemporary political theater. When the legislature is in session each spring, the building becomes an ornate playhouse, one stalked by a cast of living, breathing, back-slapping southern stereotypes of the sort Louisiana voters seem powerless to resist and by tragic bit players struggling for attention at the periphery with petitions and studies. You won't necessarily see good acting on the boards here, but the theatrical machinations are always compelling to watch, even if sometimes in the manner of a car wreck.

Louisiana travel is sometimes promoted as a chance for Americans to experience a foreign-seeming culture right here in our own country. But anyone from Louisiana looking for a deep dip into a realm of exotic folkways and customs, of dizzying differences, fascinating cultural artifacts, and queer mores need only visit the state capitol in Baton Rouge when the legislature is at work.

My most recent visit was on a late spring afternoon that happened to coincide with "Youth Day" at the capitol. Throughout the afternoon, groups of grade school kids wearing color-coordinated T-shirts noisily formed up to proceed from hall to hall under the eye of their chaperones. As I first walked up the broad fall of steps to the building's main entrance, I spied a group of children way up on the capitol's open-air, twenty-seventh-floor observation deck waving to people far below. I waved back and was craning to smile up at this future generation of Louisiana voters when something closer at hand caught my attention.

Just ahead, standing under a huge statue in honor of the state's early European settlers, was a thin, middle-aged man in shirt and tie cutting loose with a hot string of angry curses into his cell phone. He paid no mind to me—nor to the woman standing a few paces behind him, fiercely sucking down a cigarette—as he continued a monologue worthy of *Goodfellas* right there by the capitol's august main entrance.

"What the fuck? This motherfucker don't even know us, he don't even know us, and this motherfucker is bringing up this fucking shit?" the man said loud and steady, not shouting so much as spitting the words as he paced before the bank of brass doors. "He fucking don't even know us and he's fucking bringing in the governor on this? Fuck that. This motherfucker isn't getting any fucking traction on this one, fuck him!"

There are some interesting exhibits at the Museum of Political History at the Old State Capitol, and the modern capitol has a few of its own historic displays too. But this guy and his public blue streak was the living Louisiana political history I wanted to see. I could tell this would be a good visit.

* * *

Approaching Baton Rouge from the west, either on quick Interstate 10 or the older Highway 190 just to the north, you see the capitol rising in the distance like a column. You can drive toward it for a long time before it appears to grow any closer. There's no missing it, especially at night when its illuminated cupola shines like a lighthouse over the dark horizon.

The capitol was the pet project of the iconoclastic Louisiana politician Huey P. Long, who promised to build it during his campaign for governor in 1928. In its skyscraper design, you can read Louisiana's industrial ambitions rising from its plantation past or perhaps the soaring ego of Huey Long himself, whose legacy is forever tied to the place. Not only did he have it built; he was also assassinated inside its hall in 1935 while serving as a U.S. senator. He was laid to rest in a tomb sitting in the building's shadow. Still, I can't help but think the capitol's epic stature might also have something to do with the peripatetic history of Louisiana's government seat before Huey Long's skyscraper went up.

Throughout the nineteenth century, the capitol moved around so much you really couldn't blame citizens of that era if they didn't know just where to find it from one decade to the next. Since becoming a state in 1812, Louisiana has had thirteen different capitols in five different cities. The first six sites were in New Orleans, starting with the Cabildo, the old base of Spanish colonial rule that is today a state museum in the heart of the French Quarter. In 1830, state leaders decided New Orleans was too corrupt for their business and moved the capitol upriver to Donaldsonville, which they promptly deemed too boring. They moved the show back to New Orleans just a year later.

The capitol made it to Baton Rouge in 1850, when the building now known as the Old State Capitol was erected, and it might have had an uninterrupted tenure in that city if not for the Civil War. Once New Orleans surrendered to Union forces and it seemed clear Baton Rouge would fall next (which it did, a few weeks later), the state's Confederate government decamped to Opelousas. The St. Landry Parish Courthouse, which still stands, served as the wartime capitol in exile for about nine months before advancing federal troops forced another move. The next stop was Shreveport's original Caddo Parish Courthouse, now demolished, where the Confederate legislature held three sessions.

During Reconstruction, the capitol moved to New Orleans and stayed there for fifteen years but still managed to squeeze in another change of venue during that span. Finally, in 1882, it returned to Baton Rouge, where it has remained ever since, albeit in two different spots. It seems appropriate, then, that the current capitol building has the air of monumental permanence in its scale, in its lush details, and in its specific adulation of Louisiana heritage. And since its dedication in 1932, Louisiana government has enjoyed by far its longest stretch at the same address.

* * *

The Old State Capitol is an out-and-out tourist attraction, and well worth a visit, though many people who have never been still may recognize the ridicule tarred on it by no less a literary hand than Mark Twain's. In his 1883 memoir *Life on the Mississippi*, Twain described the Old State Capitol as a "little sham castle," and considered it evidence of the "debilitating influence" on southern culture perpetrated by the works of Sir Walter Scott with "their grotesque 'chivalry' doings and romantic juvenilities."

"It was Sir Walter that made every gentleman in the South a Major or a Colonel, or a General or a Judge, before the war; and it was he, also, that made these gentlemen value these bogus decorations," Twain wrote. "For it was he that created rank and caste down there, and also reverence for rank and caste, and pride and pleasure in them."

Twain linked the Scottish novelist's hugely popular tales of English feudalism, with all its pageantry and joisting, to a fixation among the South's antebellum ruling class on gallantry and valor. He wrote *Life on the Mississippi* when the nation was still filled with the Civil War's orphans and amputees, which might explain his ire toward what he saw as a symbol of prewar southern chauvinism. Now, though, with the remove of history, the Old State Capitol just seems like a grand and unusual building, a turreted, whitewashed citadel lined with arrow slits and stained-glass windows, something between a gothic Ivy League library and a Mormon temple.

Inside, the Old State Capitol's stunning architectural centerpiece is a broad, cast-iron spiral staircase. As I climbed it, my eyes were drawn up and irresistibly riveted to the kaleidoscopic bloom of a huge stained-glass dome overhead. The central iron mast of the staircase continued up to the dome, and then branched down like the arms of an umbrella carrying hundreds of small glass squares and arrowhead shapes in red, blue, purple, orange, and yellow. This constellation of color was reflected in mirrors around the open hall and played on the abundant polished woodwork and shiny iron fittings.

Louisiana's Museum of Political History occupies the building's former legislative halls and offices. It includes bits and pieces from a lot of state political history but primarily serves as a tribute to that history's foremost celebrity and lasting icon, Huey P. Long himself. It's hardly the only such memorial. There's an exhibit in the current state capitol marking the spot where he was fatally shot at age forty-two by Baton Rouge physician Carl A. Weiss. This assassin was promptly killed by Long's bodyguards a few feet away. Far to the north, in Long's hometown of Winnfield, Huey and his brother Earl—a later state governor, mental asylum inmate, and famous aficionado of Bourbon Street burlesque talent—are the star attractions for the unrelated Louisiana Political Museum. But the Old State Capitol is the place to see the animatronic Huey P. Long, a moving, winking statue that delivers recorded speeches, explains his old platforms, and trades jokes with the recorded, vintage voice of a radio announcer emanating from speakers throughout its exhibit hall, a former legislative conference room.

The lifelike robot is not merely convincing; it's downright unsettling. It was a slow afternoon when I visited, and I was alone in the exhibit room with this thing. Draped in an oversized suit and painted bronze all over, it looked like one of those human statue street performers. Most disorientating were the machine's persuasive eyes, which shone clear white from its smirking, metallic-colored face. I half thought I was being put on, that this statue would step down and shake my hand or goose me before some concealed film crew rushed out to say it would all appear on cable television soon.

Instead, animatronic Huey kept clicking and whirling away as I sat there in the empty room. When Long's recording started cycling through some repeat jokes—a trait not unknown to real live politicians—I decided to head upstairs. There, under the mottled light of the stained-glass dome, I found the "We the People . . ." exhibit, which used a series of storyboards to illustrate the basics of the democratic political process. One wall featured life-size stock photos of people identified individually as citizens, legislators, and lobbyists, complete with thought balloons explaining their roles. Their faces were left as open portals so visitors could stick their own heads through and act out that particular link in the legislative chain. This exhibit was sponsored by the Shell Oil Foundation, whose mother company has a titanic stake in the way Louisiana lawmakers might view such matters as, say, environmental legislation or taxation. I really wished a few Shell representatives were around on my visit. It would have been great to see them stick their heads through the portals and demonstrate how legislators and concerned citizens sound to their ears. Instead, I had to satisfy myself imagining the editor who parsed the text of these thought balloons.

"I am a professional lobbyist, though anyone who wants to help influence the legislature can be a lobbyist," read the balloon text above one neatly groomed but blank-faced figure. "I was hired by the citizen activist group to raise public awareness on the issue of taxes. I am setting up an appointment with a key legislator so he can learn how my group feels about the upcoming tax bill."

* * *

With such lessons fresh in mind, I headed over to the modern capitol building to see how it all might play out in real life. My visit came at the very end of the 2009 legislative session. The Louisiana budget called for spending about $30 billion in the next year. Some of that money was part of an extraordinary influx for rebuilding work after a string of hard hurricanes, starting with Katrina in 2005. But it didn't take a forensic auditor to deduce that in a state with about 4.4 million residents, a $30 billion budget had room for enterprise and ambition. As the mandated deadline of the session loomed just days away, things were getting tight for all the people who wanted a piece of this action.

I'm not suggesting every citizen who visits the capitol during the session is after a cut of taxpayer money. After all, the kids visiting for "Youth Day" were probably just as impressed by the observation deck as I had been when I ventured way up there for the bird's-eye view of the Mississippi River and the greater Baton Rouge area. But it seemed clear that many of the people I dodged and occasionally bumped into around the halls of power were there with a specific purpose in mind. They shared a look, whether they were buttonholing a legislator by the restroom door, passing a folded note to an aide, strategizing over a binder in the lobby, or staring into the blue glow of a smart phone screen. It was the look you see in news coverage of stock market trading floors, the look you see when flight information changes at the airport, and the look people can't repress while watching their home teams compete. It was the look of vested interest.

On the other hand, I'm sure I looked a bit bumbling. I was dressed like a tourist in jeans and short-sleeve shirt, and sweat was blooming through both garments after my hike up the majestic front stairs outside in the stunning June heat. I didn't have much of an itinerary and practically everyone around me did. Even the school kids were on a field trip schedule. I felt like a hick on his first visit to the airport being buffeted around by annoyed business travelers.

But I rather enjoyed the out-of-place feeling. It was like being on vacation while everyone else worked, and I settled into the corner for some prime people-watching. The capitol's main hall was a fantastic, shifting parade of striding lawmakers, some dressed in suits as white, fine, and gleaming as plantation columns and others in the sleek togs and flashy cufflinks of urban preachers or funeral directors. Ladies of a certain age filtered through, wearing conservative pantsuits and looking like members of an Elizabeth Dole fan club. There were hurrying aides, ulcerous lobbyists, and type-A citizens on missions. And there were also the people at the fringes. All over the building, convicts roamed in two-man teams, dressed in work shirts bearing their inmate numbers and the stencil of the Dixon Correctional Institution, a prison located a few towns up the highway. They waited with janitorial carts for elevators to arrive. They pushed brooms around the feet of unnoticing legislators standing stock still in the midst of cell phone conversations. They even ladled gravy and noodles from the hot lunch line in the capitol building's basement cafeteria, where a hand-printed sheet of paper posted by the cash register publicly dunned those lawmakers who owed for lunches on credit.

After a bit of this I moved to the senate chamber and found a seat on the sidelines just in time to catch a benediction delivered by a Baptist minister visiting from Lake Charles. He blessed everyone in the chamber in the name of Jesus and reminded us that "we're here on our business but it's really the Lord's business." Then we recited the Pledge of Allegiance, and the senate chamber fell back into chatter as the next chapter in the dispersal of $30 billion in taxpayer money got under way.

Citizens of Louisiana might wonder what they get for that kind of funding, but the numbers don't tell a very comforting story. C. B. Forgotston, a New Orleans attorney, gadfly, and one-man government watchdog, includes a feature on his Web site (forgotston.com) called the Louisiana Misery Index. This running list tracks national statistics where Louisiana is in the lead (murders per capita, the rate of children under age five on the brink of hunger) and where it rests at the bottom of the pile (funding for research, population gain). The press secretary for past governor Mike Foster, who presided over two very sleepy terms from 1996 to 2004, called the index "cynical to the point of being toxic." C. B. Forgotston took that as a compliment and uses the quote as an epigraph to this list.

Louisiana jockeys for somewhat higher or lower positions in these rankings with other states. But one area where the Bayou State reigns supreme is land loss. Coastal advocates say no landmass on the planet is disappearing faster than south Louisiana, thanks primarily to manmade causes. The state is dissolving—not figuratively or morally, but literally. If the coastal crisis were a military campaign, our armies would look worse than Napoleon's fleeing Russia as this front continually rolls back. The very symbols of the state engraved in the marble, brass, and woodwork of the Louisiana capitol are going away. Imagining what Louisiana will look like without its coastal wetlands, without large portions of Cajun country, without its fisheries and its current oil and gas dispositions, and without New Orleans seems to me a pretty shocking and macabre future. It's the very heart of the state's distinctive culture that is at stake, as well as the underpinnings of its economy and the cream of its natural heritage. Since Katrina, the crisis has garnered more attention in Louisiana and around the world, and while important work is proceeding in some corners it's clear that the issue has yet to claim an overriding lock of the doings of state government.

Of course, even Napoleon's field commanders must have attended to myriad matters as they were driven back over the steppe, and Louisiana lawmakers had a lot on their plates too when I visited during the 2009 legislative session. Some hot-button issues of the season included bills to reassure medical professionals that they were under no obligation to mention certain services, drugs, or information to their patients if doing so would conflict with their own religious convictions. Some lawmakers also devoted their energies to a bill ensuring that if an orphan is adopted by a gay couple, the state doesn't have to change the kid's birth certificate to acknowledge both new parents as a family unit.

Social issues are important to a lot of voters, as are the ways $30 billion of their money is divvyed around a diverse state. Still, as I sat at the edge of the senate chamber I couldn't help but fantasize about what might happen if we had some big, burly, seersucker-clad political powerhouse of the old school to whip the legislature and the state's apparatus into a single-minded focus on saving the actual, physical state of Louisiana from destruction. Lots of people around Louisiana are still in awe of Huey Long and his reputation for plowing over opposition to complete enormous public projects, like state highways, river crossings, and the very building in which I sat daydreaming. Maybe if his brassy, animatronic tribute over at the Old State Capitol was reprogrammed to recite folksy coastal restoration planks more people would listen. In fact, if a robotic Huey Long statue were wheeled around the state's campaign trail with nothing more to say than just that sort of message I'd be happy to help vote it into office.

CHAPTER 11

THE RIVER RATS

Riverine Pub Crawls Around Livingston Parish

We were roaring through swampy wilderness on Jet Skis, leaving grand rooster tails of white spray behind us and eating up the beautiful miles of still, bright, cypress-lined channel ahead. I was gripping the handles of the rear seat behind my host and brand-new friend Rob Arrington, a.k.a. River Rat Rob, as he veered around bends and shot through straightaways. Three other brand-new friends followed on their own Jet Skis, matching Rob's maneuvers. But otherwise we were all alone in the massive expanse of swamps, rivers, and channels between Lake Maurepas and Interstate 10.

The beautiful desolation of all these miles of water and cypress was so overwhelming that I almost lost track of our objective on this high-speed afternoon outing. But then a signpost up ahead pulled me back in. The sign was a simple plywood square nailed to the stump of a dead tree, with the stenciled words "Black Lake Club" and a spray-painted arrow pointing toward a turn in the onrushing channel. It proved the first in a series of such signs, staked out through the swamp like breadcrumbs, directing us right to the door of an eminently out-of-the-way barroom.

"See, they don't want you getting lost out here," Rob shouted to me over his shoulder as the Jet Ski boomed along.

A few miles ahead, we found the Black Lake Club sitting on the edge of another channel branching into the great watery maze of Livingston Parish. The club was a low, small, humble building with a big covered deck facing the water. It sported a letter board sign

En route to the next stop on a river rat bar crawl.

advertising drink specials and band schedules, not to any street traffic but rather to boaters like us cruising past.

I found it incredible that we had arrived at this remote bar by water, and that we were led to it to by signs plotted at the twists and turns of seemingly trackless swamp. What was more astonishing though was that the Black Lake Club was only one of sixteen bars we would visit that afternoon as Rob continued his tour of interconnected rivers and canals. We found all of them on Jet Skis over an unbroken, eighty-mile loop. While most are car accessible too, a few can only be reached by watercraft, and along the way we even dropped by a quiet, lovely country chapel that is similarly accessible only by river. Had we expanded the tour a bit further, we could have boosted the bar crawl to nearly thirty waterfront watering holes all within daytrip range.

This is Louisiana's most intense river rat country, and I was touring with its chief impresario, River Rat Rob.

* * *

There are college towns that don't have this kind of bar density, but here all of them were stretched along waterways and clustered in towns that barely register boldface mention on state highway maps. I had stared at and studied a detailed, sixty-four-page Louisiana road atlas for months while planning my trips around the state, going so far as to scan the thing on lunch breaks and in bed at night before sleep, looking for interesting curves and nooks to explore around south Louisiana. Places like Port Vincent, French Settlement, Warsaw Landing, Blind River, and the Tickfaw River seemed too obscure to warrant a trip, the towns appearing as little dots along country highways, the rivers just thin trickles of ink snaking through large patterns of the map's printed swamp symbols.

It turns out I was using the wrong map. I would have remained ignorant of this entire corner of riverine Louisiana had I not stumbled upon Rob Arrington's Web site (riverratrob.com), and found one of the highly specific maps he makes.

Rob, a friendly forty-something with a youthful bearing and a Deep South drawl, maintains automated sorting machinery for the postal service for a living. But his passion is to travel the inland waterways of Louisiana on his Jet Ski, and he carries a global positioning system to track down and document all the cool stuff along the way. These features include marinas, boat launches, bars, and restaurants, plus those important details like key forks in the myriad channels and go-slow idle zones often enforced by sheriffs' deputies in police boats. A few years back Rob started making maps from all this recon, superimposing his field data onto satellite images, surrounding the margins with ads from local businesses and distributing them to the boating public.

On summer weekends, and especially during the three-day holiday weekends, thousands of people crowd onto these waterways. They party-hop along the countless private camps and cabins lining the riverbanks, and they motor from the dock of one waterfront bar to another. Much like the bar stops on motorcycle runs, these establishments provide a framework for people to get together and cruise from place to place. Rob's maps are the guide to that framework, and he periodically leads his own runs with groups of two dozen or more Jet Ski riders and boaters following him to all the hotspots in the Amite River and Lake Maurepas area.

"A girl out here asked me, 'Rob, what are you, a genius or something? Did you make a lot of money with Web sites or invent something and now you just do this river stuff for fun?'" he told me, by way of explaining his consuming hobby. "Now I told her, 'No, darlin', I just do this out of sexual frustration.' Well, she just about fell out laughing at that one."

His self-deprecation aside, Rob's work making maps and leading runs has begun to stitch together a huge but largely fractured and parochial community of inland recreational mariners and the businesses there to serve them, including those many waterfront bars. In this way, he's an ambassador for a culture in which people proudly call themselves river rats.

"I've been on the river since I was four. Not this river, I only moved here a few years back, but wherever I've been it's always been near the water and I always do my best to get out on it. I think I've been a river rat all my life," Rob said. "But you know where this whole river rat thing started? It was the poorest of the poor, the white trash that had to live next to the river. No else wanted to because you'd get flooded all the time. But that's how this all started.

"There are river rats all over the place. Florida, Mississippi, Arkansas, Texas, Colorado, here. And no matter what, they all think they're the only river rats, like they made this up. Even here, you got people who think they're the only ones doing this, that their little area is the only place around for the river rat thing," he said.

Once a year, Rob holds a mass public party that is in effect a gathering of the river rat tribes. It's called the JAM (or Jonathan Arrington Memorial), in honor of his son, a talented guitarist and songwriter who died in 2006 at age twenty-four. Naturally, Rob hosts this bash on the water, usually at a place at the southwest edge of Lake Maurepas labeled on his maps as "The Sand Bar."

I assumed this was another waterfront bar. But it is actually a natural sandbar, a big, soft, barely submerged lump in the lake that proves a convenient spot where people can anchor boats and get out into the suddenly knee-deep water to party. All summer long, people converge on this sandbar, hop off their boats, and saunter around in their swim trunks and bikinis with koozie-sheathed drinks in hand, completely surrounded by the immense lake, chatting, waving, and flirting with whoever else made it out to this remote social spot.

Hundreds of boats cluster around the sandbar during Rob's JAM, bringing thousands of people. All of them stand in or float on water the entire time. There is a floating stage, complete with generators for the sound system, and Rob arranges a musical lineup as the sun-burned masses dance in the water.

* * *

I met Rob for the first time at Pirogue's Landing, a combination bar/boat launch on the Amite River in Port Vincent, a town about twenty miles southeast of Baton Rouge. He had agreed to take me around to some of the sights detailed on his map of the region, but the first hint of what was in store for the day was directly across the street at Fred's on the River. This was another, even larger, bar/boat launch/restaurant complex not fifty yards up the Amite. Already, there were options for where to launch and where to drink.

A few of Rob's friends and fellow Jet Ski enthusiasts joined us for this minirun, and I would ride along on his rear seat. I had never been on a Jet Ski before, so I received some rudimentary instructions and related commentary.

"It's a lot like riding bikes," Rob said, meaning motorcycles. "Keep yourself straight, don't lean into the curves or anything, and you'll do fine. We ride like Harley drivers do, and there's a respect thing there. The bad name with Jet Skis comes from the kids who ride them like the guys you see on the highway on those crotch rockets, weaving in and out of traffic and being reckless. Out here they're buzzing by boats, ignoring idle zones, just being dangerous, but you won't see people who know what they're doing riding like that."

With that, we snapped off down the Amite River, reaching a restrained cruising speed of about forty miles per hour through riverfront forests, then slowing when we approached long stretches of riverfront homes. Each property had its own dock or patio jutting into the water, and altogether these clusters of homes gave the image of a dense, watery village. Some of the buildings were old and disintegrating, looking like not much more than glorified laundry sheds, while others were as modern, solid, and expensive-looking as country club homes that happened to face a river rather than fairways.

As I always do while traveling through unfamiliar areas, I tried to imagine the line of work that maintained each house as we passed. This one with the tidy vinyl siding, screened gazebo, and family-friendly pontoon boat? I guessed refinery foreman or school principal. That mildewed trailer slumping in two opposing directions but with the gorgeous, multitiered deck terracing down to the river where a gleaming cigarette boat awaited action? I'd wager electrical contractor, mortgage originator, or career alcoholic with a family inheritance. And the house that looked more like a private yacht club than something built for a single family, the one with a hanger-sized boat garage and huge, onyx-coated windows? Either lottery proceeds or personal injury law.

There were some river homes that could fit in along any American subdivision and others that seemed plucked from a Mekong slum. There were even sites specially built for RVs with open-ended metal barns in which the rigs could be parked, with the dock just a few steps away.

My favorites, though, were the ones that looked like folk art constructions, places piled up with cool, rusty, and quizzical found objects. Their decks sported everything from antiquated saw blades to intact telephone booths, those twentieth century relics. And after losing count of the examples we passed, I am now convinced that half of the roadway signs that go missing in Louisiana end up tacked to poles and posts at riverfront camps.

The diversity of homes and camps is matched by the range of different watercraft plying these waters. There were speedboats that looked like they could make the run to Cuba and party barges that weren't much more than swimming rafts with outboard motors and cushioned seats. There were swamp-cruising airboats, more Jet Skis, bass boats, the occasional construction barge, and even a lifeboat from an ocean-going vessel, one of those plastic-capped, safety-orange boats designed to withstand rolling seas after a maritime disaster.

"Yeah, there's a guy who cruises all over in that thing, uses it in the boat parade we do out here at Mardi Gras," Rob said. "He can really get it going too. "

For every type of river camp and for every type of watercraft, there seemed to be a different type of waterfront bar and restaurant to match their speed and style. The waterfront bars accessible only by water tend to be the wildest. One is Blind River Bar—located deep inland at the intersection for several waterways—and another is Sun Buns—situated all the way across Lake Maurepas on the channel leading to Lake Pontchartrain. The most infamous, though, is the Prop Stop, just up the mouth of the Tickfaw River near the northwest corner of Lake Maurepas. With its two-story wooden deck, extensive use of driftwood and weathered cypress, and supremely isolated surroundings, the Prop Stop looks like a modern-day pirates' lair, and the buccaneer-on-spring-break atmosphere is stoked from every quarter. There's even an event coordinator on hand encouraging busty girls to compete in bikini hula-hoop derbies and wet T-shirt contests thinly veiled as water balloon tosses.

The bars closer to civilization are necessarily tamer, but take a lot of different forms. Some are like roadhouses facing the water while others are more like family restaurants with direct boat access. Many serve steaks and burgers and fried seafood, and some feature bands, especially outfits playing swamp pop, that neat mix of country, R&B, and Cajun-style music that cropped up in south Louisiana in the late 1950s and endures today at joints like these.

We came upon one place, PJ's Landing, near the very end of a four-mile offshoot called Bayou Francois. Airline Highway, the road that continues straight down to New Orleans and passes within blocks of my house, was just over the bank and down the road, but I had no sense of this proximity at the time. The bar seemed to materialize out of the dense cypress corridor of the bayou, and it looked like nothing more than beige metal storage building with a few windows cut in and a huge barbecue pit outside fashioned from a retired fuel oil tank. We tied up the Jet Skis, and I followed Rob inside to find an orderly, bright barroom filled with a friendly assortment of characters sipping cocktails from Styrofoam cups. It was about four o'clock in the afternoon on a Friday, and PJ's had a pretty solid crowd. One of Rob's maps was taped to the wall behind us and, along with a menu board listing pornographically named mixed drinks, this map constituted the better part of the room's décor. It seemed to occupy a place of honor in the bar. But none of the customers or the bartenders seemed to recognize or acknowledge him as we worked through a round of Bud Light and Crown Royal.

"This is the kind of place where no one's going to find you unless you want to be found," Rob said.

To me, that sounded like the whole river rat scene in a nutshell.

* * *

Wherever I went seeking out river rat culture, I felt like I had stumbled onto a part of Louisiana hidden in plain view. It turns out I had been cruising past glimpses of it for years—like the occasional waterfront bar/boat launch spotted by the side of a highway bridge or the rural speck on the map bypassed on the way from city to city—with no clue what was going down just around the bend. Once I started digging around, it was as if I'd suddenly discovered that my favorite neighborhood pub had been hosting raging parties in an unknown back room right under my nose.

There are a few small, more sedate river rat warrens closer to New Orleans at the edge of Lake Pontchartain, including one in Slidell to the east and another in Madisonville to the north. Up in Pointe Coupee Parish, near the pretty lake town of New Roads, river rats still converge on False River, which isn't a river but an oxbow lake. It was once part of the Mississippi, but this water body was left landlocked when the main stream forged a new path. Today it sits as a twenty-two-mile-long stretch of water, shaped like a boomerang, with a few bars and hundreds of private docks and patios lining each shore.

There used to be many more drinking spots and boat-run destinations along False River, but as waterfront land values climbed, many of these joints disappeared and modern homes and condo developments rose in their place. To Rob, it provides a cautionary example of what could happen along his beloved Amite River.

"Up on False River, it used to be you could go from bar to bar all day, get a beer at each one and end up having a whole case. Now, you do the same trip and you're lucky if you've had a six pack," he told me during our Jet Ski run.

If isolation is a good hedge against snazzy new development, though, the small but determined boat-to-bar scene around Lake Verret should enjoy a degree of longevity. This is another area I initially overlooked while studying my Louisiana maps, and to the unknowing motorist, fixated on roads, the area doesn't look very promising. The maps show a single road, Highway 70, cutting south from the Mississippi River toward Morgan City, surrounded on all sides by water and unmarked swaths of swamp, with lakes and bayous to the east and the levee-hemmed Atchafalaya Basin to the west. This highway—a two-lane road, really—runs through the towns of Pierre Part, then Belle River to the immediate west, and, after a stretch of about sixteen rural miles, Stephensville, a tiny cluster of camps and homes along a tangle of intersecting bayous. But as is so often the case in Louisiana, the vantage on this place from a boat is much different from the one you get from a car.

Just picture how Gros Marina looks to the families, the gangs of college kids, and the retired couples arriving by boat on a hot summer Saturday. The directions printed on the marina's business card read simply "six miles down Four Mile Bayou," and while, yes, that does sound like a line from a bad Cajun joke it still provides helpful coordinates for people showing up by boat. After a long stretch of cypress forest and slow-moving brown water, they come upon a low, metal-roofed building, surrounded by garage doors that are all thrown open to form a breezy pavilion filled with long, wooden tables and mounted deer trophies. There's a stage where swamp pop bands torch their way through bass-laden ballads while several successive generations of couples slow dance in their shorts and their camouflaged baseball caps. Beside the stage, in an enclosure that looks like it should be the sound booth, a matronly lady dishes out thick catfish courtbouillon for five bucks a plate.

As the band plays, guests duck into the combination bar/convenience store behind the stage for canned beer, frozen daiquiris, and such maritime conveniences as spark plugs and live bait. And after a spell some of the boaters head up the bayou again, past the docks of small fishing camps and onward to the next stop, Mosquitoes Bar, where they can dock again, get fresh drinks, and see who they might know hanging out in the barroom.

There are a few more waterfront bars in the Lake Verret area, including the Hook Up, right in the heart of Pierre Part, which is to say across the street from St. Joseph the Worker Catholic Church. Boats slide into the waters of Bayou Pierre Part from the Hook Up's launch under the shadow of the church's steeple, while inside the tiny joint the jukebox or DJ spins swamp pop tunes. Two miles down the street, the Spunky Monkey is like a modern sports bar that happens to double as a marina on Belle River.

Add to these places a profusion of landlocked bars—including the immense music club Stevie G's and the 1930s-vintage swamp pop dance hall the Rainbow Inn—and you have an impressive array of good-time destinations in these tiny and close-knit bayou communities. Camps line the lakes, recreational fisherman crisscross the fruitful waters, and everywhere kids cast lines from docks and piers. At sunset, I watched contentedly from the bank of Bayou Pierre Part as a father and daughter motored past in the family skiff, the girl waving to shirtless strangers outside a bar while the dad toasted them from afar with his own can of beer as he steered the outboard.

* * *

But it was back in the Amite River and Lake Maurepas area with Rob where I found the river rat habitat most prolific, and not just for the waterfront bar count. We were about halfway through our day, weaving around such colorfully named waterways as Bayou Secret, Tennessee Williams Canal, and Bayou Tent, when Rob delivered us to Our Lady of Blind River, a chapel situated miles from any road, much less a town. It looked like a very small barn with thick shingles and a short steeple. A broad dock lined with car tire bumpers faced Blind River, which provided the only access, and a collection of high-reaching cypress trees rose around it like pillars.

Our Lady of Blind River is the work of Bobby and Martha Deroche, and they maintain it with a loving hand. The door is always unlocked, and boaters are welcome to visit for some quiet time with the statue of the Virgin Mary, cloistered in a hollowed, varnished cypress trunk at the altar. No one was around on our visit, yet I still found a few blue votive candles flickering away in the corner.

Back on the Jet Skis after this quiet interlude, we were once again roaring through the swampy distance to the next stop, and again the beautiful natural scenes all around began to mesmerize. The water was so still and dark that the trees and dense growth along the banks were reflected flawlessly below. Cypress appeared to reach both up and down, and the clumps of hanging moss pointed their ragged fingers to the waterline from both directions. Dark herons and white egrets perching in the trees and balancing on floating logs heard us coming but simply stayed put, eyeing us stiffly as we cornered the bends.

The ever-vacillating Louisiana weather remained peaceful too—until the late afternoon, when it got ugly quick. We had pulled into a riverside marina and store called Thunder Bayou to refill the gas tank when I first felt a quickening in the air. The sky behind us remained bright, but all ahead low clouds loomed with purple menace. By the time we were ready to leave, the clerk was eyeing us warily.

"You're on Jet Skis? And which way are you headed?" she asked.

"Well, right into it. It'll be all right though, it's his first time on a Jet Ski," Rob said, pointing a thumb at me. "He'll be our good luck charm."

Our earlier companions had split for home while we were fueling up, but another one of Rob's Jet Ski friends, a lean, fiery woman named Kendall, joined us for the last eleven-mile stretch back to Pirogue's Landing where our trucks waited. As we set off, the clouds began to swirl, the water turned dark, and the wind picked up, making treetops by the canal swoosh and the neat canvas dock awnings flutter like flags. For a while, though, I believed Rob might be right about the good luck. We started riding up the Amite River Diversion Canal, a long straightaway lined with the most expensive-looking homes on the waters here, and while the clouds coursed overhead we felt no rain. We were making pretty good time, and the sky looked golden bright over the end of the canal we were chasing.

"Sometimes these things don't open up for a while, we might make it back okay," Rob called over his shoulder.

My career as clear-skies talisman came to a crashing halt just a minute or two later, however, as the first big raindrops arrived. They picked up as steadily as an opening faucet and soon the water all around us was roiling and jumping with splashes. Whenever we tried to drive fast, the rain hit our faces like hail. So we had to take it slow, chugging along as the water came down relentlessly.

"You're cruising with real river rats!" Kendall was yelling from her Jet Ski through the hammering rain. "This ain't like those girls out here on the party barges, coming out to the river and trying not to get wet!"

"Yeah, the see-and-be-seen crowd," Rob burbled through the water hitting our faces.

"This is when you know you're a river rat, when you love it so much you're out in this!" Kendall went on, excited, bouncing a little on her seat. We puttered on and I silently thought back to the orange lifeboat we'd passed so many miles ago. That would be nice and dry, I thought.

After about a half hour of this, the rain ceased, the birds resumed chirping in the forest on either side of us, and we found our last few miles of Amite River clear, flat, and all to ourselves. Rob and Kendall gunned it, and we zoomed back to Port Vincent.

We arrived at the boat launch soaked through, chilly, and ready for another beer. Ordering a round, I caught a glimpse of the three of us in the bar mirror, sitting there bedraggled, sunburned, and fatigued. We may have looked to all the world like drowned mice, but for my part, at least, I finally felt like a river rat.

CHAPTER 12

GONE FISHIN'

Chasing Bounty Inland and Offshore

I feel very proud about the outcome of my first offshore Louisiana fishing trip, and it's not because of the respectable catch I brought home. Rather, it's because on my very first outing into the Gulf of Mexico—my first brush with a passionate pursuit for countless Louisianians—I came away with a durable fish story about the one that got away. And I have a boatful of witnesses to back up the tale.

Like most good fish stories, this one started very early, with the predawn alarm buzzing much sooner than I thought necessary. Antonia groaned and swatted vaguely in the direction of the alarm, or perhaps my face. Sunrise was still hours away, but I had to meet my soon-to-be fishing brethren at 5 a.m., and as the greenest guy in the whole crew I certainly didn't want to be the one to show up late.

This trip was organized by my friend Mike Kerrigan in honor of our buddy Tim's fiftieth birthday. Tim's son, his brother, and an old college friend would all be along too, and Kerrigan had chartered a boat and a captain for a day on the Gulf. I knew these guys through our shared participation with the local rugby team, and to me they all were part of that work-hard, play-hard, do-the-right-thing mentality embodied by south Louisiana men at their best, guys who do well for themselves in their careers and are involved in their communities but make plenty of time for cutting loose.

"You have to look at fishing as another adjunct to the world of drinking," Kerrigan counseled as part of his invitation for me to join this outing. "You don't have to try all that hard to catch fish around

Fishing the "inside" water in a St. Bernard Parish marsh.

here, so what you have is a floating barroom with the opportunity to get that adrenalin pumping now and then when you reel something in."

So before dawn on a July day, we all rendezvoused and crossed the Mississippi River to pick up Highway 23. This is the narrow, two-lane road that runs seventy miles south of New Orleans and ends at the docks of the small fishing town of Venice, the jumping-off point to what partisans insist is some of the world's best sport fishing waters.

This rural highway also parallels the Mississippi River and passes quickly from suburban clutter around the fringes of New Orleans to green country stretches hemmed on both sides by high, even levees, which hold back the river on one side and on the other guard against water surging over the rapidly shrinking wetlands during tropical storms. We passed a refinery grinding away in the early morning darkness, a facility big enough to command its own rail spur. Next came towns like Port Sulphur, where ochre piles of sulfur trailings from a once-huge mining operation still litter the landscape. Then we were passing Empire and Buras, fishing villages where Croatian still lingers as lingua franca for the oyster trade and where Hurricane Katrina found its ground zero in 2005.

The white summer sun was finally up as we drove further south through Plaquemines Parish, and daylight revealed cattle grazing by the roadside and lone cows silhouetted nobly on the levee's crest. We were following the river to its very end, bound for one certain marina at an especially remote point in a state where most residents can count on finding reliably good fishing spots within just a few miles of home.

I had never experienced Venice, but so far I knew it was a long trip with a painfully early start and a potentially hefty bill at the end. I was told to bring along at least three hundred dollars in cash for my share of a six-man charter. As the miles ticked past, I began to wonder why we had chosen such a distant point of departure.

* * *

I'd been along for a fishing charter in Louisiana before, and it had seemed much easier and much cheaper than this outing. Of course, it was also an inland water fishing trip, which proves to have much different stripes from the offshore variety.

This earlier trip was organized as part of a friend's bachelor party weekend. We had to depart early then too, but not crazy-early. We left our city homes, took a few turns, got on a secondary highway, and within thirty minutes or so arrived at a small marina in St. Bernard Parish, the next jurisdiction downriver from New Orleans. I was startled by just how fast we went from familiar urban areas to prime Louisiana wetlands fishing grounds. The marina was crowded with idling pickup trucks, and guys were standing around eating donuts and cracking sunrise beers while small, dart-shaped bass boats and whalers slipped from trailers into the water. We found our charter captain, a friendly-looking, middle-aged man with a salt-and-pepper beard who wore the sort of billowing fishing shirt that is as common in St. Bernard Parish as pinstripes in London's financial district.

"Y'all can just call me Red Bone, everyone does," he said.

I felt this nickname boded well for us. In my starkly uninformed imagination of dockside ways, such handles were coveted and fought over by fishing guides working the same waters. If this guy was no good, he surely couldn't hold on to such a cool name. He'd be called Lil' Rob or Squirt or something else. But certainly not Red Bone. It sounded like an earned moniker.

I was so new to fishing that the smallest things impressed me deeply. For instance, whoever thought to build coolers right into the hull of the slick little fishing craft we boarded was, in my mind, a genius. One of the coolers was filled with shrimp, and it took Red Bone threading these onto hooks later in the morning for me to realize they were bait, and not lunch waiting to be prepared.

Four of us rocketed off on Red Bone's hotrod of a boat. We ran down a narrow channel through the marshland, and after a few turns we were in the thick of a beautiful morning scene. The sun was still low on the horizon, shining dusky orange above and holding down a band of cold purple at the horizon. The wetlands remained in dark shade, and they stretched on endlessly in every direction, looking like vast pastures in olive and heather hues.

In fact, this terrain is veined with interlocking passages, all narrow, often circling back on themselves, sometimes bottoming out, sometimes running deep and slow. From an airborne view, the whole area looks like a maze with countless possibilities and no clear answer. From our boat, just above the waterline, it seemed like one continuous series of twists and turns, interrupted here and there by open lakes. I didn't know yet if Red Bone would live up to his cool-sounding name and find us fish, but after a half hour of maneuvering this confusion of channels and marsh, I really hoped he could at least find our way home.

"All right," Red Bone called, throttling the boat down to a gentle glide, "let's try here."

"Here" was a patch of water, lined by the very low hedge of marsh grass in the near distance. Looking around, I could see nothing that clearly set it apart from any other potential stop over the past few miles. But this is where the captain's skills and experience come in. We hadn't just hired a guy with a boat and the willingness to get up early and drive us around the wetlands. The captain has to have a good idea of where in all this unmarked vastness to stop for a good shot at fish. We baited up with those delicious-looking shrimp and cast off. The four of us each assumed a spot around the boat, holding our rods out gingerly, not really sure what would happen next. It took a minute, but shortly our friend Stephen was hooting.

"I think I got one," he said, as his pole jerked radically toward the water.

We all watched as he reeled it in, and none of us more intently than Red Bone, who wanted to see what his chosen spot was delivering. It seemed big, and soon we saw a dark form just under the surface as Stephen brought it in.

"Aw! A cat," said Red Bone. "Don't worry about that one."

Stephen's fish broke the surface and was indeed a large, drippy-lipped catfish. I've probably eaten catfish more than any other sort of fish in my life, and I have no prejudices against it, but it was evidently not what we were after. Red Bone grasped the thing, took it off the hook and, without it ever even technically entering his boat, tossed it back into the water. Over the next few minutes our team hooked a few more catfish like this and, to my amateurish amazement, Red Bone kept throwing them back. They looked pretty impressive to me, though of course I was also impressed by the notion of a boat with built-in coolers. Moreover, they were all we seemed to be getting. If we didn't even keep the catfish, I thought, we could at least save some bait shrimp so we'd bring home something edible. Fortunately, Red Bone had other ideas.

"Lines up, boys, we're getting out of here," he called, and soon we were zooming off again.

We proceeded to an area I would call indistinguishable from any of the dozens of miles we'd already traversed, but which Red Bone called "a good hole." He idled the boat very close to the marshy bank, and explained that just below us was a deeper spot, a pool where swirling water had carved a submerged dip in the channel bed. It was just the type of spot to attract smaller fish, Red Bone said, which in turn are eaten by bigger fish, which of course were the fish we were after.

And they were there. Baited up again (don't think I wasn't keeping track of the shrimp count), we dropped our hooks and were soon rewarded with aggressive tugs. In quick succession, we each reeled in slim, long, beautiful trout. We were on, and we stayed on. Over the next few hours, Red Bone would scoot us from one area to the next, his selection and intuition always a mystery to me but always validated by more keepers. Little ones were tossed back to the water to grow up. We worked through the beers and muffuletta sandwiches we'd packed for the day, and those crafty coolers were gradually filled with our limit. The roster eventually read like the menu at a Creole restaurant: drum with thick, zigzag stripes, redfish practically begging to be grilled, speckled trout dotted with attractive black freckles. The boat coolers were impressive all on their own, but full they were downright inspiring. Soon, my fridge back in New Orleans—thirty miles and a world away—would look even better.

* * *

The prospect of bringing home some similar haul kept me from dozing off during the long drive down to Venice with Kerrigan. He'd given enough hints that I knew to expect a different type of outing, though just how different was still unclear.

"You need to bring an extra T-shirt," he told me earlier.

"Why?" I asked, taking the bait.

"Because we're going to reel in some big fuckers, okay? And when you get one of those up there in the boat, and you're ready to get your picture taken, you're going to want to hold it up against your chest, you know, really do it up to get that good picture. But it's big and it'll be bleeding all over you and getting its fish slime all over you. So you need to ditch that shirt after the picture and have another one with you, okay?"

I packed an extra shirt, and had visions of marlins mounted in fishing lodges. We finally arrived in Venice and met up with our captain, James Peters of Osprey Charters. He proved every inch the trim, sandy-blond, Croakie-wearing image of a guy who goes sport fishing for a living. Measured and knowledgeable, laid-back in conversation but intense and focused in action, he seemed like just the man to lead us on a big fish hunt. Later in the day I asked him how he got into the business.

"I started fishing as a kid, of course, and any job I ever had I just ended up spending whatever I made on fishing," James said. "But I learned it really doesn't matter how much you make, you can spend it all on fishing. If you make forty thousand dollars a year, you can spend all your money on fishing. If you make five hundred thousand, you can do it too, look at the boats out here."

The marina was indeed filled with all manner of recreational fishing craft, from modest whalers to vessels that looked ready to cross an ocean, plus boxy houseboats lashed to the docks like floating fishing camps. We loaded our boat, a wide-open, thirty-six-foot craft with a swoosh-shaped hull, and began heading out from the marina when the weather intervened. A storm had followed us all the way down Highway 23, and now the entire horizon behind us was a thick, low layer of flinty dark moving in with curling, surging motions. James parked the boat under a sort of drive-in boat garage by a series of waterfront condos and, after consulting a weather Web site on his laptop, told us to kill some time around Venice until we could gauge what Mother Nature had in store.

Venice, despite the picturesque name, is not a place to browse much. Like so many other end-of-the-road destinations in Louisiana, Venice is a utilitarian spot. It's more of a beachhead for its real purpose in support of offshore activities than the setting for anything that might happen dockside. It's battered too often by hurricanes and lesser storms for people to invest in substantial land-based commercial attractions, and the carnage of recent hurricanes was still plainly evident during this visit. We found blasted-out storefronts and concrete building slabs wiped clean. Everything standing, or rebuilt, seemed geared either to the offshore oil patch or sport fishing. We passed rebuilt motels and bunkhouses, a heliport ferrying offshore rig workers over the horizon, and streets named for their primary industrial patrons—Halliburton Road, Coast Guard Road, etc. Marinas, launches, and fuel docks lined the waterfront. Most buildings were blocky and raised up on pilings. Whether oil rig crews or fishing parties, people come to Venice to get out on the water and reap what nature provides off the Louisiana coast.

"There's not much majesty here," Kerrigan said as we drove around town. "But don't worry, there's plenty of bounty."

Finally the weather improved, James called with the all-clear, and off we went. We careened around a corner out of Venice, passing large, outbound Gulf trawlers, and then joined the main flow of the Mississippi River. We cruised out on the last few miles of the nation's mightiest waterway as it branched into its aptly named "bird's foot delta" and an area known as Head of Passes, where the titanic river forks into its final, divergent channels to the Gulf.

Our boat's huge, outboard engines kicked up a glorious trail of froth as we left oceangoing oil tankers in our wake. We passed Pilot Town, a hideout-like company camp, inaccessible by land, where the local pilots contracted to steer those giant ships up the treacherous river wait for their clients. A few miles later I spotted the South Pass Lighthouse. This white, skeletal tower is practically the only structure the hurricanes have left standing at Port Eads, an outpost marking the extreme southern tip of Louisiana and named for the engineering genius James Eads. He was the man who first devised jetties here in the 1870s that harnessed the scouring power of the river to clear channels of silt and keep the route open for steamers, enabling the Mississippi to connect the crops and products of the American heartland with the world. Those jetties were essentially levees, soon to be the favored tool to control the river elsewhere. That eventually the levee system would so thoroughly shackle the river that the coastline began collapsing around it is part of that bedeviling double-edged dynamic of trying to control the Mississippi.

Soon the last bits of the channel dribbled off into a thin string of earth, and finally we were out in the Gulf. Behind us, the flat, vulnerable Louisiana coast was a mere ribbon of green between the teal of the sea and the vast blue of the now-clear sky. With no geographic features, no buildings or immediate coastal development of any type, the shore quickly disappeared completely from view.

Ahead was open sea but also, paradoxically, our new and only landmarks: the gray silhouettes of oil rigs. They were spaced across the horizon as regular as pickets, with their stark legs, boxy upper works, and towers all distinguishable even from far off. James was driving us to some specific but invisible grid in the trackless spread of water between the shore and the rig line, and when he felt that we had arrived at that spot we got the word to bait up.

This was my very first attempt to hook a fish in open Gulf waters, and I was mentally settling in for a game of wait-and-see. I was in great company, standing in a handsome and very fast boat, now idling, surrounded by beautiful skies and calm waters. I thought I might open a beer and savor the moment, when—boom!—the tip of my fishing rod dove violently toward the water. My friends all began howling simultaneously. Within moments of each other, and within seconds of dropping our lines, we all had struck fish, and shortly we were each reeling large, fiercely fighting, stunned-looking red snappers through the surface and into the boat. It happened so quickly and in such close coordination that the whole thing felt choreographed. We each baited up again, dropped our lines, and then more were coming up, just as fast and easy. And, just as quickly, it dawned on me why the Louisiana coast is such a big deal for fishermen. The vistas may not be too grand, but Kerrigan was right about the bounty.

And then we were off again. James was flooring it toward some other unknown point in the distance, getting his boat to skip over the rippling Gulf at sixty miles per hour. We all found secure seating immediately. The wind at that speed in an open boat on the Gulf was enough to peel our ears back. T-shirts grew skin-tight, sunglasses were forced into nose flesh, and astronauts must have an easier time sipping Tang in orbit than I did trying to drink from my can of beer. Speed is big in the charter fishing game, James explained to me later, once we had stopped and we could actually hear each other speak. Big engines and fast boats mean the captain can get his clients to the good spots before other captains working the same areas, going on the same learned hunches. And you spend less time going from spot to spot when you can pound away at those nautical miles at highway speeds.

All of this horsepower rushed us toward a cluster of the oil rigs. Their industrial intricacies came into focus—the stacked decks and heavy cranes, the up-and-down network of yellow-painted catwalks and railings, the satellite dishes and dangling orange escape pods. A helicopter touched down on a landing pad above us as we skipped and bounced past.

The offshore engineering of prime interest on fishing trips, however, are the rigs' legs, the barnacled, elephantine-thick columns that extend deep below. While the BP disaster was a catastrophic example of the environmental menace these rigs can pose, fishermen have long known that the marine life growing on their columns creates incomparable fish habitat. In normal times, they function like artificial reefs. Throughout the rest of the day, James would keep us in close orbit to a succession of these rigs. We could look up to see men thudding along catwalks in heavy boots and hear the curt announcements over the rigs' public address systems.

Down below, rolling now on the waves and close enough almost to reach out and touch one rig's dented, deeply rusted legs, we were baiting up for what James promised would be amberjack, the day's main event.

"They call them reef donkeys," Kerrigan told me. "Big, tough fish and they'll fight you 'til the end."

Like the red snapper earlier in the day—and the drum and trout from my much earlier inshore fishing trip—this was a fish I knew well from New Orleans restaurant menus. This familiarity made me want to hook one all the more. It wasn't just some creature swimming around down in the unseen depths, but a recognizable entrée in waiting. Unlike with all those other fish, however, hooking an amberjack would prove the easy part, while reeling it in would be the challenge.

"Wrap this around you," James advised, handing over a belt with a rigid metal plate, which would hang like a flap of armor over the groin. It had a notch into which I fitted the largest fishing rod I have ever held, a heavy-duty number with a big, brass reel of thick line. Just how big were these amberjacks going to be?

"Probably thirty, forty pounds," James answered. "It's all in your form though. You'll do fine."

I was not aware that form was required for this trip, and I certainly didn't pack any in advance. But James and Kerrigan patiently explained the basic drill of hoisting the line up and then reeling in on the descent to eat up slack and draw the amberjack in.

"It's the same when we go after tuna," James said. "I have big guys come down here with huge arms, saying, 'Just get me to 'em, captain, I'll reel in the hundred-pounders.' And that fish will wear out all six guys on the trip, one after the other, and they still can't get it in. But then a ninety-pound woman will be out here with the right form and reel it right home by herself."

We weren't going after hundred-pound tuna, just forty-pound amberjack, but it did prove to be a real fight. Puttering in the shadow of a rig, I got one on the line almost as soon as I dropped the hook. I did my best with that form I'd just learned about—pulling back, leaning in. My forearm and lower back were soon aching, but I could see the silvery shape of the big fish shimmering just under the waves, and then it was up, flapping against the water and the boat hull and gasping through its tortured mouth. James took over, unhooked the fish and presented it to me.

Here it was, the money shot Kerrigan had prepped me for from the beginning, the trophy pose with the big, bright, still-living fish before a backdrop of open Gulf. I was Hemingway with a goofy straw hat, the Crocodile Hunter with a beer belly.

"Yeah, Ian!" my mates were chanting, clearly amused by my cherry-pop glee at winning this first big fish, succeeding in this first real physical effort to bring one in.

The camera was ready, and I took the fish.

"Hold him by the gills," Kerrigan called from starboard. "Get your hand right in there. Watch the mouth now."

I held the thing to my T-shirt, one hand near its tail, the other looking for some purchase under its gill flap. And then it all went wrong. The fish shook in frenzy, its slick, scaly body slipped on my sweating forearms, and off it bounced, first against my carefully provisioned T-shirt, next against the gunwales of the boat, and in an instant back into the water, all in a flash.

There was a stunned silence, during which I saw the freed fish darting off through the water, and then the boat erupted into laughter and howls.

"I knew it, you're a conservationist!" someone shouted from the bow.

"He's too soft! He couldn't go through with it!" yelled another.

There was no possible retort. I was posing with a big fish just a few feet away from the very cooler which should have taken it to dock, to James's fish-cutting table, and eventually to my grill at home.

But that day's luckiest amberjack slipped the noose and was back swimming again with a pierced lip and a new lease on life.

The ribbing died down, and James good-naturedly set me up for another try. This one came into the boat in much the same manner, though this time I used infinitely more care in the final stages. It was only the second live amberjack I had ever touched, but I doubt any other amberjack has ever been held tighter.

Chapter 13

LAFOURCHE THE LONG WAY

The World's "Longest Village Street" and Houma Headquarters

As Antonia and I drove down Highway 90 from New Orleans toward Bayou Lafourche, I felt the usual sparks of excitement that precede a trip to a new destination, and especially one with the promise of outdoor adventure. My father-in-law, Don Keller, is an avid kayaker, and nearly every year he takes part in a four-day group paddle and camping trip called Paddle Bayou Lafourche. Antonia and I decided to join him for the Saturday leg of this marathon journey, and I was eager to get out on the water and explore what I was sure would be interesting sights along the bayou route.

But it became clear very quickly on this trip that the mere presence of our group paddling Bayou Lafourche in canoes and kayaks was, in its own way, every bit as novel and noteworthy as anything we would spot from the water. Throughout the day, people on the bayou banks would alternately wave to us, snap our photos, cheer, stare bemusedly, and, in two cases, throw parties in our honor.

About forty minutes outside of New Orleans we met Don and about a hundred other intrepid paddlers at our preselected rendezvous spot. This was the Plaisance Fruit Stand, a roadside shack run by Cleveland and Virginia Plaisance between the towns of Thibodaux and Raceland. Cleveland and Virginia live directly across the street from their stand in a modest, white-paneled ranch house. The front of the house faces the bayou, and behind it a spread of farmland reaches back nearly to the horizon. There were people milling around everywhere, including easily identifiable paddlers in their outdoor

A grave in Plattenville, along Bayou Lafourche.

gear and a collection of people from around this rural area who had come by to join the party. Passing motorists honked their car horns, waved excitedly, and hooted out their windows.

A group of musicians played Cajun accordion, fiddle, drums, and guitar in the shade of the farm stand, and across the street the Plaisance family garage was filled with a buffet of aluminum pans and Tupperware containers holding alligator sauce piquant, jambalaya, potato salad, and enough desserts to stock a bake sale. We found Don, who explained that this entertaining stop had become an annual tradition along the four-day paddling route.

"The first year we ever did this trip, the idea was we would stop here and buy fruit and get some refreshments along the way, and it was all arranged ahead of time and they knew we were coming," Don said. "Well, the next year, the Plaisances said, 'It's not going to be about you all buying stuff, it's going to be about us having a party for you.' All their relatives and their friends cook all this food and bring it by, all for the love of people who come out to use their bayou like this."

After a portion of potato salad for Antonia and a few repeat servings of alligator sauce piquant for me, we prepped our borrowed canoe for departure. We found the bayou down a steep slope immediately behind the fruit stand, and a small crowd of the Plaisances' friends lined the high bank, sitting in folding chairs to watch us set off like spectators at a regatta. Most of them sat up there quietly smiling, though a few shouted encouragement from above.

"Good luck!" someone yelled.

"Thanks for doing this, God bless you!" called another.

Genuine hospitality is a well-practiced custom in south Louisiana. But there was something else behind the welcome and the interest on display here for the Paddle Bayou Lafourche group, though I hadn't quite figured out what it was as we paddled down the bayou's still, brown path.

* * *

It took Antonia and me a few minutes to reacquaint ourselves with the teamwork of tandem canoe paddling, by which I mean I steered us straight into the reedy banks time and again while Antonia was soon able to confirm that, yes, the canoe could survive a T-bone collision with another canoe. But at least there was no perceptible current to negotiate as we got situated, and Don eagerly shared paddling advice while he deftly circled our bobbling craft in his sleek kayak. When we weren't inadvertently exploring the reeds, the easygoing pace of the bayou also allowed us to admire our new surroundings at leisure.

I admit that for a long time I thought "bayou" and "swamp" were basically two different words for the same thing. Now I've learned that a swamp is an unmoving mass of stagnant water while a bayou usually just looks like an unmoving mass of stagnant water. When Byron Almquist led us around the moonlight canoe trip through Manchac, we covered swamps—which were dense with trees, dark, and barely navigable—and bayous—which were broader, lined with cypress, and strung with Spanish moss. Those bayous still looked pretty swampy to me.

But Bayou Lafourche is a different type of bayou. There were no swamp scenes here at all. Rather, Bayou Lafourche is like a small, dozing, tobacco-colored river sitting beneath high, thick banks with overhanging trees and piles of brush. Most striking of all though—especially for anyone mistakenly thinking he was headed for a cypress forest swamp tour—the bayou is bordered on each side by narrow but densely settled villages separated intermittently by the geometric divisions of neatly planted sugarcane fields. There is the occasional urbanized town, but development isn't so much intense as it is steady, marching in thin belts along either side of the bayou.

Bayou Lafourche ("the fork," in French) was named by European explorers who saw it prong off from the Mississippi River at modern-day Donaldsonville. From there, it wends a path roughly shadowing the Mississippi's southeastern course for seventy miles until, at the appropriately named town of Cut Off, it snaps south and continues down to empty into the Gulf near Port Fourchon and Grand Isle.

But as recently as seven hundred years ago, around the time Dante was writing *The Divine Comedy* in Europe, Bayou Lafourche was the main stream of the Mississippi River. Without modern levees, the Mississippi tends to fan around, with gravity and hydrology perpetually seeking steeper, more direct ways south. During Bayou Lafourche's shift as the main stream, soil deposits from normal seasonal flooding built up the land on either side, creating natural high ridges and spectacularly rich soil all along the way, just as the Mississippi did along its present course.

As European settlement accelerated in south Louisiana, farming and fishing communities developed along the bayou, clinging to the narrow bands of high ground. It was the continuity of this small-scale development that inspired New Orleans writer Harnett Kane to dub Bayou Lafourche "the longest village street in the world" in his 1943 book *The Bayous of Louisiana*.

Don and the other paddlers who committed to the multiday long haul of Paddle Bayou Lafourche started their journey in Donaldsonville on Thursday, and they would finish on Sunday at the industrial port and fishing town of Lockport, covering about half the bayou's total length by the end of it. Antonia and I would see only a portion of this route on Saturday, but on another occasion I did spend a day driving the length of Bayou Lafourche on Highway 1, which closely parallels its course. It took me more than four hours to make the trip from headwater to outlet, allowing time for a few stops along the way, and all the while I marveled at how well the old "longest village street" handle still fit.

The driving route took me from the riverfront refinery area around Donaldsonville past high sugar country and through small villages with ornate brick churches, like the mossy, gothic Christ Episcopal Church in Napoleonville and the Assumption Church in Plattenville, where a cemetery of raised crypts was surrounded by green walls of tall cane. Settlement remained tight and consistent between the towns too, with a mix of Acadian-style homes on brick piers and tumbledown clapboard cottages with rusted tin roofs. Many of them, humble and proud alike, had the most gorgeous, thickly developed live oaks erupting from their yards like dark lawn sculpture. Always, the bayou sat on one side, while fields stretched back behind the homes.

The bayou runs clear through Thibodaux, by far the largest town along its route. The water bisects downtown's orderly grid of pretty Victorian homes and passes along its impressively intact and coherent historic business district, where many bars and restaurants serve the crowd from nearby Nicholls State University.

The village pattern resumed again as I followed the bayou out of Thibodaux, and I passed a steady mix of homes and businesses, plus many small houses where lawn signs advertised business services offered on premises. One hand-painted plywood sign read "on-site oil change by grease monkeys" and another claimed "ironing done here," but it was the simple sign for Verdun's Meat Market near Raceland that made me stop to visit. The sign stood before what looked like a perfectly ordinary suburban house with a beige brick façade. But I pulled open the front door to find a gleaming white workroom where a woman in a blood-splotched apron greeted me with a quiet smile on her face, a large knife in one hand and a freshly trimmed rib eye in the other.

"We got Whole Foods meats at Wal-Mart prices," said the butcher, Anita Verdun, who continues the bayou-side business her father started here a generation back.

She said the grass-fed cattle for her inventory were grazed out back and that they were slaughtered on premises at this very old-fashioned butcher shop. When I ordered a few sirloin steaks, Anita asked me how thick I'd like them and then cut them before my eyes with her butcher saw. She wrapped these up in paper, along with a few links of garlic sausage. As usual, my compulsive habit of bringing an ice chest along for the drive paid off.

As the bayou continued south, its stream grew wider, and soon its banks were lined not just with homes and businesses but also with docks and large fishing boats and oil companies' metal-hulled service craft. Through the towns of Lockport, Cut Off, Larose, Galliano, and Golden Meadow the string of these trickle-thin villages formed an unbroken line of hulls, masts, docks, homes, and strip malls, plus signs for more curious home-based businesses, such as "Eliane's Tuxedo Service and Tomb Portraits." I stopped in Golden Meadow to admire the Holy Mary Shrine, an open-air, waterfront grotto to the Virgin, and then walked across the road to chat with a man who was pulling twenty-five-pound redfish out of the bayou and made it look as easy as scooping goldfish.

These "line villages" fell away for the last few miles of Highway 1 to Leeville, however, as erosion became extreme and the giant swooping bridge to Port Fourchon and Grand Isle began its ascent.

* * *

Along the entire drive of Bayou Lafourche the occasional roadside fishing interlude was the only sort of water recreation I found. Coeds at Nicholls hold canoe races on the bayou each October during homecoming week, but otherwise it seems that very few people access the region's ubiquitous waterway besides commercial fishermen and offshore crews headed to work. That's what made the spectacle of our hundred-plus canoes and kayaks setting off from the Plaisance Fruit Stand so unique, and, I learned, that was just the point of the outing.

The annual Paddle Bayou Lafourche trip is organized by the Barataria-Terrebonne National Estuary Program (BTNEP), a congressionally mandated conservation group. The canoe trip started in 2000 as an antilitter campaign, one based on the simple hope that if locals enjoyed and appreciated the bayou a little more they wouldn't toss quite so much garbage in it. The program quickly morphed, however, and now it serves as an awareness effort for the land loss crisis eating through the very estuary the agency was created to protect. Locals still participate, but now many of the people who sign up for the trip each year are outdoors enthusiasts visiting from around the world.

There are twenty-eight similar national estuary advocacy programs around the country, but none has such a big job as BTNEP. The local agency says the Barataria-Terrebonne region, which is nominally nourished by the fresh water and sediment carried by Bayou Lafourche, is disappearing at a rate faster than any other area, and it's a key fault line in Louisiana's overall coastal land loss crisis. BNTEP is among a host of regional organizations trying to marshal political muscle for the water-control policy changes needed to reverse that loss. So with the attitude that every little bit helps, they host this springtime paddle along Bayou Lafourche to give interested parties a personal perspective of the crisis.

It doesn't take much to visually demonstrate the extent of Louisiana land loss. Satellite images comparing the coast today with its condition just a few decades ago pack enough then-and-now punch to arouse astonishment and foreboding. Viewed from the air, the straight, linear hash work of oil and gas canals stands out clearly against the lacy, wandering patterns of natural bayous, and everywhere the coast looks frayed and blown out. Dark water has infiltrated deep against green wetlands, leaving skeletal outcroppings around the edges. It all looks alarmingly cancerous, like the infected lung diagrams used in anti-smoking ads.

BTNEP's paddling trip doesn't show this dramatic deterioration from the waterline, nor does it try to. Ground zero for the coastal crisis begins many miles beyond the range of the four-day trip Antonia's dad would complete, way down by Leeville and Port Fourchon. Anyway, from a boat the watery scene isn't all that dramatic unless you know what was there before. Louisiana fishermen often lament how many of their coastal navigation landmarks have disappeared in just a few years, leaving them occasionally disorientated in the waters they thought they knew by heart. But to someone bobbing around in a canoe the empty vistas might not make such an impact.

So instead of an end-of-the-line journey, BTNEP's paddling itinerary shows the culture and the places that are still relatively intact farther inland. In this way, paddlers bear witness to what may well vanish if water-control policy stays the present course.

* * *

Sometimes, a stretch of boardwalk dipping into a nature refuge is enough to help people appreciate a massive resource in their back-yard. To appreciate Bayou Lafourche in a new way, all I needed was twelve feet of plastic canoe hull and a paddle. As we departed the Plaisance family farm stand, we moved through a still, low gulch lined by pretty, lush, wild-growing water plants. We saw nicely landscaped backyards and looked up to see rooflines of bayou-side homes as we passed. Our colorful flotilla of canoes and kayaks whished along, and we continued under the low, timber and iron bridges that crossed the bayou at regular intervals. Floating green bouquets of hyacinth drifted beside us, and the whole of Bayou Lafourche ahead seemed like one slow and low watery path leading into a silvery horizon of clouds. The scene felt timeless, but things were once much different here.

Bayou Lafourche remained a potent force long after it lost its status as the Mississippi's mainstream. It certainly impressed the pioneering woman travel writer Catharine Cole (the pen name of Martha Field) when she took a steamboat trip down Bayou Lafourche in 1892. Her journey coincided with a time of high water, and she related to readers of her column in the New Orleans *Daily Picayune* newspaper that the bayou was "booming in its banks 17 feet above the level of the fields and country roads."

"The current is something tremendous," she wrote. "It sweeps along like a millrace. To ride over its surface high up in the air look-ing down on the earth-world as one may look out of a fifth story window, is indeed a curious experience."

I found her description quite curious myself after paddling along today's trickle-slow, ravinelike bayou. The reason for the dramatic change once again comes back to that vital but vexing pendulum swinging over south Louisiana: flood control.

The same historic flood cycles that built up the land beside Bayou Lafourche, enriched the soil, and made it the best place around to build and to farm also threatened that development with periodic inundation. It's the same dynamic that plays out on a larger scale along the Mississippi. The federal government's answer to protect communities along the Mississippi was to build the high, thick, modern levees in the 1930s that now so effectively steer the river down to the Gulf. For Bayou Lafourche, the answer was a dam built in 1905 at its headwaters in Donaldsonville.

By one estimate, Bayou Lafourche previously drew off 12 percent of the Mississippi River, or about forty thousand cubic feet per second. The dam closed that flow like a faucet. Thirteen years after Cole described practically flying over the Lafourche landscape above adjacent rooftops, the bayou was reduced to a gully. By 1955 a pumping station was built at the old bayou entrance in Donaldsonville to allow a controlled flow. Today, that flow is all of two hundred cubic feet per second, or at least two hundred times less than what Cole experienced during her 1892 flume ride.

The Mississippi levees keep most of the river's good, salt-fighting fresh water and precious, land-building sediment trucking on down to tumble into the open Gulf. The dam at Bayou Lafourche makes sure hardly any fresh water or sediment makes it to the suffocating marsh around Leeville and Port Fourchon. In both cases, the end result is the continued withering of Louisiana's wetlands.

BTNEP has been campaigning federal authorities to redesign the Bayou Lafourche dam structure to release more of the Mississippi's flow. In addition to building new coastal land, the group believes the added fresh water would stabilize the Lafourche region's drinking water supply. About three hundred thousand people draw their water from Bayou Lafourche, but the flow is so meager now that this source has become less than reliable in the southern areas as salt water creeps in from the Gulf.

The state began engineering studies for such a structure in 2006, though when I paddled the bayou three years later this paperwork had not made the bayou any less slow or low. The plans are of course reliant on federal approvals and federal funding, so the purpose of BTNEP's Paddle Bayou Lafourche has grown into a recruiting junket to convince anyone at all to become an ambassador for the coastal restoration cause.

"All the things you see and the people you meet on this paddle, these are the places and the culture that are threatened, this is what's all washing away," said Shelley Sparks, the BTNEP manager for our trip.

The music, the food, and the open-armed hospitality during the party at the Plaisance Fruit Stand showed one facet of Cajun bayou culture imperiled by Louisiana's environmental meltdown. Down the bayou we would encounter another part of the state's cultural equation that in many ways is the most vulnerable of all.

* * *

After a few hours of paddling past more pretty yards and beneath more low bridges we came to the Raceland home of Dr. Mike Robichaux, a local physician, and his wife, Brenda Dardar-Robichaux, who is chief of the United Houma Nation. This would be the last stop of the day, so we landed our boats, and the whole group of paddlers stretched their legs and backs and headed across the road and to the broad, oak-lined lawn of the Robichaux house.

There was a lot of activity outside the big, two-story, contemporary house. Men were prepping a huge, cast-iron cauldron in which they would cook an al fresco jambalaya for the entire paddling crew, while at another outdoor cooking area women were making traditional Houma fry bread, which are puffy disks of fried dough. A little closer to the house, a few Houma craftswomen had arrayed displays of jewelry, including many pieces made from the armored, spade-shaped scales of the big, toothy, fearsome local garfish. Across the lawn, people were assembling tents under a canopy of spreading oaks. The Robichauxs were throwing this party for the Paddle Bayou Lafourche crowd, our second fete of the day. Those paddlers continuing the trip on Sunday would spend the night camping on their property, which also doubles as the nerve center for the entire United Houma Nation.

When we thanked Brenda for her spectacular hospitality, she brushed it off and explained how happy she was that this group of travelers was interested in the area's land loss struggle and her people's plight because of it.

"The people on this trip are the kind of people we need, they're people who will see this and understand what is happening and they'll tell our story," she said.

The eighteen-thousand-member United Houma Nation is the largest Indian tribe in Louisiana, but the Houma don't get much recognition, and especially not the type they most desperately want. Though Louisiana recognizes the United Houma Nation, the federal Bureau of Indian Affairs does not, and that means no Houma-governed reservation lands and no federal money for social programs. The Houma have sought official Indian status from the government since 1979, and Brenda continues the effort to explain and interpret her people's story for federal officials.

The name Baton Rouge is a reference to red-painted poles that seventeenth-century French explorers found by the riverside at the site of the future state capital. These poles marked the border of Houma hunting territory, and at the time the tribe was spread throughout these relatively dry upriver areas. But as waves of European settlers arrived the Houma were pushed farther and successively farther from these coveted agricultural lands. Eventually, they ended up along the sodden periphery of Lafourche and Terrebonne parishes, and today most members of the United Houma Nation reside in the deepest bayou country.

The Houma tribe was not terribly bellicose in the days of early European settlement and expansion. Since there were no big battles with Europeans there were no treaties to end hostilities and thus no early documentation of their tribal identity. Further, they long ago traded their native language for French, and there was widespread intermarriage and family building between Houma and European people.

Brenda said one of the most frustrating factors standing against Houma recognition is the distance between communities the tribe claims when counting its members. Many Houma people live in tiny communities and settlements spread across southeast Louisiana. But Brenda argues that these areas only seem far apart to people trying to travel between them by car. Since being pushed to Louisiana's fringe, the Houma evolved a lifestyle to make a living from these watery surroundings. Many Houma support themselves as fishermen and plenty still get around by boat.

"We could not get them to understand," she said, referring to federal officials. "We offered to take them by boat and show them how our people traditionally connected, how the bayous tie all these communities together much more closely and much faster than the roads and highways. But they wouldn't go."

Of course, this traditional lifestyle on the edge of the water now puts the Houma people on the frontlines of coastal land loss. Race-land, where Brenda lives, is a very small town along the state high-way between Morgan City and New Orleans, yet it is a metropolis and consumer's dream compared with the settlements where many Houma people live farther down the bayou, places like Pointe-aux-Chenes, Dulac, and Isle de Jean Charles. When storms come, these are also among the most exposed and vulnerable spots on the dis-solving Louisiana map.

After Hurricane Katrina hit the region, more than eight thousand of the Houma people were displaced, and finding them again was an especially desperate effort. Even if the federal government won't recognize the tribe, it seems segregationists had them pegged for a long time. Houma people were barred from regular state schooling until the 1960s. As a result, illiteracy remains pervasive among their older generations and many of the tribe's elders speak only French. This was not a good formula for maneuvering the bureaucracies of disaster relief, insurance, and state recovery programs after Katrina, that web of paperwork and automated call center loops that drove the most educated and analytical in south Louisiana to frustrated tears. A full year after the storm, Brenda could not account for nearly one in five Houma people displaced by the hurricane. Many remain officially unaccounted for still, though she believes these people are living in the bordering states of Texas, Arkansas, and Mississippi, waiting to see what will become of south Louisiana.

As a group, the Houma are among the poorest and least educated people in the state. They have no official federal identity. They were driven from their original homeland, and their adopted homeland is being eaten away at the steady, ceaseless pace of rust because no one in power has figured out how to restore the ruined Louisiana coast in a hurry.

In the year after Katrina, the Robichauxs hosted countless teams of college students who had volunteered to canvass the area and deliver aid packages of clothing and food to the far-flung pockets of Houma families that had returned to sort through the wreckage. The students slept in tents on their lawn under their oaks and feasted from the Robichaux camp kitchen at night. When our happy flotilla of Paddle Bayou Lafourche canoes and kayaks pulled up to their home, we received the same welcome and hospitality. That wasn't because we did anything special for their people. It was just because we thought enough about their bayou to get on the water and explore it.

Since that canoe outing I've crossed Bayou Lafourche many times and driven along its banks on my way to other travel destinations around the region. But after that paddling trip down the bayou, and after that night at the Houma headquarters, I can never again see the waterway as a mere line on the map.

Part II
WEST OF THE ATCHAFALAYA

Dancers and ceiling fans spin at the Black Pot Festival & Cookoff.

CHAPTER 14

CAST-IRON CAJUN CULTURE
Acadian Journeys and Jam Sessions

It's one thing to value tradition, to applaud efforts to preserve regional ethnic customs, and to generally respect your cultural forbearers. And it's quite another to be in the midst of a swirling manifestation of Acadian folkways in south Louisiana and be utterly turned on.

This was how I felt one October night standing at the edge of the thumping, bouncing plywood dance floor in an open-air, barnlike pavilion on the outskirts of Lafayette. I was listening to the Red Stick Ramblers whale away on stage with singer Linzay Young crooning French lyrics I couldn't begin to follow, and I was watching beautiful, smiling women in print dresses, pigtails, and cowboy boots dance close with lean young men under whipping ceiling fans. I'm not sure if my mouth was agape, but certainly my eyes were wide open.

Yes, it's one thing to appreciate tradition and it's another to feel it bumping through the tight points in your circulatory system, making you feel alive and eager to participate, which is just what these kinds of Cajun cultural close encounters always do to me.

I finished the beer I was clutching as one Ramblers song ended, and I found a dance partner as the next tune began, which was as easy as offering my palm to a stranger as if to shake hands. When the band's two fiddles hit again, I was clumsily but enthusiastically shuffling my way around the dance floor, along with a few hundred people for whom such scenes are just another example of home-grown fun on a Saturday night.

This was the climax of the South Louisiana Black Pot Festival & Cookoff, a weekend of dancing, drinking, cooking, eating, camping, and jamming with a tight-knit group of Cajun, zydeco, and bluegrass musicians, along with their friends, their families, and a smattering of awestruck onlookers, like me. The setting was the Acadian Village, a menagerie of vintage Cajun cottages and barns arranged around a little white chapel and a meandering bayou. This model village is run as a folk life museum and tourist attraction, but during the Black Pot Festival no exhibit placards, no artifact guides, and no costumed reenactors were necessary to convey the region's heritage. The modern rendition was plain to see on the stage, around the dance floor, and in the campsites later on in the night.

The whole event was the creation of a group of twenty-somethings from the local roots music scene, led by Linzay Young, fellow Red Stick Ramblers player Glenn Fields, and Jillian Johnson. The Red Stick Ramblers, a five-man outfit playing a mix of Cajun, gypsy jazz, and western swing, happens to be one of my favorite bands, while Jillian is the singer of her own band, the Figs, a charmingly cheeky all-girl group playing vintage string band sounds. This seems like promising DNA for a roots music festival to have at its conception, and they and their friends recruited a roster of like-minded bands and diverse performers from around the region to take part. What helps make the Black Pot stand out amongst so many other, much larger musical festivals, however, happens away from the stage.

The festival got started in 2006, and it was still quite small and intimate when I first found it in 2008, with about twenty-two hundred people attending over the course of two days and two nights. It seemed like most of them knew each other. But even for someone like me, rolling in without introduction, the festival had so many opportunities for interaction that it felt more like a big social gathering than a commercial enterprise or even a cultural showcase. Many musicians and festival attendees camped on the grounds for the duration, and together they created an after-hours party of impromptu jam sessions around their campfires long after the scheduled performances wrapped up. The next morning, some of these people became cook-off contestants and broke out their well-seasoned cast-iron skillets and Dutch ovens—the festival's namesake "black pots"—to start prepping an outrageously delicious catalogue of gumbos, stews, jambalayas and fricassees under tailgating tents. They spooned out samples for the cook-off judges, and then they shared generously with anyone who cared to try their entries. I cared very much.

*   *   *

Like most Louisiana festivals, the Black Pot is an all-ages affair, and I watched many young children, preteens, high school kids, and people who looked like their grandparents dancing and socializing there. What I found so distinguishing about Black Pot, though, was the youthful energy spiking the air here. If folk festivals sometimes have a nostalgic feel, or the purposeful solemnity of preservation, this one had the vigor and boy-meets-girl tension of a culture very much in active use.

The Red Stick Ramblers tour widely, and I was a big fan of their music long before I started really exploring south Louisiana. But prior to discovering what the Ramblers and their contemporaries have going on, my impression of Cajun music was tragically pigeon-holed to the creaking stuff you hear in the background at some New Orleans gift shops or the tunes that automatically light up when you visit swamp tour Web sites. It was hokey, gray, and distant, and though that impression wasn't fair I just didn't know any better.

The Ramblers helped lift the veil. This band formed in 1999 when its founding members were enrolled together at LSU in Baton Rouge. They built their first fan base playing at college bars for college crowds, and when they started getting gigs in New Orleans they turned up at the music clubs my friends and I frequented. Their sound was traditional, but their shows were flat-out hot. Who were these crazy young Cajun guys, we wondered? Who were these guys, sounding so good, playing fiddles and upright bass and steel guitar, dressing sharp in coats and ties, drinking hard and making all of our New Orleans girls want to dance? I immediately admired them, and considered them a harbinger of some new wave revival of fading Cajun roots.

Once I started traveling the Acadiana region though, I saw more and more examples of how people of different generations were united by their ideas of a fun time on a Saturday night rather than separated by them, and how this dynamic worked through their music. The Ramblers were not so much a revival as the natural succession of community traditions transmitted between generations in Acadiana. Eventually, Linzay Young helped clue me in.

"The thing is, everyone's living it. There's really no generation gap. Sure, young people still go to Lafayette to go clubbing and do all that, but then they always return to hunting and fishing, going to the Cajun dance, being with their families and doing all the things we do here, they always come back to it, and music and food are always right there, you can't miss it. So there's always been an undercurrent of young musicians picking it up and carrying it on," he told me.

"The Cajuns are a tough people. They've been through a lot through their history. There's an expression 'lâche pas,' which means 'don't let go,' and that's how people embrace our culture here. They hold on," he said.

The Cajuns—or Acadians, more properly—have had to hold on for a long time. The tale of how they wound up in Louisiana to cultivate what shines today as one of America's most intense and durable subcultures is one caught up in global politics, diaspora, reunion, and an ongoing tug of war between tradition and assimilation. There are a lot of points in the Cajun story where they could have slid under. But they didn't let go.

*　*　*

The roots of today's Cajuns go back to the religious warfare that raged between Catholics and Protestants across northern France in the late sixteenth century. Dr. Carl Brasseaux, an Acadian historian and director of the Center for Louisiana Studies at the University of Louisiana at Lafayette, writes in his book *French, Cajun, Creole, Houma* that the common people of the region "had to be constantly on guard against marauding bands of religious fanatics, foraging mercenaries and brigands capitalizing upon the breakdown of local law enforcement."

Naturally, they grew mighty sick of this, and some saw France's nascent New World territories as a chance to start a new life. They began shipping off for the colony of Acadia (L'Acadie, to the French) on the Bay of Fundy in modern-day Canada in 1632, not long after the first Pilgrim settlements were gaining footholds in New England to the south. This rugged, coastal Acadia was an unfamiliar land, but these pioneers were at least surrounded by a lot of familiar faces. Dr. Brasseaux estimates that up to 70 percent of the original Acadian settlers came from one single estate in the Pitou Province of France. From its very roots, Cajun culture was marked by extraordinary group cohesion.

They cultivated lands and for the next century evolved their own agrarian culture in an isolated outpost on the north Atlantic coast, far from the internecine strife that continued to roil France. They had much more contact with the local Micmac Indians than the European world they had left behind. But international politics eventually caught up with the Acadians, as they had come to be known.

Britain acquired their territory from France through treaties to end the War of Spanish Succession in 1713. Acadia was renamed Nova Scotia (Latin for New Scotland) and two decades of uneasy negotiations began between British colonial administrators and their new, French-speaking subjects. In 1755, while England and France were once again fighting each other around the globe in the Seven Years' War, the British military decided to settle the matter of the Acadians. Red Coats rounded up as many of the settlers as possible, razed their villages, and pressed the suddenly dispossessed refugees into ships for uncertain exile. What's remembered by Cajuns today as "Le Grand Dérangement," or the great upheaval, had begun.

Some of the exiles were spread around other British colonies, some were shipped to internment camps in Britain itself and others were returned to France, where, after a century of Acadian pioneer culture overseas, they must have felt quite out of place. The rough transport and years of displacement that followed were catastrophic for the Acadian people, and at the time France and Spain accused Britain, their perpetual enemy, of genocide.

"It was their version of the final solution," Dr. Brasseaux said of the British, during an interview. "At least half the Acadian population died during that time, and it took two generations for their numbers to return to what they were in 1755."

After nearly a decade, however, the first ships of Acadians arrived in Louisiana, beginning in 1764 with a boat carrying just twenty men, women, and children representing four families. They were followed the next year by nearly two hundred Acadians, including Joseph Broussard, the resistance leader known as Beausoleil. More were fast behind them. Their first villages were along the Mississippi River upstream from New Orleans. Other Acadian settlements appeared along the bayous on the western side of the Atchafalaya River, beginning at a French military post on Bayou Teche called Attakapas, which later became the town of St. Martinville. Hardships continued as these new pioneers tried to establish homesteads in a jungly, ferociously hot land. By the end of the first summer, nearly three dozen of the Attakapas settlers had died of fever, including Beausoleil himself.

The Louisiana colony was essentially bankrupt at the time. But officials were eager to populate the area, and so they encouraged the Acadians to stay along the Teche by allowing them to take over land grants previously given to French military officers. It was a meager start, but the survivors of deportation, exile, and frontier rigors were finally building a new Acadia for themselves. In 1766, Jean-Baptiste Semer, age eighteen, wrote to his father, who was still exiled in France, explaining that a "person who wants to devote himself to property and make an effort will be comfortably off in a few years. It is an immense country; you can come here boldly with my dear mother and all the other Acadian families. They will always be better off than in France."

It was the sort of news the scattered Acadians were pining to hear, and thousands more would soon beat a path to Louisiana.

* * *

Visitors to Acadiana can dig into the details and pathos of this story, and catch a few doses of photogenic cultural mythology, during a quick visit to St. Martinville. Built around the large square of St. Martin de Tours Catholic Church, which claims the honor of "Mother Church of Acadiana," the small, bayou town has become a repository for the Acadian tribal memory. Its attractions include one site for education, another for photo opportunities, and a third for remembrance.

The main educational resource is the Longfellow-Evangeline State Historic Site, which was opened as Louisiana's first state park in 1934. It includes historic Cajun buildings and a museum with exhibits explaining the Acadian diaspora and reunion in Louisiana.

What I had heard so much about, however, was the photo op, the Evangeline Oak, and that was my first stop when I visited in the middle of a summer Saturday. The Evangeline Oak grows in a tiny park by the bayou and behind St. Martin de Tours. It's pretty, with thick, twisting limbs and a bushy dome of dark green leaves, though it's not extraordinary all on its own. What makes it perhaps the most photographed tree in Louisiana is its connection to Henry Wadsworth Longfellow's 1847 epic poem *Evangeline*. This fictional tale concerns a young Acadian woman, Evangeline, separated from her betrothed Gabrielle during Le Grand Dérangement. The poem was immensely popular in its day, and like a lot of other hits it inspired a number of spin-offs and reinterpretations. One of these was a 1907 novel by St. Martinville's own Judge Felix Voorhies in which Evangeline is reunited with Gabrielle under an oak by Bayou Teche only to learn he has found another love. She goes mad with grief. Even though things didn't end well for this Evangeline, her character has been held up by generations of Acadians as a symbol of cultural fidelity, and her namesake tree has become a tourist attraction.

I dutifully snapped a few pictures and continued along a short bayou boardwalk to the Acadian Memorial, a cultural center and secular shrine to difficult history, family lineage, and ancestral hopes. Examining the educational tributes inside, I got the sense that the memorial might be for modern-day Cajuns what the Ellis Island museum is for descendants of later American immigrants. Inside, a richly detailed painted mural stretching thirty feet long pictures some of the first Acadians to arrive in Louisiana, including the hero Beausoleil and the young Jean-Baptiste Semer. Across the hall, a collection of tall plaques bears the names of the three thousand earliest documented Acadian refugees. I watched a mother lift up her young son so he could get a good look at the bronze lettering above his head.

"See, that's us, Arceneaux," she told him. "See how they spelled it different? We got the x at the end later, you see?"

* * *

While Cajun culture thrives in south Louisiana today, it wasn't always so venerated. The twentieth-century American urge toward assimilation took a heavy toll, and in the push for increased literacy at the beginning of the 1900s the Cajun French language was trampled. In 1921, Louisiana effectively prohibited students and teachers from using any language but English in the classroom. Generations of Cajuns were taught that speaking French was a sign of ignorance. Cajun tour guides, waitresses, and shopkeepers of a certain generation all have shared stories with me about being punished for speaking French as they grew up. There were powerful economic motivations to ditch French as well. For instance, when the oil business came to town, it was run by people from Texas and Arkansas. Cajun farmers found they could make much more money working as roughnecks, provided they could speak English and communicate with the new bosses.

It's hard to say just when the turning point occurred after decades of cultural deterioration. One popular story maintains that Acadian soldiers who had served as frontline interpreters in France during World War II returned home with new pride and respect for the language they were taught to disregard, and that these veterans began digging into their heritage anew. But when I asked Dr. Brasseaux about this he dismissed it as an overblown tale.

"If that was true, the culture wouldn't have been on the brink of extinction in the 1960s," he said. "I think it had more to do with a backlash, with people just having had enough of the denigration and being sick of the self-loathing."

Whatever its spark, by 1968 the state government recognized the cultural revival then under way by creating the Council for the Development of French in Louisiana, or CODOFIL, which was tasked with preserving Acadian culture. In 1974, CODOFIL hosted the first incarnation of an annual autumn cultural celebration that today goes down in Lafayette under the name Festivals Acadiens et Creoles.

The intergenerational transfer of Cajun culture happens on hunting trips and at fishing camps, in kitchens and campsites, at music jams, in horse stables, during Mardi Gras, and at family gatherings, from weddings to funerals. That's where the deep fermentation happens. But for the traveler, a good festival like the Black Pot or the Festivals Acadiens et Creoles is a chance to watch it all bubble over the top. While plenty of visitors turn up, these festivals are attended primarily by locals from Acadiana communities. I am convinced that watching people who share a heritage party together gives a pretty good read on their living culture. After all, what you choose to do with your leisure time and how you part with disposable income says something about what you value and desire. Above it all, though, these events are just so much fun. I was starved for some Louisiana fun the first time I made it to Festivals Acadiens et Creoles, which was in the fall of 2005 just a few weeks after Hurricane Katrina.

* * *

I fled New Orleans before the storm hit and would spend two months marooned in Baton Rouge before I made it back to my destroyed neighborhood to begin rebuilding. I had been living in a motel room for about a month when I heard Festivals Acadiens et Creoles (then called simply Festivals Acadiens) was happening less than an hour's drive down the highway. I decided it was time for a break, and I was hardly alone. The Katrina levee failures all but emptied New Orleans and scattered its people about the country. Many were staying in Lafayette or, like me, in places within easy driving distance, and after weeks of watching from afar as cable news documented the agony of our city we were dazed, depleted, and itching for an excuse to let loose a little.

Immediately after arriving at the festival grounds in Lafayette's Girard Park, I began spotting friends and familiar faces from New Orleans. Together there in the grass between music stages and food booths we hugged, backslapped, and stifled a few tears we didn't think we had left in the tank. We had been feeling like refugees since the flood, and these Lafayette festival grounds had become an unplanned reunion site. In the emotion of the day, I couldn't help but feel some special affinity with that year's Festivals Acadiens programming theme, which commemorated 2005 as the 250th anniversary of Le Grand Dérangement.

As usual, admission to the Festivals Acadiens was free, the Francophone-centric music was glorious, the cans of beer were inexpensive and ice cold. The food, with its main ingredients of crawfish, shrimp and pork manipulated into about sixty different varieties of handheld meals, was righteous. And, that year, the crowd was filled with New Orleanians letting go of their many worries on a dance floor made of grass and dirt.

The pulling, rhythmic sounds of Cajun music and driving beat of zydeco demand dancing with a partner, and wherever these types of music are being performed a dancing partner is never hard to find. At the first notes of each song at the festival, people reached out for hands and found them—the hands of friends, spouses, strangers—and together they moved into the mass of dancing couples.

A man danced with his toddler son held on his shoulder, both of them bare-chested in the heat and wearing matching bandanas on their brows. A woman in denim shorts who looked about my mother's age shook her skinny white legs in a fun dance with a portly black man wearing farmer's overalls, Ray-Ban sunglasses, and a straw hat. A father danced with his two blond-haired, grade- school daughters in a triangular waltz. Kids were bopping everywhere, dancing in the dirt and racing around the crowded festival grounds like giggling sprites in a forest of adult legs.

The day was exceptionally hot, so I greeted a bank of dark clouds overhead with relief. The main stage featured another of my favorite Cajun bands, the Lost Bayou Ramblers. This band takes no prisoners. They sing in French, with Cajun accordion and fiddle leading the way, but they also swagger like rockabilly studs with a highly charged sound and a stage presence to match. The bassist, Alan Lafleur, is known to climb up on his large, sturdy instrument and balance on it like a surfboard as he continues playing while the crowd cheers him on. This approach has been known to baffle audiences when the band hits the national folk festival circuit, where people might have more conventional expectations for a Cajun act. But the Lost Bayou Ramblers are the kind of band you want on stage when the rain starts falling on an outdoor crowd. This was no time for a waltz, and as the rain picked up so did the tempo of their music. Puddles formed in the grass and dirt and people danced right through them, splashing muddy water up their legs as they juggled cans of beer with the hands of their dancing partners and slicked their hair back from smiling eyes. I did not exactly forget about Katrina during all this, but I was very pleasantly distracted for a while as we danced, drank, and hollered in the rain.

* * *

You don't need to visit Acadiana during the fall and spring festival seasons to experience today's Cajun music. This sound is the foundation for a lively nightlife, and the music calendars for bars and dancehalls in the region routinely feature the best-known names beside the up-and-comers. My favorite such spot in Lafayette is the Blue Moon Saloon, possibly because I tend to get carried away when I'm in the heat of this scene and the Blue Moon Saloon doubles as a guesthouse. I can get carried as far away as I want and then carry myself to bed a few paces from the dance floor.

The Blue Moon itself looks like a cape-style house that would be at home in any Massachusetts suburb. Inside, it's cut into a series of guestrooms. There's a shared kitchen and showers down the hall, making the place feel like a Bohemian hostel, though with more comfortable beds and a noble if not too fussy stab at décor. In the rear, a covered, wooden deck that clearly grew by spurts and spans serves as the dancehall, and as show time approaches it fills to bursting. Antonia and I visited one spring weekend, and we arrived to find the place already crammed with a friendly Saturday night crowd dancing under blue and red lights. We squeezed in and danced together while the band, the Pine Leaf Boys, ripped into fiddle and accordion music and set everyone on the deck moving in tight, two-step fashion.

"I love that we're staying here, it's like we live at the bar!" Antonia yelled, once the appeal of having a hired room within steps of the dance floor became clear. After a day of driving, after a Lafayette seafood dinner earlier that night, and after a few more hours of dancing, we walked exhaustedly from the crowded deck, across the

Blue Moon's deserted kitchen and turned in for the night as the Pine Leaf Boys kept the young Cajun night owls dancing for hours more.

When this local roots music fuels a party, the party tends to carry on. At the Black Pot Festival in particular there seemed to be no end to the music or the partying. The official programming of Cajun music and zydeco wrapped up at about midnight, and the crowd filtered through the dark Acadian Village and its bayou-clustered cottages. About half of the people drove away, while the other half returned to their campsites and began digging around for things in their tents and RVs. Phase two of the night was just starting, and I could hear the tuning sounds of countless acoustic instruments everywhere as people warmed up for the after party.

I strolled the irregular paths that separated campsites, following my ear from one jam to the next and sometimes just trailing groups of players as they traveled around like troubadours looking for collaborators. Christmas lights and festive lanterns were strung along the outstretched awnings of campers, making them look like the cheerful entrances to clustered bars in some honky-tonk dream. Another campsite was lit by candles set inside mason jars, and their orange, flickering light played on the shiny undersides of a pair of fiddles played by two girls. These fiddlers watched each other and alternated the lead while young men and women sat around them on a ring of ice chests and camp chairs. Some just listened, others sang along when the tunes called for lyrics. Suddenly an accordion joined the fiddles as another little musical band arrived at the circle, slipping in from a dark passage between parked RVs. In a moment, the whole candlelit gathering was singing in French, and I watched as four friends sitting close on a tailgate swayed into each other and bellowed as if doing a karaoke send-up of a Queen anthem, rocking the truck on its axles.

When I called it a night a while later, my tent wasn't as comfortable as the bed at the Blue Moon Saloon, and I didn't have Antonia with me, but it still felt as fun as living at the bar. I'm supremely grateful the Cajuns live up to their "lâche pas" motto. I would never let go of this culture either.

Chapter 15

HORSING AROUND ACADIANA

Of Jockeys, Knights, and Racetracks in the Rough

It was a crisp Sunday in October when three of us traveling from New Orleans arrived in a broad field in Ville Platte to find signs of a vigorous afternoon of tailgating in full swing. The grassy spread was packed with pickups and RVs. People holding beers and big plastic cocktail cups strolled from one group to the next, visiting friends who were hanging out under sun canopies and within roped-off perimeters by the side of their vehicles. Smoked meats hit portable grills and the aroma hung everywhere. LSU sports banners flew from RV antennas and radios crackled with eager AM-band commentary.

But the event that had brought us out here was something closer to feudal Europe than the football gridiron. We had come to this town at the northern reaches of Acadiana for the Louisiana Tournoi, a fascinating local tradition melding medieval anachronism, the region's enduring horse culture, and the insatiable impulse in south Louisiana to build a party around events and public gatherings of any sort at all.

The stars of the day were not quarterbacks or coaches. The stars here were men dressed in knight costumes, mounted on horseback, and equipped with sharp, short wooden lances. Over the course of the afternoon, these men would race each other to see who could spear the most brass rings in the least amount of time in a thundering competition fueled both by deep heritage and light beer.

I traveled here with my brother-in-law Donald Keller and his wife, Sarah Bailly, and we bounced their Jetta over deep ruts in the field

A contestant prepares for a heat at Ville Platte's Louisiana Tournoi.

to add one little foreign auto link to the chain of pickups and RVs parked around this temporary racing ring. We tuned in the radio commentators to catch some precompetition color.

"Well, how about that Boyd Landreneau? He was our champion last year, you like him this year, maybe do it again?" said one of the announcers.

"Oh yeah, we'll be looking for him," said another. "But it's a shame Jody Fontenot won't be here today. Had a little farm accident, so still nursing that, but he won the two years before that and back in '03 too. So there's a void there. We'll see who steps up today."

The excitement was building, though we didn't know quite what to expect at our first Tournoi. We made the nearly three-hour drive out here based on a tale I had heard from a New Orleans friend who grew up in Ville Platte. It was a story that involved horses, lances, knights, armor, beer, and smoked sausage, but not too many specifics about how they all came together.

Before our trip I gleaned that the event was part of the Louisiana Cotton Festival. I read that there would be a parade downtown before the crowd moved to a nearby industrial park for "the running of the Louisiana Tournoi." The local story holds that the Tournoi, or tournament, is a transplanted vestige of jousting competitions from the days of French knights and kings. Rather than tilt at each other in the jousting ring, today's local horsemen use their lances to try to capture seven brass rings suspended from a succession of wooden scaffolds as they race around the half-moon track in timed heats. The rewards are bragging rights as the year's Tournoi Champion and membership on a panel of past champions who select the Tournoi Queen each year from the ranks of eligible young women.

* * *

We arrived in Ville Platte just in time for the parade, which made its way down the town's small, single-story cluster of shops and offices. This procession had the standard features of most small-town Louisiana parades, beginning with various officials and dignitaries cruising past in convertibles and public safety vehicles, followed by flatbeds filled with kids from church groups and school clubs waving and tossing bits of candy to the thin but steady line of onlookers along the street. Next up was the float of visiting festival queens, a collection of rosy young royalty from towns across Louisiana. As part of the duties, girls anointed with the honor of representing their hometowns as festival queens traditionally tour the harvest festivals in other communities during the year of their reign. This float was a menagerie of pretty young women symbolizing their towns' delicious wildlife or most famous dishes. So we waved to Miss Cracklin's, the Crawfish Queen, the Duck Festival Queen, Miss Etouffee, and a dozen or so others all wearing their gowns, crowns, and sashes, smiling brightly and clasping metal support brackets as a tractor pulled their float down Main Street.

Naturally, Ville Platte's own Tournoi Queen, selected by champions the year before, was a center of attention. She was conveyed on a horse and followed by her Knights of Cotton, the twenty or so contestants of the upcoming Tournoi. They were all clad in costumes of silver fabric armor and black capes and they rode mounts draped with crimson saddlecloths. They clopped along at a stately pace, waved to the spectators, joked with each other behind their sunglasses, and looked delightfully incongruous before all the down-town signs for insurance brokers and take-out restaurants.

The riders' costumes and medieval theme are part of some glee-fully embraced role playing, though the Tournoi is no renaissance fair or gothic fantasy fest. These riders had earned their spots on the day's roster through successive rounds of competition held earlier in the year, and the contest that would follow the downtown parade represented the championship bout in a tradition entwined specifi-cally with Ville Platte heritage.

* * *

According to the town's official history, one of its first citizens was Marcellin Garand, a retired adjutant major from Napoleon's Con-tinental Army. He immigrated to Louisiana late in the eighteenth century and acquired one of the earliest land grants in Ville Platte. If his surviving portrait hanging in the Ville Platte City Hall is a fair measure, the major was keen to borrow some luster from his for-mer boss. Pictured in his military coat and brassy epaulets, he looks wan and grave, as if imperial decisions would see his attention just as soon as his portrait artist finally wrapped things up. His hand is even tucked into his white, buttoned vest, in a pose familiar from the most famous portraits of the French emperor himself.

The story of the Tournoi maintains that Major Garand was a stu-dent of the old chivalric traditions of feudal France and that he set up the local version as a sporting event in his new home. Tournoi his-torians believe the early contests were very popular, drawing specta-tors by buggy and horseback from all over the region. But these meets faded into obscurity sometime in the 1880s, which the Tournoi his-tory blames partially on the rise of such novel amusements as base-ball. Community leaders decided to revive the tradition for a Fourth of July celebration in 1948, however, and two very old men who remem-bered the contests from their youth advised on how it should be oper-ated, right down to the ball held after the races to pick the event's queen. It's been run every year since, and once Ville Platte started its Cotton Festival in the 1950s the Tournoi championship became part of the town's overall autumn harvest celebrations. In a little mingling of traditions, the seven brass rings the knights aim for on their turns around the track now represent the seven enemies of cotton, which anyone from cotton country should be able to recite on demand as being flood, drought, boll weevil, bollworm, silk, rayon, and nylon.

Like so many regional Louisiana customs, this one remains vibrant because everyone involved makes sure that, in addition to being a tradition, it is a really fun time. The ball following the races is now a BYOB affair of wheeled coolers, country music dancing, and exhausted but merry Tournoi knights and their families throwing down at the Ville Platte civic center. And while the races themselves looked fiercely competitive, the pressure to perform didn't seem to keep any of the knights from partying between heats.

Once Donald, Sarah, and I parked and collected our bearings, we set off to wander the tailgating scene for a while. We visited a concessions tent where the local sheriff's office sold canned beers from a cooler and smoked sausage from a grill. Thus provisioned we joined a steady flow of people in purple and gold LSU sportswear and camouflage sweatshirts for a circuit of the grounds. The track itself was little more than a groove worn into the turf of the field, and its sidelines were defined by a solid line of tailgating tents and clusters of people sitting in folding camp chairs. Race officials sat at the center of the track under a tent, and an ambulance was standing by, and together that was about the extent of visible Tournoi management. After the event, the whole Tournoi scene could be folded down, packed up, and rolled out, and the field of competition would be completely empty once again.

Knights and their mounts had arrived in their own horse trailers, which were parked by the side of the track to form makeshift stables. I sidled up to a small group of riders who were sucking down beers and comparing observations on the results of the first heat. I approached one knight who was idling high above me on his horse.

"So what's it take to be good at the Tournoi?" I asked him.

"Well, I tell you what it takes," he said in a thoughtful tone, looking over my head and toward the track. "You need to train that horse, yes you do, and you need to train your liver too, boy, see?"

The other knights by the horse trailer started busting up at that line and we all swigged down a little more beer. While these riders warmed up their livers, others warmed up their horses in the make-shift infield, trotting them around with their lances pointed toward the sky like flagpoles. A bugle blare announced the next rider's turn, and he approached the starting line. An official gave the signal and off he went, whipping around the half-moon track with a wake of dust flying off the horse's hooves. Approaching each of the seven scaffolds, he raised his lance to shoulder level like a rifle, pointed it toward the ring dangling ahead, and an instant later the crowd either cheered to the sound of the brass clanging onto his lance or groaned in unison if he sailed wide. By the end of the lap he had five of the seven rings stacked on his lance and a smile on his face. Officials read scores through a public address system, the radio announcers kept issuing updates for the folks listening at home or through the radios of their trucks parked around the ring, and others in the tailgating crowd marked their favored knights' progress on the crib sheets provided in their official Tournoi programs. Then a bugle blared again, the next rider approached, and in a moment all eyes were on the galloping hooves, flashing silver tunic, and speeding lance.

* * *

The costumes and feudal trappings of the Tournoi sure seem different, but at its heart the event draws from a widespread horse culture in south Louisiana, one that has spawned some interesting travel destinations and even led a few locals to the highest levels of praise and glory in the sport of kings. This culture is the reason sportswriters around the country commonly refer to south Louisiana as the "cradle of jockeys," and that reputation is backed up by some championship stats.

Calvin Borel, a native of the small bayou town of Catahoula, won the Kentucky Derby in 2007 and again in 2009 and 2010. Kent Desormeaux of Maurice won in 1998, 2000, and 2008, and he set the current record for the most wins in a single year when he rode to victory 598 times in 1989. New Iberia native Eddie Delahoussaye won the Kentucky Derby in 1982 and 1983 and racked up close to 6,400 other wins before retiring in 2002. There's Ronald Ardoin of Carencro, Ray Sibille of Sunset, guys like Curt Bourque, Randy Romero, and Shane Sellers, all from Erath, Robby Albarado of Lafayette, and many others who are heralded in horseracing circles as part of a winning tradition of "Cajun jockeys."

But these men share more than their Cajun heritage. They grew up working horses, starting as early as age five in Borel's case. They learned about horses "from the hoof to the ear," as some of them say, and they had plenty of opportunities to ride them and race them competitively long before their contemporaries from other regions could get such experience.

"We can get off a horse and know exactly what was wrong with him," Kent Desormeaux said in a 2007 interview with sportswriters. "That means a lot to a trainer. We wrapped bandages and groomed them and rode them in match races before we were ten years old."

Those "match races" were held at bush tracks, a collection of unsanctioned rural tracks that proliferated around south Louisiana for more than a hundred years. They may have been rooted in traditions from the old plantations, where planters would keep horses, organize their own races, and indulge the gambling bug. Even in modern times, some bush tracks were just oval courses cut through sugarcane fields, and others were straightaways marked on pasture by little more than barn barrels and hoof-worn paths. Desormeaux's father operated one in Abbeville called Cajun Downs, and there was Patin's in Henderson, Broussard's and Acadiana in Maurice, Huval's in Youngsville, and the Quarter Pole in Rayne, among others.

If south Louisiana is the cradle of jockeys, these bush tracks were the incubators. For instance, the jockey Mark Guidry of Lafayette mounted up for his first race at a sanctioned track when he was sixteen, the minimum age to get a jockey's license. But by then he already had seven years of experience racing at bush tracks, starting at age nine. He went on to win more than forty-seven hundred races before retiring in 2007.

The bush tracks were also proving grounds for horses whose owners hoped they could make the leap to legit tracks and big money purses. The owners recruited their young sons or nephews as ultra-lightweight jockeys in races where rules were often determined on the spot.

"Really, it was an anything-goes kind of time," said Ronald Ardoin, who had retired as a jockey and was working as a jockey agent when I caught up with him.

"My dad started putting me on horses at those tracks when I was seven," he said. "They'd have you strip down to your underwear to get as light as possible and if you were too small they'd tie you on that horse so you'd stay up there."

He said the one consistent requirement was to have "live weight," meaning either a rider or something that would move with the horse and simulate the effect of a mounted rider during the race. Meeting that requirement at bush tracks could take some wildly unorthodox forms.

"They'd put beer cans on the horse, bags of rocks. They'd tie fighting roosters to the horses sometimes and when the roosters got flapping up there, boy, the horses would really go," Ronald told me. "I've raced against horses ridden by monkeys. Picture that one. They'd just put monkeys in the saddle and off they'd go. All I could do was just hold on in a race like that."

Alas, the age of the bush track seems over. The modern American realities of liability insurance began catching up even with the less freewheeling operations in these once-isolated Cajun and Creole communities. Meanwhile, the rise of sanctioned racing at new licensed tracks nearby siphoned off the talent and the betting money. The bush tracks quietly reverted to field and pasture, one by one.

Today, the modern, professional horse track Evangeline Downs in Opelousas is the center of racing action in Acadiana during its thoroughbred season from April to Labor Day. Delta Downs in Vinton out near the Texas border picks up the season from October through March. Both double as casinos.

Driving toward Evangeline Downs for the first time, I saw that the place looked like any other large suburban or rural gambling operation housed in its huge, boxy building, surrounded by sprawling parking lots and fed by a long access road. Altogether it took up more acreage than a community college campus. The track was still at the heart of it though, and, while there certainly would be no circus scenes of half-naked Cajun children bound to horses, a considerable flavor of the region still seeps through the otherwise mundane casino setting here.

I am no gambler, and I find the stats and figures involved in horse handicapping particularly daunting. My favorite part of the racing form is always the column listing the names of the horses. That's the information on which I base most of my betting decisions during annual visits to my hometown track, the Fair Grounds Race Course in New Orleans. If a horse name strikes me as odd, ominous, or clever, that's the one I'm most likely to endorse. So horses like Idealien, He Dances Backward, Mymamastillstandin, and Almost Impressed drew my penny-ante bets at Evangeline Downs, regardless of whatever their records may have been.

But even for people like me who leave it to dumb luck, there's an allure to betting on live horse races that can never be matched by slot machines and even table games. It has something to do with the various outdoor and indoor areas of the track, each with their function. It relies on the build-up and the fermentation time between races, the ticking clock to place a bet, the constant, colorful interplay of people, and the many matters of personal preference, habit, and flair bound up in prebetting rituals. All these subtleties of the track experience go beyond winning or losing a bet, and they provide confessed voyeurs like myself with plenty to eat up between our hopeless, long-shot bets.

It seems like the paddock is where gamblers most ardently hunt for their tips and inside reads at any track. This is where the horses are paraded around in circles, usually with the jockey already mounted, and rail birds can be found here hungrily watching the body language of the horses or trying to gauge the moods of the jockeys as they depart for the track, looking for anything at all that might tickle some intuition of success or failure in the upcoming race. At Evangeline Downs, though, I noticed something I hadn't seen at other tracks, at least not to quite such an extent. It seemed that every other person hanging along the paddock fence called out to this or that jockey, hailing them by nicknames to strike up apparently casual conversation or pass on some trivial piece of information.

"Hey, Chess, man, yo, you got that truck running yet?" one guy yelled out.

"Oh no, not yet, I got to see you about that next week maybe," the smiling jockey answered.

Another guy asked a jockey if he was coming over to his place on Sunday, and down the way a jockey was gabbing with a woman leaning against the rail. It seemed like they were all just chatting at the hardware store. The bush tracks are gone, but the jockeys, breeders, trainers, and racing fans milling around the Evangeline Downs grandstand and paddock all still seem to share in a tight-knit local culture.

Lots of kids ran around the whole time, climbing on the railings by the track, perching on their fathers' shoulders, yelling for the horses during the race and scampering around with their siblings between the slow-moving drifts of adults lost in racing forms on their way to the betting windows.

The kids looked pretty excited to be there and I bet anyone who went around offering to let them mount a horse for a quick run around the track would find plenty of enthusiastic takers. Of course no one was proposing that at Evangeline Downs, which is no bush track. And, for the record, neither is Metro Soileau Downs, the next chapter in my south Louisiana horse country education. But it sure looked like one when I showed up.

* * *

Metro Soileau Downs is as rural and bushy a track as I can imagine finding anywhere in the world. It is a tiny, utterly untailored, friendly, ramshackle operation surrounded by miles and miles of rice fields in Allen Parish, about an hour west of Opelousas.

Antonia and I drove out there to meet our friend Kristian Sonnier. He's a public relations executive in New Orleans, where he certainly puts on a good show of being the smart, ambitious urban professional. He was raised on his parents' rice farm in Allen Parish, however, and with the slightest provocation—the chance to operate heavy machinery, say, or perhaps shoot a varmint—his roots as a Louisiana country boy come surging to the surface.

He and his girlfriend, Emery, were spending an August weekend helping bring in the family crop, and the plan we'd worked up back in the city was to meet for a few races in Soileau during a break in the harvest. Directions to find the track boiled down to driving past unbroken miles of rice, taking a right at a collection of silver-colored rice silos and then keeping an eye out for the dust cloud kicked up by races in progress.

Though these directions initially sounded vague, they turned out to be as precise as possible in this area of few roads and spread-out farms. We had no problem spotting the beige cloud hanging over the waving green fields, but after pulling off the road and bouncing down a dirt path I had a moment of doubt that we had arrived at the right place. All we saw was a collection of small stables, a metal building, and a scattering of farm equipment, plus about a dozen pickups and horse trailers parked here and there.

"This is it?" I said.

"This can't be it," said Antonia. "How can this be it? Turn around!"

At that moment we saw two horses coming around a bend in the dusty strip that proved, in fact, to be the track. They were tiny horses pulling sulkies, or chariot-like, two-wheeled carriages carrying low-slung riders. They seemed to be coming straight for us, but then they veered to follow the curve of the track right in front of our wind-screen. We had basically turned off from the country highway and straight onto the Metro Soileau Downs racetrack itself.

My cell phone started ringing. It was Kristian calling, and once I focused I could see him waving to us from the side of the metal building across the track.

"Yeah, we're already here and we see you pulling in," he said.

"Okay, but, ah, I think we came the wrong way, I think we're right on the track," I said.

"You are, but that's the right way," he said evenly. "Just wait until this next lap is over and come on and park over here, we got some Natural Light for you."

In a minute we were tapping beer cans together and settling in for the next race among the other spectators. The "Metro" part of this track's name seems like a bit of a joke. Soileau is a black Creole farming community that is so small it doesn't rate mention on most state maps. Its closest neighboring towns are nearly as obscure, but at least residents of Duralde can claim a few homegrown zydeco stars, like Bois Sec Ardoin and Beau Jocque, that huge, handsomely mustachioed accordion player who dominated the zydeco scene in the 1990s before his untimely death.

But Soileau does have horseman Andrew Cezar, who was born and raised here, spent some forty years working in the horse business in the Midwest and returned home for semiretirement in 1998. A trim, tall, lanky seventy-something, Andrew and his wife, Olivia, now operate Triple C Ranch and also the property's alter ego, Metro Soileau Downs. Here they run what are known as trottingbred harness races, with meets held roughly every other Saturday from April through October.

"He brought it back when he moved home, just because he loved it," his nephew Alfred Cezar told me as we watched the next race cruise through its second lap. "For a while it was just me and him out here, then a few other people started turning up and we had a little crowd."

It is indeed a little crowd. The track's grandstand was one of those low, four-tiered bleachers you find on the sidelines of junior high school sporting events, with maximum seating for maybe sixty people. Only a third of that number were here on this August afternoon. Admission was two dollars a head, and the lady who came around to collect it in a round cookie tin explained it covered a "horse feed fee." Eventually we were invited to pony up a few bucks for a 50/50 raffle—in which the winner gets half the pot and the house keeps the rest. This was again collected in the cookie tin. Otherwise, any bets going on were discreet, hand-to-hand affairs. It didn't seem like anyone was getting rich or going broke at Metro Soileau Downs.

There was no starting gate, no replay, no photo finish, and no winner's circle. Andrew Cezar scribbled the race schedule into a spiral notebook by hand. He updated the list throughout the afternoon as the next horse trailer pulled off the main road in an annunciation of dust and a new man emerged from the cab to say he wanted a race. The "race booth" was a collection of patio furniture and undersized grade school chairs arrayed in the shade of a lean-to by the side of the track. To call a race, Andrew used a microphone plugged into a boom box, which was wired to a set of speakers rigged to the metal roof over the bleachers. He followed a race's progress by looking over his shoulder, and he maintained a commentary I found completely incomprehensible on the other end of the loose, squawking, blown-bass sound system. Soul and zydeco singles from a local radio station played more clearly through the speakers between races, however, and the small crowd responded by snapping their fingers and singing along to the French lyrics of familiar songs.

After we dispatched our first beers, I followed Kristian into the track's clubhouse for another round. This was essentially a plywood and metal garage crammed with the kind of clutter to be found in any country grandparent's shed. The walls were lined with metal shelves holding hand tools and batteries still sealed in dusty packages, cans of bug spray, piles of worn leather saddles, and plastic thermoses. The bar itself was a plywood counter where a matronly lady served light beers from a cooler for one dollar per can. At the back of the clubhouse, past the combination restroom/mop closet, I saw a rice cooker and a big, lidded black pot steaming away on a household stove. After the races, people would leave the track with foil-wrapped suppers of rice and gravy, which were spooned straight from the pots like the leftovers from a family meal. Outside again, I chatted with a few elderly men relaxing in tattered armchairs that had been plunked in the shade next to the bleachers, like a cozier VIP area. I had the feeling I was in someone's backyard, watching races from a family porch.

"It's like a club, but a very open club and that comes from just having a common interest," Alfred Cezar advised. "If you're interested, you stay. And if you're not and you act that way then you're invited to leave."

To be clear, Metro Soileau Downs is not a bush track, at least not in the manner of the operations from the Cajun jockeys' wild old tales. But when I inquired about that status the question raised some hackles.

"No, it ain't no bush track," Andrew snapped, but then soon mellowed. "Some guy came here once asking me to do one like that, but you know I'd have to change it all up. This is about trottingbreds, that's all we want to mess with now."

These trottingbred horses are part of a miniature breed developed in the 1960s. They usually measure a full foot shorter and weigh one-third less than your average thoroughbred. During trottingbred races, the horses' legs are harnessed with leather hobbles to keep them at a natural trot. It was an odd sight at first, like watching Olympic speed walkers keeping their curious pace. It's a crawl compared with the pulling gallop of thoroughbreds. But speed and pageantry aren't the only things to look for in a horse race experience.

Charles Wicker, one of my neighboring spectators on the Soileau bleachers, explained that the sport's appeal comes from its ease.

"It's easy to do it, and it's easy to love," he said.

Young kids can handle the horses and control the chariot-like sulkies, and so can old timers. There are no big purses for trottingbreds, so the horses aren't too expensive. For the price of a used pickup you can expect to buy a horse, a sulky with related gear and a trailer. With that, you'd be ready for weekend races.

"There aren't a lot of ways I know of to get yourself on a horse track this easy," Charles said.

Soon he stood up and excused himself, saying it was "about his time." I assumed he was leaving, but instead I watched him stride across the track to take the reins of a horse. He was wearing shorts, a cut-off shirt, and cowboy boots, and with the mere addition of a helmet and a pair of goggles he climbed onto a sulky and led a mare out to the starting line for his turn on the race schedule. He won the race, and about five minutes later he was back sitting with us in the bleachers, covered in dust, victorious and completely easygoing about it, washing the track grit down with a Natural Light as we watched the next race together. I was quizzing him with more questions about race strategy and sulky handling when he suggested I just take a ride with his horse and see for myself.

"We're not going to race you, don't worry about that. We'll just have the horse run the opposite way around the track. That way she'll know it isn't a race and she'll keep it slow for you," Charles said.

There was a lull in races anyway, so everyone agreed it would be good fun to stick me on a sulky for a spin the wrong way around the track. I clamored aboard the little chariot, sinking into the riding position with my legs spread and suspended in stirrups, feeling vaguely as though I was about to undergo some kind of compromising medical exam. Once we got moving, however, the ride was elementary and exhilarating. The horse trotted along, slower than ever but still plenty fast enough for me as I very gingerly used the reins on the turns. The horse kicked up a new dust cloud. It drifted off toward Antonia, Kristian, and Emery, who were hollering support from the clubhouse shed. The cloud carried on toward Andrew and Alfred Cezar, who were smiling and pointing at me from the lean-to race booth. And the dust continued over the golden, late summer rice in the fields beyond.

I sure didn't feel like a Tournoi knight. The elegant races of Evangeline Downs seemed very distant too. And if it ever came to it I would never recommend putting money on me in a race against the youngest grade school jockey, or even a horse-mounted bag of rocks from the old bush track days. But I was feeling pretty big in my dusty britches by the time I hopped off the sulky and thanked Charles for the ride. This Louisiana horse culture is so accessible, I thought, even a city-dwelling neophyte can run the track backwards.

CHAPTER 16

ZYDECO'S TIGHT SQUEEZE
Creole Music's Dancehalls and Dynasties

Mere minutes into my first zydeco experience in southwest Louisiana I found myself totally perplexed. This was during a 2001 road trip to Lake Charles with my friend Christopher Blagg, a music writer. Explorations of my new state before that point had barely led me outside New Orleans, so this trip out to the far western end of Acadiana brought me to quite unfamiliar territory. I was having some trouble decoding the local customs.

Blagg and I arrived at a small downtown nightclub and found the Lake Charles zydeco accordionist Chris Ardoin on stage and the dance floor filled with couples moving together to his music. Deadly handsome and tremendously talented, Chris Ardoin was just twenty at the time. Already, though, his reputation in the zydeco world was big enough to draw Blagg across the state to check him out on his home turf on an assignment for the New Orleans music magazine *Offbeat*. I was along for the ride and doing my best to catalogue as many varieties of boudin as possible during our trip.

Chris Ardoin was laying down some great sounds in the club, and the room was responding with energy. But as soon as the song ended, the dance floor emptied. It was clear the band would launch into another number in just a moment, but everyone had immediately quit the floor and moved back to the edges of the room. It sure seemed to me that the crowd liked the band, but then they collectively turned their backs on them and all but hid in the corners.

Zydeco scion Chris Ardoin rocks El Sid O's Lounge in Lafayette.

Shortly, Chris started up again and, once the next song was solidly along, the crowd was back out, dancing now with new partners.

I was accustomed to a different sort of fan response at barroom music nights. At most rock shows I've been to, for instance, appreciative audiences signal their interest by pressing close to the stage and basically holding that space for the duration. But throughout the rest of the night, this zydeco crowd continued a cycle of dancing for a song, then emptying the floor entirely and then returning again for the next number. It turns out my confusion began by having the wrong terminology in mind. I was under the impression this was a zydeco show. But of course it was a zydeco dance and, as at any dance, the interval between songs was a chance to regroup and change partners.

* * *

When radio DJs announce an upcoming zydeco gig, they often call it a dance, and I found that zydeco fans in southwest Louisiana are as likely to say "I'm going to the dance" as "I'm going to the club."

Zydeco sprang from the house party dance tradition of rural black Creoles in southwest Louisiana, who first called it "la la music," a term that still crops up occasionally today. It's also sometimes called "Creole music," in much the same way that some Cajuns will call their own folk songs "French music." The unusual modern name is said to come from a vocal alteration of the French word for beans, les haricots, which entered the lexicon via a seminal zydeco number, "Les Haricots Sont Pas Sales," or "the snap beans aren't salty," a song about being so poor you can't afford salt meat to season the beans. Zydeco made the jump to dancehalls and now its performers headline music festivals.

Creole accordion player Amédé Ardoin, a distant relative of Chris Ardoin's, is credited with cutting the first zydeco, or la la, records, beginning with recording sessions in 1928 with Cajun fiddler Dennis McGee. Those early recordings sound a lot like classic Cajun tunes of the same period, and they are vastly different from the songs that Amédé Ardoin's modern relatives now perform. That's because different forms of black music have worked their way into the zydeco mix over the generations, and the evolution has only accelerated in recent years. Since recording his first albums as a teen in the mid-1990s, Chris Ardoin has been a champion of the so-called "nouveau zydeco," a style alternately mixing in elements from hip-hop, R&B, and reggae. His older brother Sean Ardoin played in that nouveau style for years, but this brawny, gregarious, roaring cannonball of a performer later took up "Christian zydeco," adding gospel sounds and religious messages to the mix.

Whatever form zydeco takes, it remains, at its heart, accordion-led black Creole dance music. Its central identity springs from a driving, highly rhythmic beat, and no matter what other filter is put over the music, no matter what contemporary interpretation its practitioners might apply, that beat is still there and that beat demands dancing.

Sometimes zydeco sounds like R&B, with the firm, steady drumbeat in back, but there's a rubboard and accordion up front leading the dance step. Sometimes zydeco sounds like a hip-hop number, with electronically filtered vocals and samples mixed in, but still there's the rubboard and accordion leading the dance step. And sometimes it sounds like you've been pushed through a time warp back to the days of Creole farmers' la la house parties, especially when the young, mesmerizing talent Cedric Watson plays his mix of traditional waltzes, driving acoustic funk, and Francophone a cappella ballads.

Much like their Cajun contemporaries, modern zydeco bands perform for fans who are more interested in partying, making the scene with their friends on a weekend, and flirting with the opposite sex than solemnly saluting their cultural past. Being a badass on the accordion or rubboard in southwest Louisiana is akin to playing a rocking electric guitar in other parts of the country. Here, accordion players are bandleaders, studs, and heroes.

"In this era, with this pop culture we have, it's amazing to me that the pop culture of southwest Louisiana still is Creole culture," said Dustin Cravins, a twenty-eight-year-old zydeco promoter whose family has long been involved with the scene. "It's cool to be into country music here, and not just for white guys from the country. Our music is Creole country music."

Today's typical zydeco crowd, whether assembled for a festival, at a dancehall, or in a club, will be predominantly black, with a varying representation of appreciative fans in other hues. The range of ages will begin at whatever minimum is set by the particular venue (which can mean eighteen-year-olds at some dancehalls or infants at the festivals) and then stretch all the way up to those who appear near the end of their dancing days. The fashion expressions on the dance floor will cover everything from the urban motley of hip-hop styles to crisp, tight western wear to preppy mall clothes, all of it mixing and merging as dance partners switch off between songs. This is music that cuts across a lot of turf in south Louisiana.

* * *

For visitors, the surest and quickest way to get a sense of the Creole country music scene is at a festival. Two of the biggest are held around Opelousas at opposite sides of summer. First up, on Memorial Day weekend, is the Zydeco Extravaganza, now held at the Evangeline Downs racetrack and organized by Dustin Cravins.

On Labor Day weekend, three months later, a melon field outside Opelousas becomes accordion and rubboard central during the Southwest Louisiana Zydeco Music Festival. Different folks put on each festival, but both events were born from a revivalist urge for zydeco in the early 1980s, a time when the future of the music seemed in doubt even in its cradle. Today these festivals attract thousands of people, drawing the zydeco community out of every prairie city and bayou town in south Louisiana and putting fans from Houston to Florida on the road for a trip back to the heartland of black Creole music.

The first year Antonia and I joined them all at the Zydeco Music Festival was during a drizzly and predictably sticky-hot early September weekend. We cruised through downtown Opelousas, the business center of the Cajun prairie, and minutes later we were traveling along a country road lined by crumbling barns and lush fields. We shared this rural route with fast-moving pickups tricked out with chrome rims and tinted windows. By "sharing the route" I mean I nudged us to the shoulder as these bass-thumping trucks shot highbeam warnings and then blew past us every thirty seconds. But the trail of dust they kicked in our windshield assured us we were on the right path, and soon I found the obscure turnoff for Zydeco Road, a gravel farm trail that led to the gates of the festival grounds.

We parked in a wet field among the ranks of the same trucks that had passed us on the way, we paid admission at a gap in the rail fence marking the adjacent field, and we stepped through damp clods toward the center of action. Festival fans had built small shelters of canopies and tarps all over the grounds, preparing for either a downpour or a potential breakout of the equally oppressive September sun. Off to the side ran a line of food booths where families sold several competing styles of jambalaya, pork chop sandwiches, and various smoked or grilled meats on sticks, all advertised on handwritten signs tacked to posts. People sold beers from ice chests in the shade of a metal barn, and up ahead the open-sided pavilion over the main stage looked as if it might double as a shelter for farm machinery outside of festival season.

Curley Taylor was leading his band through some hot numbers up there. He was dressed in plaid shorts and a white T-shirt, and he held his accordion low on his hip as he played and sang. A plywood dance floor had been laid over the field's wet turf, and it was packed with a dancing tangle of moving denim, sliding boot heels, shining belt buckles, sweaty T-shirts, and bone-white cowboy hats pivoting with practiced rigidity. People clustered all around the little plywood floor, watching the dance or waiting for a dance invitation. Beyond them, mothers and grandfathers herded little kids who ran playful laps around their little canopies. And past all of that, and surrounding the whole festival, were the expansive, green, soggy acres of the farm, with darker clusters of live oaks out at the property line. The original la la music dance parties surely never saw such designer denim shaking to its rhythms, but the rustic setting still seemed to evoke the past.

Curley Taylor wrapped up and a festival announcer took the microphone to address the crowd in French. I had no idea what he might have said but at least I had no cultural guilt about it. Others in the zydeco crowd, however, may have felt stung when he returned to English.

"Yeah, that was French and no, I'm not going to translate it for you," the announcer clucked. "That's the language you should have learned when you were kids but you didn't. Maybe your parents didn't teach you because they could use the French to talk about things in front of you they didn't want you to understand, things that go on between adults, things behind closed doors that little kids don't know about yet, okay? Maybe you should learn French though, it is part of your heritage."

Like the harvest and seafood festivals all across Louisiana, the Zydeco Music Festival crowns a queen. It also crowns a king, which is less common. But this is a dancing festival and a queen can't be expected to dance by herself. So there was a coronation ceremony for two young adults, Danielle Metoyer and Clarence Stagg, who appeared as proud up there on stage as valedictorians. Tiara and crown were bestowed, and then the couple celebrated their ascent by dancing together to the rattle of rubboard, the bump of bass, and the rev of accordion as the next band launched into its set. The subjects of their zydeco kingdom danced below on the slick plywood, surrounded by the thick, hot country mist.

* * *

The crowning of festival royalty is a tradition in Louisiana communities akin to homecoming courts in some others, so this musical ceremony seemed especially appropriate at a festival that was launched in 1982 as a way to get younger generations interested in traditional music.

The Zydeco Extravaganza sprang from the same impulse in 1986, when Dustin Cravins's father, Don Cravins, and his uncle, Charles Cravins, first organized the event inside a Lafayette auditorium. The crowds were thin in the beginning, but the Cravinses believed it would develop, and eventually it did become a major happening for the region. Since 2003 it has been held at Evangeline Downs, where today bands play by the racehorse paddock and crowds dance in a bricked courtyard by the rails.

Early on, the festival included a contest featuring young accordion players, often of grade school age. They competed for the applause and approval of a community audience, with the aim of boosting their self-esteem and their confidence as players. At the same time, the Cravinses were bringing zydeco to people who hadn't yet started coming out to festivals and dancehalls.

In the early 1980s, Don and Charles started what has become the area's longest-running zydeco radio show, the Cravins Brothers Show. Don Cravins is mayor of Opelousas at this writing, and he can still be heard Sunday mornings on the local station 105.9 FM, hosting his show, broadcasting shout-outs and birthday wishes to friends, playing zydeco tracks, talking up dances, and putting in plugs for economic development projects and other city hall business along the way. Also back in the 1980s, he and his brother, Charles, began a weekly television show devoted to zydeco, which featured bands performing at local clubs. The show became a local sensation, in no small part because people could prattle about who they had seen dancing with whom on TV. There's nothing like social gossip to get a pop buzz going, and that's as true in Creole Louisiana as it is in Hollywood.

"Those shows really helped make it cool for a whole new generation," said Herman Fuselier, a music writer whose Lafayette-based newspaper column and radio show, *Bayou Boogie*, cover zydeco. "That showed a lot of people that it wasn't just old folks doing this zydeco thing, and it showed them how the sound was changing."

* * *

Some years ago, while looking for a good starter kit to learn about zydeco at the incomparable French Quarter record store Louisiana Music Factory, I picked up a 1992 compilation from Arhoolie Records titled *Zydeco Champs*. Naturally, this anthology included several songs from Clifton Chenier, who was known as the "king of zydeco" until his death in 1987. The Opelousas native is credited with popularizing the addition of R&B and blues strains to zydeco, and at times he could work his accordion solos like B. B. King on his Gibson.

Zydeco Champs also lists tracks from three different generations of the Ardoin family—Amédé, Alphonse "Bois Sec" Ardoin, and Lawrence "Black" Ardoin—and songs from John Delafose and Preston Frank. Each of these men played in a distinct style, and the liner notes for the compilation explained that the selection of artists made the collection an overview of zydeco's evolution. Though the producers could not have known this in 1992, their picks also proved a foretaste of what would come. Today, the compilation plays like a musical family album of those who would assume the zydeco mantle in the next generational shift.

The album's "champs" of yesteryear were the patriarchs of zydeco families, and their progenies are big names on the zydeco circuit today. Bois Sec Ardoin was Black Ardoin's father, and Black is the father of Chris and Sean Ardoin. John Delafose's son Geno Delafose is one of the hottest up-and-coming acts in the region, and Preston Frank's son Keith Frank is probably the biggest and most reliable draw for zydeco crowds in southwest Louisiana today. Clifton Chenier's son C. J. Chenier has followed in his pioneering footsteps. If only Nathan Williams were included in *Zydeco Champs*, the collection would be an even more comprehensive preview of today's zydeco leading lights, since his son Nathan, Jr., a.k.a. Lil' Nathan, is beginning to pack the Creole dancehalls himself.

These guys and their local peers hit the national festival circuit to varying degrees and some can get gigs overseas. They make periodic trips to New Orleans to play at the combination bowling alley/music club Rock 'n' Bowl, where during Thursday's regular zydeco night it can seem like every black man in the Crescent City who feels at ease in a cowboy hat and western wear turns up on the dance floor. But the basis of the zydeco scene for today's young guns is close to home in southwest Louisiana, where the local fan base routinely fills a circuit of venues in the musical golden triangle between Lafayette, Ville Platte, and Lake Charles.

One of the most important of these venues is a 1940s-vintage dancehall along a dark stretch of Highway 190 in Lawtell, a miniscule farming town just outside Opelousas. Until 2006 it was called Richard's, and in Louisiana-speak that's "ree-shards." But the place was shuttered after a family ownership dispute, sold, and then renamed the Zydeco Hall of Fame, since the name Richard's was off limits as part of the family dustup. But everyone still calls it Richard's, including, occasionally, Dustin Cravins, one of its new owners.

"Let's face it, the place still lives on in everyone's hearts as Richard's," Dustin said.

Like other rural Louisiana joints, and especially the zydeco dancehalls, this place looks rather decrepit by day or whenever it's not in use. But on the weekend nights when dances are scheduled, an illuminated roadside arrow sign snaps on and trucks begin parking along the gulley-lined shoulder of the country highway leading to the place. The club itself looks like a rural veterans hall. It's large, spare, and quite rudimentary. There's no air conditioning, which in Louisiana should disqualify a room as a dance venue for most of the year. But such is the draw of this dancehall that crowds turn up, get soaked to the skin in the close, breathy sweat of the place, and appear to love every minute of it.

"I don't know many cultures in America where you'll find three generations of the same family dancing to the same music at the same club on the same floor, and the beauty of it is the oldest generation of those three probably was dancing on the same spot back when they were kids," said Dustin.

A similar scene takes shape at Slim's Y-Ki-Ki, a dancehall right in downtown Opelousas. The ceiling here is so low that tall men in Stetsons look like they'll skim it as they dance. On a summer

Friday night, though, what really caught my eye was the gaggle of very young-looking men and women stalking the edge of the dance floor. Between songs, the guys were hanging out together, laughing and smiling like they were telling embarrassing jokes. About ten paces away the girls were also hanging out together, occasionally touching their hair, holding their arms over their chests and positioning themselves at just the right angle to allow them to keep an eye on the guys while ostensibly watching the zydeco band across the room. As the night went on and the crowd built, clusters of middle-aged people alternately took over the bar and packed the dance floor, while these kids kept up their nervous displays to each other. It was just like any other late-teen social scene, except these kids were acting it out in the view of a few successive generations—with aunts on the dance floor and grandma getting whiskey and water at the bar—while the zydeco band kept up a live soundtrack that all of them wanted to follow.

In Lafayette, right off the interstate and nestled in a working-class city neighborhood, El Sid O's looks a lot more like a lounge than these older, roadside dancehalls. Cars and trucks were parked everywhere when I pulled up. Some were cramming the grassy overflow parking lots around the place and others were boosted up on the edge of sidewalks. Members of a black-clad private security team were shining flashlight beams here and there around the perimeter, evidently looking for something.

Chris Ardoin was playing inside. It had been eight years since my first trip to see him in Lake Charles. He was no longer the underage prodigy but now was a seasoned veteran of the circuit. His draw had remained as strong as ever, and the dance crowd at El Sid O's was pressed from one painted cinderblock wall to the next. More people were hanging off the stools and the lounge chairs by the bar, wiping their sweaty brows with handkerchiefs and ordering drinks four at a time to ferry back to their friends. Chris looked as confident, buff, and cool as ever as he sang to the crowd in English and worked his accordion. His rubboard player whirled about on stage like a live wire, keeping the rattling rhythm and urging on the dancers with side lyrics and call-and-response shout-outs that were eagerly returned by the excited crowd.

The crowd danced, downed beers, and threw their fists in the air, pumping their arms and cheering. This was a local sound, it was their sound, and it was distinct from all of the rest of the world, yet it was also keyed to the compulsive allure of the modern and the hip. I got the impression El Sid O's was the place to be for this crowd on a Lafayette Friday night, just as surely as the hot clubs in New Orleans or Atlanta or New York were the hubs for the music happening there.

By the time I made it to El Sid O's I had been to a lot of different zydeco scenes in the years since that early Lake Charles road trip with Blagg. Here was Chris Ardoin playing again, but this time when he paused between songs the dancers didn't quit the floor. This time, the crowd was too thick for them to go anywhere at all.

Chapter 17

"ISLAND" HOPPING IN IBERIA PARISH

Exploring the Salt Domes and the
Old Spanish Trail Through Teche Country

Salt domes really should be compelling enough all on their own. After all, wherever one of these geological oddities appears, it augurs a mind-bogglingly immense deposit of salt, a colossal subterranean mountain of the mineral left behind from another epoch that can plunge miles deep into the earth.

The Gulf Coast is riddled with these salt monoliths, the remnants of evaporated seabeds shaped and molded by geologic pressure through the ages. They are normally concealed underground, but sometimes their dome-like tips protrude above the surface. Where this happens in south Louisiana these mounds stand out with such landmark prominence above the flat surroundings that they've been dubbed islands. Hilly and green, covered with topsoil and vegetation, these undulating rises of overgrown salt do indeed look as consciously different from the landscape of marsh and plain as an island on the sea. Iberia Parish is home to several, including Avery Island and Jefferson Island—neither of which is surrounded by water.

These salt dome islands are rare and exceptional, but evidently in south Louisiana that isn't enough. Rather, both Avery Island and Jefferson Island have collected a host of interesting attractions and unusual history as if through some kind of geological magnetism. Food culture and hard industry, mesmerizing botanical beauty and prolific wildlife, a Civil War incursion, a pirate tale and theater legend, and even a stunning engineering disaster variously paint the

The Buddha temple on Avery Island sits above it all.

stories of these inland, landlocked islands of Acadiana, and they have anchored them as enduring visitor destinations.

* * *

I was familiar with Avery Island long before I'd ever heard of a salt dome or had even visited Louisiana. That's because Avery Island is the famous home address printed on the labels for Tabasco, the hot pepper sauce produced there by the McIlhenny Company to the tinkling tune of up to 720,000 diminutive glass bottles per day.

Tabasco sauce had something like cult status in my Rhode Island family while I was growing up, and that wasn't because we ate lots of spicy food. Quite to the contrary, my maternal grandmother had administered the hot sauce to chasten her children—my mother and my aunts and uncles—for unacceptable language or some other transgression. In her household, a stinging spoonful of Tabasco stood in for the bar of soap used for punitive mouth washing. My aunt Kate would later mount a framed print of the Tabasco label on her wall, like the totem of a hardship overcome. Perhaps this unconventional application of Tabasco helps explain why spicy food was such a rare part of my childhood diet, though in bean-and-cod New England that's not so unusual.

South Louisiana, on the other hand, has a reputation for fiery food. But in truth it's neither as uniformly nor as intensely spicy as some newcomers first imagine, and Tabasco may bear a share of responsibility for this exaggerated but widely held notion. Some bedrock Louisiana dishes are indeed inherently spicy, like the stew so expressively called sauce piquante, and other staples do call for alarming amounts of hot pepper, like the seasoning mix used for boiled crawfish. For the most part, though, getting a really spicy meal here is a matter regulated at the table with judicious applications of hot pepper sauce over the region's smothered meats and stews, omnipresent fried seafood, and countless rice dishes. Tabasco is by far the most prominent of the options in this department, and it has become an iconic brand of Louisiana, a red symbol of the state's food culture. As a readily transportable, shelf-stable consumer item, Tabasco has had a long reach. The upshot is that people who will never make a roux, that flour-and-fat foundation for so much Louisiana cooking, know that a shake or two of the famous Louisiana hot sauce can make even the most dismal cooking palatable.

To me, nothing speaks to the penetration of the Tabasco brand quite like an experience I shared with many New Orleanians in the weeks after Hurricane Katrina. This was during the time when a warm meal was hard to come by in most parts of our devastated city. But from the tailgates of National Guard trucks and from Red Cross relief stations my neighbors and I were able to collect military-issue field rations, known in army parlance as MREs, for Meals Ready to Eat, which were completely sealed up in thick plastic pouches. We broke open these meal kits in our ruined New Orleans homes to find Tabasco rolling out in tiny, thimble-sized bottles, thoughtfully provided by the federal government to improve the freeze-dried victuals originally intended for combat troops deployed around the world. This post-Katrina period of loss and frustration was a time for prolific foul language, and in the midst of it I had to think back to my late Rhode Island grandmother and how she might have approved of government-sponsored Tabasco in the MREs lashing our offending tongues.

Fortunately for the McIlhenny Company most people buying Tabasco seem to use it to enhance flavor rather than to correct disorderly children, and the popularity of the brand has made its production facility on Avery Island a major tourist attraction. Busloads of visitors turn up for the daily Tabasco factory tour, which is advertised on highway billboards around the region. The tour itself is free, but it is short and disappointing. It begins with the screening of a promotional video extolling the many uses of the hot sauce ("Try it on pizza or hot dogs!") and continues with a brief stroll down a glass-lined corridor looking into the plant's packaging area, which was idle on my weekend visit. A room of interactive, Tabasco-themed electronic games and a few historical displays complete the tour, which ends at a large gift shop stocked with everything from aprons to golf tees, all bearing the brand's famous logo. Were this tour all that Avery Island has to offer, it would not be worth the two-hour drive from New Orleans. But I found the trip rewarding enough to make repeat visits thanks to the salt dome's other prime attraction, the splendid and sprawling Jungle Gardens, and for the pleasure of simply getting there along one of Louisiana's great scenic drives.

* * *

Leaving New Orleans on an early spring morning, Antonia and I crossed the Mississippi River and headed southwest, passing the deep swamp country around Houma and then continuing through Morgan City and over the Atchafalaya River to enter the Bayou Teche region. This is where we left the modern, four-lane Highway 90 behind and diverted up to Highway 182, an older, slower route with a less direct path between points but a more direct view of the geography and history that defines this area.

Between Morgan City and New Iberia some fifty miles away, Highway 182 roughly matches the twisting course of Bayou Teche, which takes its name from the local Chitimacha Indian word for snake. Brown, slow, pretty, and twisting, this waterway does seem to slither through the rural landscape, though its languid pace belies this bayou's mighty past. Like Bayou Lafourche to the east, Bayou Teche too was once the mainstream of the Mississippi River, some twenty-eight hundred to forty-five hundred years ago. When the course found a steeper, faster route, the Teche was left as a slow-moving trickle lined by mounded banks of high ground, the sediment leavings of successive river flooding from the distant past. What Bayou Lafourche is to the communities leading down toward Grand Isle, Bayou Teche is to the region strung between Lafayette and the Atchafalaya River, where the Teche now empties. All of the towns formed along its banks, and long, narrow bands of farmland radiate out. Once busy with steamboats and barges bearing sugar and timber harvests, the Teche was the main street and the prime shipping highway for the area, and it also served as an umbilical cord for early Cajun culture, which grew and spread along its course.

As Antonia and I drove west in the gathering heat of this spring day, Highway 182 led us along a repeating pattern of agriculture and town centers all ordered along the path of the bayou. We saw vast fields of sugarcane edging right up to the roadside and spreading to the distance. The fields were low and just beginning to grow at this stage in the season, and on later trips over the same territory, in the fall, I'd see these fields being shorn of mature cane. Later still, the stubble left behind would be set alight, a postharvest practice that scents the autumn air and makes dark towers of brownish smoke visible for miles over the countryside.

The roadside fields in these rural stretches are broken by the occasional mill, then stately stands of live oaks, and then a gradually increasing frequency of old homes that resolve themselves into bayou towns. These towns developed in a linear manner, fastened to the course of the bayou, and at intervals Highway 182 will cycle into its role as each town's Main Street. In Franklin, our path was staked by a center row of white iron lampposts and was lined on either side by majestic homes, many of which sported high, white columns, broad porticos, and yards full of sheltering oaks. A wave of settlers of English descent arrived here after the Louisiana Purchase in 1803 when Franklin was developing as an important inland port, and their wealth and sensibilities give the small city an enduring Anglo ambiance that still stands apart in the heart of French Louisiana.

Names like Trowbridge, Burroughs, Baker, and Palfrey are attached to the historic homes these families built, which are now highlights for self-guided walking tours of the town's dense, lushly shaded, and refreshingly intact historic district.

Past Franklin and after another stretch of cane fields we soon entered Jeanerette, a small town with an old business district of brick storefronts, 1950s-era pharmacies, and a landmark bakery. LeJeune's Bakery, founded in 1884, is one of those classic businesses that endures on the strength of intense specialization rather than diversification or trying to keep up with trends. Its loaves of French bread and flat gingerbread "stage planks" are worth a stop. Even on a hot day the allure of bread still warm from the oven is impossible to resist, and so a great many plain, unbuttered loaves from LeJeune have become spontaneous car snacks along this route.

The pace on Highway 182 is slow and ambling as it wends through towns, and it can feel downright pokey if you get stuck behind a laden sugar wagon clattering in from the fields, dropping sticks of cane on the road as it goes. But this old route was originally a leg of the Old Spanish Trail, a first-generation transnational highway. Stretching from Florida to California and built between 1915 and 1929, in the era of the Model T Ford, the route was the precursor to Interstate 10, which now covers much of the same coast-to-coast turf in a vastly speedier fashion. Purpose-built for cars, this "trail" owes its romantic-sounding name to an early highway marketing scheme loosely based on the Spanish colonial history shared by the states the road traversed.

"While there was no actual cross-country historic Spanish trail, the modern highway ran roughly parallel to the expedition routes of De Soto, De Vaca and De Navarez, as well as mission trails in Florida and Texas," writes John Murphey, a historian and founder of Drive the OST, a Santa Fe, New Mexico–based group that now tries to promote the old route. He writes that travel brochures issued in the 1920s "made the contemporary driver feel as though they were following the 'footsteps of the padres and conquistadores.'"

Travelers in south Louisiana won't find the sort of Spanish colonial architecture or deep cultural imprint they'd see in San Antonio or Tucson farther west along the trail. But as the route crosses Acadiana it does visit a bastion of the heritage that colorful Old Spanish Trail tag was meant to conjure: New Iberia, the next stop along Highway 182, a town originally formed as part of Madrid's hopelessly patchy efforts to Hispanicize the region.

Spain acquired the vast Louisiana territory from France by treaty, but the French settlers and native-born Creoles here did not simply relinquish their cultural loyalty nor their hearts' allegiance with the exchange of flags over the halls of colonial power in New Orleans. Spain's new Francophone acquisition also was a region bordered by the holdings of its longtime European enemy and constant New World rival, the British. It's no wonder then that the Spanish administrators felt the need to seed their new territory with bulwarks of friendly fellow countrymen. It would have taken a massive migration campaign to seriously challenge French culture in Louisiana, and that didn't happen. But vestiges do remain today in areas where the Spanish government focused its energies.

In 1778, a group of colonists from the Spanish-controlled Canary Islands off the Moroccan coast were sent to settle in St. Bernard Parish, an area of farmland and marsh just downriver from New Orleans and named for Bernardo de Gálvez, Louisiana's Spanish governor at the time. Their descendents are still known as Isleños, or islanders, and they maintain tight-knit communities in tiny—and increasingly storm-battered—fishing villages there, end-of-the-road places like Delacroix, Reggio, Shell Beach, and Yscloskey.

The following year, Governor Gálvez sent some Isleños and a band of sixteen families recruited from Spain's Andalusia province to settle along the banks of Bayou Teche. They farmed, laid the groundwork for the town of New Iberia, and today their descendents fill up the local telephone directory with Iberian—or lightly Gallicized Iberian—surnames like Romero, Rodrigue, Segura, Domingue, and Migues.

As was the case with German settlers in Côte des Allemands and other ethnic pockets around Louisiana, this kernel of Spanish identity was eventually absorbed by the dominant French culture, and modern-day New Iberia looks, sounds, and tastes like a large Cajun town. As Antonia and I drove in, the Old Spanish Trail once again became Main Street, and this Main Street was again arched over by the dark, thick twists of oak limbs and lined with pretty, historic houses. There's a compact, dense business district by the bayou banks, where fans of New Iberia novelist James Lee Burke can pick out landmarks featured in his hardboiled crime fiction, like the deco-style Victor's Cafeteria and the Iberia Parish Courthouse.

Among the downtown tourist attractions, the most curious is the Conrad Rice Mill, which produces Konriko brand rice. This is by no means the largest rice mill around, but after some ninety years in business it is the oldest one still in operation in America, and its appearance in New Iberia signals an agricultural shift in the surrounding countryside, where cane fields begin to give way to rice farms. The brief tour here began with a laughably outdated slideshow about Acadiana, presented in a cluttered storage room behind the company's folksy retail outlet, the Konriko Country Store. Produced by a New Orleans ad firm in 1981, and evidently left unedited since, the slide show was replete with narrated references to "Negroes" and adoring shots of bikini-clad Cajun girls partying at festivals. Next came a stroll through the creaking, groaning, fully functional old mill building, which on my visit was accompanied by several cats that perched freely on the machinery and leapt after moving shadows among the hollows of the old structure. Archaic but honest, the rice mill tour makes a trippy diversion for forty minutes or so, and it does give a view into the production of the staple ingredient for so much Acadian cooking.

Over the tracks and a few blocks away back on Main Street, Shadows on the Teche is the town's significantly more highbrow attraction. Situated between Main Street and the bayou, yet deeply cloistered behind a tall hedge of bamboo and a curtain of moss-draped oaks, this mansion-turned-museum was built in 1834 by sugar planter David Weeks. Its unique architectural style combines the exposed brickwork and towering columns of Georgian Revival with elements more common to French colonial design. Most strikingly, the floor plan has no corridors, and all rooms are accessed by wide galleries and exterior staircases. Union troops billeted here during the Civil War and the home fell into decades of disrepair. In the 1920s, however, William Weeks Hall, a descendent of the original builder, restored the place and entertained such illustrious visitors as author Henry Miller and director Elia Kazan. Many of the celebrated callers were invited to pen personal messages on a door of the mansion, as a sort of brazen guest log, and their words are still on display as part of the Shadows on the Teche tour.

After New Iberia, Bayou Teche makes a dramatic turn and loops back on itself before heading due north through towns like St. Martinville, Breaux Bridge, and Arnaudville. This turn is where the Old Spanish Trail branches off from its bayou course and continues through the urban heart of Lafayette. But here Antonia and I took a different turn, the one that heads south from New Iberia to its most famous attraction, Avery Island.

* * *

A lone, slim blacktop road covers the six miles from town to the front door of Avery Island, and it can seem like one long driveway. There was nothing else around as we approached but cane fields and black tank cars idling above us along a rail line embankment. Through the windshield, we saw the green, tree-covered salt dome moon up like a broad, low bubble pressing over the flat distance.

A moat-like bayou runs alongside Avery Island, and after crossing it and paying a one-dollar bridge toll to an old man waiting on the other side in a roadside shed I felt as though we had entered a self-contained kingdom. The entire island is owned by the Tabasco-making McIlhenny family, and it is divided into areas that are either open or off-limits to visitors. Our first stop was the Tabasco factory, a campus of large, quiet, brick buildings set behind its own levee system and looking like a trim military academy. Other parts of the island are dedicated to growing the heirloom seed crop for tabasco hot peppers, a variety native to Mexico that the McIlhenny Company took for its brand name. Elsewhere on the island, past the "no trespassing" signs, there are McIlhenny family homes and residences for company employees. There are also oil wells pumping away at petroleum deposits, which nature reliably plants near salt domes, and there is the groundside infrastructure for salt mines that plumb the unseen depths of the island.

Artifacts found on the island indicate Native American people gathered salt here for centuries, and European settlers discovered and utilized briny springs flowing from the island's surface. By the nineteenth century the Avery family of Baton Rouge ran a sugar plantation on the island, then called Petite Anse Island, and around the outbreak of the Civil War they discovered huge quantities of rock salt just under the surface. A large-scale mining operation developed, and the Avery plantation quickly assumed strategic importance in the supply chain for the Confederacy's salted meat rations, a vital commodity for sustaining nineteenth-century armies in the field.

"[T]his activity transformed the Averys' obscure retreat into a military target," writes McIlhenny Company historian Shane K. Bernard in *Tabasco: An Illustrated History*. A first attack by Union gunboats late in 1862 was repulsed, but by April 1863 the island and its salt works fell to federal forces.

After the war, it was one-time New Orleans banker Edmund McIlhenny, the husband of an Avery daughter, who decided to convert tabasco peppers growing on the island into a spicy condiment. He blended the small, potent red peppers with vinegar and the island's own salt and devised an aging formula that called for barrels of this pepper mash to be sealed up with still more Avery salt. The details of that process are explained on the short factory tour, during which visitors can't help but get a noseful of the ambient pepper hanging in the air all around the facility.

The more absorbing part of our Avery Island visit, however, was a journey through the Jungle Gardens, a 250-acre collection of flourishing exotic plants, tides of seasonal flowers, abundant and unafraid wildlife, water features, and sacred statuary draping a corner of the salt dome. Credit for all this belongs to Edmund "Ned" Avery McIlhenny, a scion of the hot sauce family who in the late nineteenth century established himself as an Arctic adventurer and conservationist before setting out to build a magnificent showpiece garden around his Avery Island estate.

We paid a modest entrance fee at the gardens' welcome center and picked up a map of the property, showing its main attractions all connected by a thin, winding road. Instantly, I wished we had brought bicycles to pedal around this parklike property, but instead we covered it in the truck, keeping a slow, observant pace and getting out at the hotspots to walk around a network of footpaths. The first stop actually was right at the gates—a grove of live oaks, planted so close together that their limbs mesh overhead. A few families were eating picnic lunches beneath this shady, majestic spread, which looked more like a mosaic of spreading, dark trunks, young, green leaves and intertwined shadows than an orchard of individual trees.

Everywhere, springtime explosions of soft-colored camellias and azaleas bathed the landscape in color and fragrance. We passed lagoons where we could see the flat heads of gators silently bobbing up and saw more of them down the way resting in muddy banks. There were landscaped tunnels of Chinese timber bamboo and a sunken garden of low, unfurled sago palms. One highlight was the Buddha statue, housed in a glass-walled temple above a silent pond and overlooking a network of footpaths, rock bridges, and mounded hills. At another stop, we descended a steep decline down a set of stone steps to Bird City, a wildlife refuge begun by Ned McIlhenny in 1895 to protect snowy egrets, which had been hunted to the brink of extinction for their then-fashionable mating feathers. McIlhenny established a colony of a handful of surviving birds over a manmade pond on his island. From this humble start the population grew to thousands, and today the sanctuary still teems with the graceful creatures. We climbed an observation platform and watched for a while as their white forms threaded through the air, jostled with each other on landing pads over the pond, or perched motionless in distant oaks like white lanterns strung from the limbs.

But perhaps the most exotic feature of all for Antonia and me was the simple presence of hills, ruts, and hollows across the garden grounds. This sort of topography just doesn't happen in the soft, alluvial soils of south Louisiana, so to travel over ridges, to actually crest a sharp land feature, was an unaccustomed thrill. All of this is due to the uneven texture of the massive salt formation just beneath the surface, though since it was out of sight, and so unfathomably huge, it was hard to keep the actual mineral deposit's presence in mind. Photos included in the Tabasco factory tour show vast, echoing halls carved from the salt over the years, and these at one time were open for tours. It seemed a pity that at least part of the mine wasn't still accessible to the public, since walking through that underground world surely would give a fuller appreciation of this beautiful, but also busy and productive, salt dome island. But then, after learning the story of Jefferson Island, a sister salt dome thirteen miles away, and the tale associated with it known as "the Catastrophe," simply staying above deck with the flowers and sunshine had renewed appeal.

* * *

Like its much more famous salt dome neighbor, Jefferson Island features its own exotic gardens, the Rip Van Winkle Gardens, which are open to the public for a fee. A legend about the place holds that the Louisiana-based pirate Jean Lafitte buried some of his treasure here and that in 1923 a laborer unearthed pots of Spanish and Mexican coin while digging beneath an oak. More lasting renown for the island came from actor Joseph Jefferson, who was famous in the nineteenth-century American theater world for his portrayal of Rip Van Winkle, a role he adapted from the Washington Irving tale and reprised thousands of times (and which of course inspired the modern gardens' name). In 1870, he bought Jefferson Island—then called Orange Island for its citrus orchards—and used the property as his winter retreat and hunting lodge. He built a mansion in the steamboat Gothic style on the island's highest rise, and this country home, dripping with gingerbread and topped by a crownlike cupola, is open for guided tours as part of the garden attractions.

I made this trip by myself in the springtime, when abundant azaleas seem to carpet the gardens and even the roadways around Iberia Parish. The flowers were out in their glory atop Jefferson Island, which I found at the end of a long access road flanked by ranks of huge oaks. Passing through the welcome center/gift shop, I stepped onto the grounds and straight into a big surprise. I hadn't done much homework on Jefferson Island before turning up at its door, so I didn't even know that this salt dome was situated directly on the shore of Lake Peigneur. But there it was, the beautiful, broad, denim-blue spread of water sitting below the gentle backside slope of the island. There was a light breeze and I saw a white sailboat tacking on the lake. The vista reminded me of a seaside bluff, and the whole peaceful, breezy scene looked like a postcard picture from another state, certainly somewhere far from flat, marshy south Louisiana.

Covering twenty-five acres, the Rip Van Winkle Gardens were arrayed like a series of manicured botanical chambers connected by ambling footpaths. Something different appeared around each bend or rise on the rolling landscape, from a shady alcove modeled after Moorish gardens to a Japanese tearoom behind screens of bamboo. Peacocks stalked the walkways, and periodically the plantings would break to reveal a blue view of the lake. I couldn't get enough of the beautiful combination of Lake Peigneur against the Jefferson Island landscape. But as I learned during a dramatic video screening in the gardens' welcome center, the salt dome and the lake once combined in a most uncanny and breathtaking fashion, leading to the momentous "Catastrophe."

The mineral mountain beneath Jefferson Island bred a salt mining operation, much like the one on Avery Island. This too was once open for public tours, and writers employed by the federal Work Projects Administration described a visit under the island in the 1941 book *Louisiana, a Guide to the State*.

"Rock salt walls rise to a height of 80 feet and salt pillars support the roofs of the 'rooms' formed by previous excavation," the guide recorded. "The underground chambers stretch far back into the semidarkness, and under long lines of electrical lights men and machinery are busily working in the dry atmosphere."

Since salt domes and profitable oil finds usually go hand in hand, drilling rigs soon joined the work going on around Jefferson Island. So it was that an exploration rig hired by Texaco was out on the lake in the predawn hours of November 20, 1980. Drilling down more than twelve hundred feet, the rig's bit became stuck, and, after some time spent trying to dislodge it, the crew noticed that the entire drilling platform was listing to the side. They quit the rig, fearing it would sink, and from the shore they watched it slip under the lake's surface. They must have been relieved to be off the rig, but surely also mystified by what they were witnessing. Lake Peigneur at that time was very shallow, no more than ten feet deep, yet their entire, towering rig had slid under the surface. That's because, far below, Lake Peigneur was rapidly growing much deeper.

The rig's fourteen-inch-wide drilling bit had apparently pierced the wall of a salt mine beneath Jefferson Island. While the bit was stuck in the rock salt, fresh water from the lake began pressing in around it. It must have begun as a trickle around the sides of the bit, but at an inexorably accelerating rate the lake water would have dissolved more and more of the salt, expanding the fissure, letting in more water and setting into motion a chain reaction of stupendous magnitude.

Mine chambers collapsed, sending more water bursting in and widening the hollow beneath the lake. On the surface, a giant, sucking vortex formed. All of the miners working underground managed to escape, and they joined others watching from the shore as entire barges loaded with trucks and salt mining equipment spiraled down and disappeared beneath the surface. The Delcambre Canal, a waterway that normally flows very languidly away from the lake and out to the Gulf, abruptly reserved course as lake waters plunged down into the growing salt cavity. Fishing boats and tugs on the canal were drawn backwards against their full-throttle engines and men had to jump from their decks to safety on the banks. It must have seemed biblical.

Amazingly, no one was killed, but the force of the sinkhole sheared off some sixty-five acres of land from Jefferson Island, including ancient oaks, huge pecan trees and the contemporary home of the property's owner, John Bayless, Jr., the man who had first built the island's formal gardens. The brick chimney of that house still juts up from the lake, now a good distance from the new shoreline. It took several days before the Delcambre Canal could refill the lake, which remains significantly deeper and saltier as a result of the eco-industrial drama.

All was very peaceful on a fully restored and elegant Jefferson Island when I visited, and in fact that afternoon the lovely grounds were being prepared for a wedding. Guests were beginning to arrive as I made it back to the welcome center by the parking lot, and rows of folding chairs were arrayed on the lawn overlooking the blue lake. White ribbons fluttered in the breeze from the backs of the chairs and from the sides of a podium where the ceremony would take place.

I had no idea who would be married there that afternoon, and by the time the bride and groom arrived I'd be driving away from Jefferson Island, heading back down the ranks of live oaks, eventually to pick up the Old Spanish Trail again and cruise the cane fields on my way home to New Orleans. But before I left I gazed over the grassy slope leading to Lake Peigneur again and, as you do at weddings, silently wished them luck in their married life together. They had certainly picked an unforgettable place to begin it.

CHAPTER 18

SADDLE SOUNDS

Dusty Dance Floors and Creole Trail Rides

Finding the way to my first Louisiana trail ride wasn't easy. But once I spotted it, there was no doubt I was in the right place.

Along a rural road near Cecilia, a small town just north of Interstate 10 and just west of the Atchafalaya Basin, it was impossible to miss the evidence of the big zydeco party that my friend Geoff Coats and I had set off from New Orleans to find. After traveling many rural miles, we suddenly came upon a grassy field crammed to capacity with pickups, SUVs, sports cars, and, most of all, horse trailers. Riders on horseback roamed the grounds, and a team of people at the head of a dirt driveway collected admission under a hand-lettered poster reading, "You Fight, You Go To Jail. No Exceptions!"

The trail ride, in its south Louisiana incarnation, is a roving, horseback party set to a zydeco beat and hosted by the many small, black-run riding clubs around the region. These regular Sunday events draw hundreds of riders, sometimes thousands of riders, plus their relatives and friends and random zydeco fans. One riding club usually hosts each trail ride, and the members from many others show up to participate, rolling in with convoys of horse trailers and RVs.

I had only the sketchiest idea of what these events might be like, an impression based mostly on teaser references dropped by zydeco musicians during a few interviews I'd conducted. They described Sunday afternoon outdoor parties with tons of beer, boudin and pork chop sandwiches, an all-ages crowd, urban cowboys everywhere, and hour upon hour of dusty-boot dancing in fields and barns to zydeco

An open-air zydeco dance floor after a trail ride in Cecilia.

from the best players around. To me, their descriptions made the events sound like rural, zydeco- and horse-based versions of the second line parades I had discovered with such utter glee back in my adopted home city.

In New Orleans, a profusion of black membership groups called social aid and pleasure clubs host wildly fun parades through the city's neighborhoods, also traditionally on Sunday afternoons. The events include thumping, foot-moving music from brass bands, jubilant dancing in the street, a come-one, come-all attitude, and club members duded up in wardrobes of brightly colored suits and sashes, with bowler hats and feathered fedoras for the men and swooping bonnets for the women. Altogether, the second line parade melds the pomp of deep-running tradition with the spontaneous energy of a block party, albeit one that moves a block at a time. I was very eager to experience anything even remotely resembling this good time in zydeco country.

I later figured out that the best way to get the most information about upcoming trail rides is to find one in progress and then review the rainbow of various flyers stuffed under your truck's wiper blade by the end of the day. An alternate strategy is to hit a few butcher shops in the towns around Lafayette, Opelousas, and Lake Charles and look for the same flyers stacked next to the boudin steamer at the counter. These handbills give all the details, including whether a particular trail ride is a benefit to fund a child's hospital bills, a celebration of a club's anniversary or, as a few claim, "the biggest trail ride ever."

Of course, that's the kind of thing I learned only after I'd been to one. A troll through the Internet for trail ride details turned up only the most basic information about this Cecilia event, namely that it would be held at a place called Club LA, that the zydeco star Keith Frank and his Soileau Band would perform and that the whole shindig was hosted by a club called the Grandwood Riders. As with so many other joints in rural Louisiana, though, Club LA's online profile is decidedly submerged. Geoff and I would have to wing it with no address. Fortunately, once in Cecilia we found a banner staked in a weedy lot advertising the trail ride. There was a phone number penned along the bottom of the banner, which Geoff dialed while I drove.

"Okay, yes, we're just coming up to the Piggy Wiggly now," I heard Geoff say to the lady who answered his call. "Okay, so U-turn here, back to the banner, take a left, right up the road. Got it, thanks!"

I have faith that whenever you can cold-call a public event and get customized driving directions based on the vectors of a Piggly Wiggly grocery store, that event will be fantastic, and my first trail ride experience was no disappointment.

* * *

Our final approach was guided by a queue of chromed-out trucks and Dodge Chargers filtering into the already-packed field of parking. Past row after row of vehicles we spotted Club LA, a whitewashed ranch house sitting back from the road amid grassy acres. The guys at the entrance gave us tickets the size of business cards to pin to our shirts, proof that we'd paid the eight-dollar admission, and they told us the band would start shortly after the mass of horse riders returned to the grounds. The riders had departed around noontime, and for the past few hours they had been clopping around the rural Cecilia route under the full brunt of a sweltering summer day with zydeco playing from wagons rolling along beside them.

We made a circuit of the grounds, where people were dressed in an even split of crisp western wear and hip-hop fashion. There was a stage in a clearing separated from an adjacent soybean field by a row of trees, under which clusters of families and groups of friends held down every piece of shade. It was clear everyone was waiting for the main event to begin. Keith Frank and his band were still tuning up on a tiny plywood stage that was so small and crude it could have doubled as a roadside farm stand.

Geoff and I headed inside Club LA, where we found droopy-draw guys shooting pool, an empty dance floor, and a few bare bulbs casting sickly yellow light on a meager lineup of liquor bottles and foam cups. Fans blew the air around, but it wasn't much cooler beneath the bar's metal roof than under the outdoor sun. We had a polite drink and soon were back outside wandering by horse trailers parked behind the club, where the faint whiff of smoldering pot mingled with the ambient aroma of horse pies and hay. That's when we crossed paths with a short, heavyset woman walking purposefully across the field and carrying a sloshing, steaming stew pot with both hands. It was clearly quite a load, but still she stopped when she saw us. She rested the pot against her belly and beamed a big smile our way.

"You're the boys I talked to on the phone?" she asked.

"Yes, ma'am," said Geoff. "Thanks for the directions!"

"Well, we're glad you're here. Hope you have a good time!" she said walking off, putting that big pot of food in motion again.

"How do you think she knew it was us?" I asked rhetorically.

Earlier, in our first pass through the grounds, Geoff and I had noted that with the exception of the Soileau Band's guitarist we were the only white people around. This never became uncomfortable, and if anything we benefited from the hospitality that decent people show newcomers and unfamiliar faces. But there was no doubt we stood out, a point driven home by the children who stared at us with looks of unedited bewilderment beneath their oversized cowboy hats.

"Kids don't lie," Geoff chuckled after a crowd of preteens had gaped in silence as we walked past them. "They look really surprised to see us."

We bought cheap cans of beer from a makeshift bar under a tree by the stage and started settling in to the scene when some commotion broke out by the entrance to the grounds. We rubbernecked and heard the security staff hollering at a guy in a silver BMW who had caught gravel and peeled out on the dirt road while all around him coursed a collection of very happy but exhausted men on horseback. The trail ride was coming back in, and we rushed up to the main road to watch.

What followed was a spectacle of collective horsemanship that had stretched on for hot miles, had been going on for ceaseless sweating hours, and was now galloping back to roost in a final burst of friendly bravado. I abandoned my attempt to count the horses after just the first few dozen, and I had to estimate the final total at something north of three hundred. Most riders were men in their twenties to fifties, though there was a solid contingent of women riders as well. They were at the end of a very long ride down blazing country roads, and in this final stretch they urged their horses to a last lunge, like a posse roaring back into town to celebrate a successful mission.

The horses pranced, sauntered, and high-stepped their way off the road and onto the grounds, which soon became a dusty confusion of bouncing riders weaving through rows of parked trucks. Young kids in gleaming white cowboy boots and matching hats ran up to meet their parents, who pulled them up to ride on the saddles with them for victory laps around the busy field. These sons and daughters looked as proud to have the reins of the family mount as the kid given the helm on his dad's boat for the first time.

* * *

Soon the Soileau Band's drum, bass, and guitar began laying down an opening pulse, and Keith Frank stood poised at the edge of the stage, framed by two-by-fours holding up a tin roof. He's a big man with a huge following of zydeco fans, and he looked like a country king standing there in an open plaid shirt with his wooden-box accordion hanging at ease on the leather strap over his shoulder. Before him were all the generations of this trail ride crowd, and in a moment they would turn this patch of leafy country field into a raging dance floor of dust, boots, and couples locked in the loose but deliberate steps of zydeco rhythm.

But first, as the band kept up a slow-rolling beat, shout-outs were in order. At least every third person in the crowd wore a T-shirt emblazoned with the logo of his or her riding club, and the members cheered as Keith Frank belted out their names. The tiny sampling of the clubs I could scratch down in a notebook there in the jostling crowd included our hosts, of course, the Grandwood Riders and also the Big Body Riders, the Eunice 51/50 Riders, the Breaux Bridge Riders, the Unexpected Riders, the Paid In Full Riders, the Gutta Girls Riders, the Good Girl Riders, the Straight Up Riders, the Young Stud Riders, the Fighting Fille Riders, the Freetown Riders, the Crazy Hat Riders, the Chocolate Cuties, the Avenue Riders, the Bad n Bossie Riders, the Hip Hop Ghetto Riders, the Cecilia Brunk Riders, the Southern Platinum Riders, the Muleman Riders, and the Lee Boy Riders.

This random list doesn't do justice even to the number of clubs present at this single trail ride. As I scribbled down their names, it became clear how the great number of these organizations could populate an entire calendar with weekend events around the area.

Any tradition so thoroughly ingrained and vigorously practiced must have some serious roots, and New Orleans writer Michael Tisserand makes a convincing case for one origin theory in his book on zydeco culture, *The Kingdom of Zydeco*. Tisserand describes trail rides as a revival and modern interpretation of a country tradition dating back to the nineteenth century boucherie, that communal butchering of a hog.

In the days before refrigeration, it was a matter of vital economy for farmers in a small community to get together each weekend, butcher a hog, and divvy up the resulting groceries for each household to consume more or less fresh through the week. Naturally, people arrived at these meat fests on horseback back then, and the gathering of country neighbors was bound to become social. As electricity and fridges made individual farms more independent, the ritual boucherie fell by the wayside. But, Tisserand writes, "there remained a desire for the weekly gatherings, and by the late 1960s, country people had begun meeting on horseback, retracing the routes to the boucherie that was no longer there, in general agreement that the trail itself was worth the ride."

* * *

It took me a few months to get out to another trail ride. Again, my directions were vague, and I might have missed this party completely if not for a small plywood sign tamped into the ground with the words "trail ride" written in orange spray paint. The sign pointed me down the frontage road running parallel to Interstate 10 near Welsh, a small town on the long prairie stretch between Lafayette and Lake Charles. After a few miles I came across a second, identical sign, but I also saw the first of what proved a steady trail of horse pie clumps. These steaming markers guided me directly down a dirt road just off the highway to J & J's Place, a country ranch and the site of the Bareback Riders' party.

I was running solo on this outing, but after the trip with Geoff to that Cecilia trail ride I felt I knew the ropes. Sure, the men at the ranch's all-but-hidden entrance looked a little surprised to see me, but at least this time I knew they'd charge an eight-dollar admission, hand me a paper ticket stuck with a safety pin, and tell me where to park. I was already well ahead of last time's blank slate.

I approached a low, open, red-painted barn across the grassy grounds, and I heard its metal roof rattling with the heavy bass of contemporary zydeco. Inside was a scene much like the outdoor dance floor that materialized under the trees in Cecilia. At one corner of the barn, the Zydeco Nubreeds were led on accordion by J. Paul Jr., a young, lean Houston native with tattoos stenciling his muscular forearms and a crucifix tied at his neck. They kept the all-ages dance party moving before them. Big girls and skinny men, kids and their aunts and peers, trim cuties and handsome teens were all coupled off, and they switched partners with each new song. The front of the dance floor was owned by a group of voluptuous ladies in matching green tank tops, which identified them as members of the LTC Riders. They confidently grabbed partners twice their age or half their age or they just danced with each other, grinding and posing and goofing on the dance floor, but they always kept dancing. Everyone slugged down beers, crushing the discarded cans under their feet and kicking stray empties across the floor as they danced. Others passed around bottles of sweet, blue Boone's Farm wine, which were sold from iced bins at the bar in the back of the barn. In the shade of a nearby stable, women sold palm-sized sweet potato pies and pork sandwiches on white bread.

A few ceiling fans wobbled along high above but made no impression on the dusty, late-summer heat inside the barn. Smart dancers kept bandanas in their rear pockets to wipe the sweat and grit from their faces but everyone soaked through their clothing anyway.

Again the riding club T-shirts were everywhere. I was busy making a mental catalogue of them—noting the Cadillac Riders, the Southern Studs, the 747 Riders, the Bounce Back Riders—when I spotted a familiar face in the crowd. Across the barn, dancing with one of the gregarious LTC Riders, was Irvin Bernard. Tall, bronzed, and weathered, Irvin is my own father's age, and he must be as passionate a trail rider as they come. Geoff and I had met him at the Cecilia party a few months earlier.

"My name's Irvin," he told us, then after a beat added, "Irvin Cowboy."

We laughed at the pun, but he stayed stone faced. I thought for a long, nervous second we had misunderstood and offended him. But then his face cracked into a big smile. He knew he got us.

"Yeah, ha ha!" he hooted. "Irvin Cowboy. That's how they all know me here, boys, and everywhere I go, it's Irvin Cowboy."

We shared a beer and he gave us a little crash course in trail ride culture, explaining that he never missed one if he could help it. Here in Welsh, he was dressed exactly the same as he had been at the Cecilia party, wearing faded blue jeans and matching denim shirt and the same tattered cowboy hat festooned with dozens of pinned tickets and buttons from past trail rides. This hat was like a rag doll bouquet of old tickets, all dangling like thick confetti, and the sheer number of them spoke to his trail ride attendance record. I waited for a break in the music and then approached Irvin to say hello.

"Hey, you're here!" I said. "You really do come to all these, huh?"

It took Irvin a moment to recognize me, but when he did he smiled and grabbed my forearm, squeezing it as tightly as if grasping a hammer's handle.

"It's like I told you and your buddy. If I miss a trail ride, I really miss it, you know?" he said in a voice that sounded worn from a day of happy shouting. "I don't care if it's raining even. If it's raining when I leave my house, guess what? It's probably not raining where the trail ride is. I always go, man. The trail ride is it."

J. Paul Jr. was still playing a while later as I made my way through the field to find my Toyota hidden where I'd parked it between the much larger trucks and horse trailers. Looking down the ranch's dirt lane and past the access road, I could see cars and semis rocketing along the interstate, which I would soon join for my long drive back to New Orleans. I glanced back toward the barn for a moment and saw a flock of kids in matching riding club T-shirts walking together, dragging their boots through the dust and giggling at some joke. Just behind them, a young woman in jeans and a white halter top led her horse in a solitary lap around the grounds, weaving between parked sedans and pickups. Her long black hair bounced and swayed with the animal's stride, and soon she was past all the vehicles and silhouetted against the dark tree line at the edge of the grounds. It seemed for just a moment like a timeless country vignette, even as the zydeco bass and rubboard rattle shook the roof of the nearby barn. The image of this lone woman and her horse taking a moment apart from the fun commotion of the party stayed with me, and I thought about her as I went toward the highway. I imagined her heading home later on, putting her horse up, calling it a night, then going to work the next morning, a Monday, and waiting out the week until the next trail ride weekend.

Chapter 19

HENDERSON'S WILD SIDE

Over the Top in an Atchafalaya Levee Town

I awoke just after sunrise in a rented bed in Henderson, lurched out to the deck in my boxer shorts and undershirt and groggily went through the checklist of my senses, trying to bring them each online. Rubbing sleep from my eyes, I saw the narrow, uneven dock stretched out on water that was covered with a motionless crust of floating green algae. Over the trees just ahead I saw the rusty wheat color of the dawn haze. I heard the paper bag sound of some unseen but presumably large bird moving its wings in the brush behind me. I smelled the wet, mossy-sweet air, and sensed the barest, warm breeze over my skin, since I was, of course, still in my sleeping skivvies.

I wanted to soak in every detail of this wetlands sunrise, which was a new and mesmerizing experience for me. And yet it also was only the latest in a series of interesting discoveries around Henderson, a small town of about fifteen hundred residents and the hub for a most gratifying variety of Louisiana lodgings, the swamp houseboat for hire.

Antonia and I had pulled into Henderson the day before and ended up staying on one of these rented houseboats, which in design terms fall somewhere between a cabin and a floating tool shed. Small, cozy, and clean, ours was lashed to the rickety dock beneath McGee's Landing, which is a prime example of accumulated Cajun enterprise. On one waterfront property it combines a boat launch, a swamp tour operation, a gift shop, a houseboat motel, a restaurant,

Boats come in, and the nightlife gears up, on the edge of the Henderson swamp.

and a bar and music venue. All of that is perched on the very western edge of the Atchafalaya Basin, on the "wet" side of the basin's massive levee, giving unfettered access to—and direct views of—the largest swamp in North America.

Antonia lay sleeping during my brief morning reverie, and after standing around out there for a few minutes more I rejoined her in the houseboat and promptly fell back to sleep. I wanted to see my first swamp dawn, but I also needed more shuteye. After all, we had been up pretty late the night before partying along the strip of bars that runs down the same levee just behind our houseboat.

Henderson is a gateway to the natural splendor of the Atchafalaya, a wonderland for outdoors enthusiasts and anyone interested in Louisiana wildlife. But this tiny town along the swamp also boasts a robust nightlife, one full of quintessential Louisiana good times. Within two miles of our houseboat's berth that night there was the Atchafalaya Club at Pat's, with a dancehall the size of a convention center; then a crazed, hopped-up marina bar called Turtles; another huge dancehall dangling over the water, by the name of Angelle's Whiskey River Landing; and, just above us at McGee's, still another venue where a swamp pop drummer had serenaded us the night before while his band slow-rolled through power ballads and the bar crowd waltzed in little circles with easygoing, beer-buzz grins. When we were done for the night, Antonia and I left through a side exit by the bar, walked down a ramp to the dock and slept in our little houseboat as the muffled swamp pop tunes from upstairs gave way to the croaking, splashing, clicking sounds of the swamp itself.

Some bar scenes rely on a nearby college or sports stadium, some on urban population density, and others on beaches or other tourist draws. The lively Henderson bar scene relies on the Atchafalaya levee, as does so much else in the region.

* * *

Levees are a constant in some parts of south Louisiana. They are so large and green and integrated with their surroundings that they can seem like geological features rather than massive works of government engineering. Back home in New Orleans, the Mississippi River levee is essential to daily survival. Its role in the city's life is invariably driven home for me anew each spring when the northern thaw swells the river level and, while motoring down Tchoupitoulas Street, I can look up to see the hull of a massive, ocean-going tanker moving several stories above my car. But to look at, the levee is just a long, regular lump of earth covered with grass and weeds, and it seems so elemental, so present—so there—that eventually it just feels natural. Certain stretches of the New Orleans levee system, the literal life ring for the vulnerable city, are popular places for people to bring their dogs to exercise, and I know a few jocks who run "inclines" up its slope, trying to get their calves accustomed to hills while living in a region with so few natural rises. It's like the levee is a part-time, linear park whose fulltime job happens to be keeping the city from oblivion.

In addition to its design-specific roles, the Atchafalaya levee in Henderson also provides egress to all that waits on its wild side. Of the aforementioned bars and dancehalls, only Pat's is on the dry side of the levee—the side that faces town—but it still hangs over water, in this case the slim, gentle Bayou Amy sitting parallel to the levee.

Pat's is a huge place that is hard to miss once you get close, but the other venues on the other side of the levee took me quite by surprise the first time I went looking for them. They are all but invisible from the meandering levee road, with only signs and arrows pointing visitors up and over the hump of the levee to reach them. When I first drove up the gravel path allegedly leading to Angelle's Whiskey River Landing, I had no clue what would be on the other side of the rise. I just slowly drove on, kept to the right of the narrow trail, and hoped anyone coming unseen from the other side would do the same. When I reached the peak, the view through my windshield was like that of a watery valley vista, with a sprawl of cypress and calm interweaving channels cut through by slow-cruising boats. And just below me, as the signs had promised, sat Whiskey River Landing. It looked like a large, drab waterfront warehouse, but one trembling with a zydeco bass line, while above it cars and trucks were parked at precarious, brake-testing angles on the levee's downward slope.

* * *

That Henderson's social life should reside on the levee feels appropriate, since the town owes its very existence to this mighty flood control structure and the disaster that spawned it, the Great Mississippi River Flood of 1927. Levees have been used along the Mississippi River practically since New Orleans was built on its banks, and the word levee itself derives from the French "to raise."

They started as low, rudimentary bumps to keep predictable seasonal flooding at bay. But throughout the nineteenth century, as planters developed the dark, fecund riverside lands into profitable agricultural enterprises, the levees had to rise higher and spread farther up and down the banks to more reliably protect the area. Thus commenced the essential paradox of Louisiana's relationship with the Mississippi, the river that formed much of the state with its alluvial deposits, made the soil rich and profitable for development, and wants continuously to keep flooding and moving around even after we've built so much around it.

As early as 1814, some engineers were advancing proposals to use spillways and other manmade outlets to reduce flood risk, but levees remained the method of choice. Eventually, the U.S. Army Corps of Engineers assumed responsibility for these levees, which would stretch along the Mississippi from Illinois to its Gulf outlet at the bottom of Louisiana, the giant spout for a funnel-shaped river system draining 41 percent of America's lower forty-eight states, as well as a smidgen of Canada. After weathering a few flood stages without incident, the Corps assured the American public in 1926 that levees were enough to hold back the river, come what may. The answer to this hubris wasn't long in coming.

Later that same year, torrential downpours in the north swelled the Mississippi's many tributaries, sending unprecedented water levels along to the main stream. A first levee break, or crevasse, happened on April 16, 1927, in Cairo, Illinois, and as the massive flood stage moved downriver it would bust levees in seven states. Eventually, the floodwaters unleashed by these crevasses covered some twenty-six thousand square miles, an area equal to Massachusetts, New Hampshire, and Vermont combined. Hundreds of people died, and by the time the water had spread out some seven hundred thousand Americans were rendered homeless. Thousands of people spent days awaiting rescue on the crests of intact levee structures, the only high ground around above the flooded fields and towns, and many more would live in refugee camps for months. It was a humanitarian catastrophe abetted by a human rights crisis in shattered communities. Reports surfaced of abuses in the camps, especially the conscription of black residents into work gangs to begin plugging the crevasses.

This national disaster carried far-reaching consequences, as writer John Barry describes in his fascinatingly detailed book *Rising Tide*. He links the flood's tumult to an acceleration of black migration from the Deep South to the north, part of one of the century's great demographic shifts. In Louisiana, populist candidate Huey P. Long rode a wave of postflood discontent among working-class voters into the governor's office during an election held just a few months after the disaster. In Washington, D.C., commerce secretary Herbert Hoover became the head of the federal government's recovery effort after the flood, and he parlayed all the publicity this post brought him to win the White House for the Republicans in 1928. But John

Barry also illustrates how Hoover manipulated southern black leaders in the flood's aftermath, reneging on promises of greater political access he made to them during the crisis months. He argues that resentment over this betrayal helped sever historic links between black voters and the Republican party—the party of Lincoln—adding a seismic political shift to the demographic one brought on by the flood.

And in Acadiana, one somewhat less momentous result was the eventual formation of Henderson, setting the stage for today's great, levee-side bar scene to develop along its edge. When the Mississippi broke through levees well north of Baton Rouge in 1927, the water came barreling down the river's natural distributary, right through the Atchafalaya River and its flood basin. Small fishing villages in the basin, like Pelba and Bayou Chene, were wiped out. Refugees piled up in Lafayette, living in tent cities or wherever else they could find shelter. Eventually, though, new and vastly larger levees were built, both along the Mississippi River and along the Atchafalaya Basin. When these latter structures were completed, many of the displaced people from the erased basin villages settled in new towns along its western—or dry—side, and they planted the roots of modern-day Henderson.

The town would remain a quiet, small Acadian community for the next few decades, and it was only incorporated as a municipality in 1971. Two years later, the final section of Interstate 10 in Louisiana was completed with an eighteen-mile-long causeway that crosses the swamps and river of the Atchafalaya Basin and hits dry land again right at Henderson.

Ramping down off the highway exit today, Henderson looks like any other small, crowded pit stop along the rushing American interstate system, with multiple gas stations and chain restaurants all configured with parking lots large enough to accommodate tractor-trailers. But with just one turn from this feeder road, the scene shifts to the narrow village of Henderson, with modest homes, quiet side streets, and one main drag leading to the levee. It's the front door to the massive natural heritage of the Atchafalaya Basin, and it's just a few minutes off the seventy-miles-per-hour zoom of the state's busiest highway. Even from the interstate, you can look south over the cypress-studded swamp and see the metal roofs of a few of the levee-side boat landings and clubs in the distance.

* * *

I had heard about the dancehalls and houseboat rentals in Henderson, but as I traced out travel routes on my maps I was surprised to see a road verging off from the levee to continue along a big loop through what looked like the middle of the Atchafalaya Basin itself. How could this be? I had assumed the basin area, the territory now hemmed between the western levee at Henderson and the eastern levee near the hamlet of Ramah, was a wet warren of river and swamp. But here was this road trickling through it with a dot plotted about halfway along its run to mark a town. This was Butte La Rose, and upon seeing its name on the map I was intrigued.

I had pitched a Henderson road trip to my intrepid traveling buddy Geoff Coats as a chance to go barhopping along a rural levee and, once I had him out there, I threw in the little side excursion of an unknown and unlikely drive within the basin's levee confines. A road sign for Butte La Rose directed us over the levee, and upon reaching the crest we looked down to see that the road continued along a bridge built from what looked like telephone poles, railroad ties, deeply rusted girders, and large pulley wheels. It looked like a mechanical artifact from the early days of the Industrial Revolution, or even a drawbridge apparatus spanning a moat, but in fact it was a pontoon bridge carrying the one and only road from Henderson to Butte La Rose.

Once on the other side we looked in vain for a town center of any type. We found only an unbroken string of camps and homes that fronted a brown river and dipped their own little docks into its waters. We passed a clapboard chapel, an RV camp, a single stop sign, and a bar called Kate's, where we joined a small Sunday afternoon crowd refreshing themselves with Bud longnecks and playing country tunes on the jukebox.

I got the impression that Butte La Rose is a leisure town for people on weekend getaways and the year-round home for people who like living close to their immediate neighbors but way off the beaten track to anything else. For us just passing through, it proved to be an interesting drive across a part of the Louisiana map I had previously regarded as a wild blank between destinations. We were only about twenty miles from Lafayette, the big city in this part of Louisiana, but once we crested the levee and crossed that creaking pontoon bridge we were on a frontier to wilderness. It made me think of what the lost villages of the basin might have grown into were it not for the 1927 flood.

* * *

While Butte La Rose feels remote, a principal charm of Henderson is how accessible it makes quintessential Louisiana scenes, both of the natural and cultural variety. I had driven past the town on the interstate countless times wondering where I would eat down the road or where I might find some good zydeco or Cajun bands playing in a genuine-feeling setting, when all the while plenty of restaurants and music clubs sat here just off exit 115.

When you're in a rush to get from Baton Rouge to Lafayette, or vice versa, the basin seems like a long expanse to get beyond. But to another way of thinking, this highway span is an astounding tour over an intersection of habitat and engineering. The Atchafalaya River stretches north to south for about 135 miles, emptying into the Gulf just below Morgan City. It starts about 60 miles to the northeast of Henderson near the town of Simmesport, Louisiana, found at the confluence of the Red River and a canal called Old River, which connects to the Mississippi just seven miles away.

As a distributary of the Mississippi, the Atchafalaya has historically drawn off part of the main river's flow, and the volume of that flow had risen steadily, year after year, as the scouring water progressively deepened and widened the Atchafalaya itself. Left to its own devices, that dynamic should have caused the Mississippi to reach a tipping point and jump from its current course to the Atchafalaya sometime in the 1970s. That would have meant the end of New Orleans as a river port, and left all the industry on the Mississippi between Baton Rouge and the Gulf marooned on a silt bank.

If it sounds far-fetched for something as massive as the Mississippi to up and change address, remember that it's happened many times as the ancient flow of the river moved around, forming the wide coastal plain of today's Louisiana. Bayou Teche and Bayou Lafourche, both such sleepy waterways today, each had stints as the Mississippi's mainstream during the centuries before European settlement of the area. The writer John McPhee explains this whole process with startling clarity in his book *The Control of Nature*, which details the engineering efforts that have just barely prevented a similar shift to the Atchafalaya in recent decades.

The briefest explanation for why this jump hasn't occurred is embodied by the Old River Control Structure, a fortress of a faucet built by the U.S. Army Corps of Engineers and completed in 1963. The structure is a gigantic valve constantly maintained by the Corps to divert approximately 30 percent of the Mississippi's flow to the Atchafalaya River and keep the remaining 70 percent coursing on down past Baton Rouge and New Orleans and out to the Gulf—the path to which modern Louisiana and all the upstream interests are accustomed.

Once you get on the other side of the Atchafalaya levee, the basin experience of the lakes, rivers, bayous, and swamps can seem like nature in full, though the entire life of the habitat here is dependant on the intense and omnipresent influence of the Old River Control Structure to the north. When seasonal high waters swell the Mississippi, the Corps releases more of it through the Atchafalaya, in mimicry of the fluctuating levels nature once sent down this distributary path. That means taking a swamp tour, going out fishing, or even staying on a Henderson houseboat are different experiences at different times of the year. In the spring, with the waters running high, the cypress forests are inundated but also quite healthy, with water reaching up to their high limbs and green growth everywhere. In the winter, with the northern water locked up in ice, a tour reveals much more of the habitat's undercarriage, including the graveyards of cypress stumps left behind by the logging industry.

* * *

The levee-side scene for music and nightlife remains pretty reliable throughout the year, however, and for a very small town Henderson sure has a lot of options. After finishing the Butte La Rose loop, Geoff and I embarked on a mission to hit all of the bars and dancehalls along the levee. We missed McGee's Landing this time, perhaps because we blinked while passing its sign on the tame side of the levee, but Antonia and I made that up during our later houseboat visit.

The biggest draw in Henderson is Pat's Fisherman's Wharf, which was just a levee-front hamburger stand when Pat Huval took over the business in 1952. Huval became Henderson's first mayor at the time of the town's incorporation in 1971, and he held the post for seventeen years. His business has grown enormously, and it now resembles a campus of interconnected buildings comprising a dancehall, a restaurant, a motel, and a series of outbuildings that are all designed to look like contiguous storefronts. There's a short water tower rising here, overhead power lines stretching there, and a decorative, full-size lighthouse by the entrance to the always-packed parking lot. Altogether, the place has the feeling of a Wild West movie set.

The biggest part of the operation is the Atchafalaya Club, a huge room in a metal building with enough floor space for two indoor soccer clubs to practice simultaneously. Geoff and I paid the cover and walked into this hangar-like building to find local Cajun music favorites Steve Riley and the Mamou Playboys performing on stage while couples waltzed together on the smooth and shiny dance floor. Chandeliers, fans, and potted ferns hung down from the distant ceiling and a bar done up in decorative woodwork stretched along one wall for about half the length of a city block. We made it outside to the deck overlooking Bayou Amy, and sitting there for a spell we could simultaneously see diners framed in Pat's restaurant windows, hear Steve Riley playing through the metal walls of the dancehall, and watch a group of teenagers trying to hook catfish in the bayou with simple rods dangling over the deck rail.

Our itinerary next took us over the levee to Turtles Bar, part of a marina and houseboat complex called the Atchafalaya Basin Landing. The sun was sinking, and boats were returning to the landing at a steady clip. The bar itself looked relatively small, and initially it seemed rather quiet too, as if everyone had hauled their boats out of the water at the end of a Sunday and just headed on home. Not so.

I opened the door and Geoff and I stood there for a split second as the threshold exploded with Allman Brothers jukebox music, happy cackling sounds, and swaying, sunburned figures in golf visors and beach wraps. It felt like we had opened a hatch into some levee party vortex, and in an instant we were pulled into the bar as if by a powerful vacuum. The little place was rocking. It was packed with people fresh from their boat outings and fishing trips, and they were not letting this Sunday evening off the hook so easily. The cluttered décor was somewhere between pirate lair and country store, with lots of fake fishnets and knickknacks crowding the walls, and the crowd was swaying, roaring and addled. It didn't take them long to make us out to be newcomers.

"Hey! You! Where you from?" called one weaving, welcoming, sun-singed redhead.

"New Orleans!" Geoff said, hollering over the jukebox guitars.

I braced for the disparaging or boastful response that the mention of New Orleans so often elicits in other parts of Louisiana. I was ready for her to tell us that this here was the real Louisiana, and how New Orleans might be okay and all but that people who think New Orleans is the real Louisiana are fools, and on like that. It had been a predictable pattern elsewhere. But the welcoming redhead was thrilled.

"New Orleans! Who dat! Yeah!" she screamed. "I love New Orleans! Frenchmen Street, French Quarter, I love it! Bobby! Bobby! Check it out! They're from New Orleans!"

Bobby edged through the crowd, and he was equally excited to hear the news.

"Fucking hell, right, man! New Orleans! Woo!" he yelled, smiling, and held his palm up for a high five.

Geoff and I dispensed a round of hard high fives and then crushed against the bar for a drink with our new friends. The whole place seemed to be this enthusiastic—not about us or about New Orleans, but about being in Turtles at the end of a hot Sunday out on the water, drinking beer and cocktails, smoking up a storm, and shouting along to Steve Miller lyrics.

"Yeah, take the money and run!" Bobby was singing, smiling broadly and nodding his head to the classic rock beat.

Soon we were off to what has become my favorite Henderson spot, Angelle's Whiskey River Landing. It sits further down the levee from Pat's and Turtles, though its atmosphere and mood is somewhere in between them.

Angelle's is a huge music venue, though not as big as Pat's. And it has a lively air, with lots of people dancing and horsing around and hanging out at its two long bars, which sometimes double as elevated dance floors. But I've never seen the place quite as manic as what we had experienced at Turtles. Sunday afternoon and early evening is the only time Angelle's is normally open, but this tail end of the weekend shift is alive with an all-walks-of-life crowd of people who make the special trip down levee and over the top to party with zydeco and Cajun bands.

Zydeco star Geno Delafose and his band French Rockin' Boogie were playing during my visit with Geoff, and we could hear his accordion and the accompanying bass line even as we walked down from our steep levee parking spot above the club. Houseboats and tour barges were beached here and there along the water's edge, and we passed an outdoor cart where a guy was grilling up burgers and sausages for sale by Angelle's door. Inside, the plywood dance floor was already packed with dancers moving to the band's pulling rhythm.

The song ended and the dancers split up as per usual and cleared the floor until the next tune and the next invitation to dance. Geno started working his accordion, making warm-up sounds, and the other musicians watched him closely, waiting for him to identify the song. The crowd was waiting too, but soon it became clear Geno would slowly ease us all into the next number, building his introductory notes into a solo. And he held us all there for a few moments, his band and the dancers alike, gradually raising the momentum, like an old locomotive stoking up. The band got the idea, and the drummer added a tapping rhythm. The crowd got the idea too, and men and women started taking hands again, forming dancing pairs and moving together slowly, just lightly touching.

Geno was inflating a tense bubble of sound over the room, and with a nod over his shoulder to his drummer he let it burst. The full zydeco sound poured down. The tempo of the dancing couples immediately shifted up, and the entire room seemed to breathe together in mighty inhalations and exhalations, like the deep pulsing of bellows as Geno's accordion carried us along. The hair on my forearms stood up as I felt the kinetic oomph crash through the place. The big windows just behind the band were dark, though I knew the whole basin was out there just beyond the pane, sitting still and stoic as the plywood room around us surged with energy.

CHAPTER 20

A CAJUN WAKE-UP CALL
Music on a Louisiana Saturday Morning

Saturdays in Acadiana for me are fun, sweet, and frustrating all at once. They are fun because Saturdays offer reliably amazing Cajun and zydeco music opportunities across a slate of easygoing and varied venues. They are sweet because an itinerary to take in just a slice of the regularly scheduled gigs on that day implies a tour of some of the region's most essential small towns and its pretty countryside. And they are frustrating because I am afflicted with a rare disorder that positively retards any attempt I make to dance to this region's beautiful music.

I can dance at weddings when "Footloose" comes on, and during that whole cigar-martini-pinstripe-swing dance phase in the late 1990s, when America remembered that trombones existed, I was considered a game dancer in some circles for my ability to pump a partner's arm back and forth while jogging in place—a combination that, at least in a crowd, appeared to resemble dancing. The standards are a bit higher in Acadiana, where people dance to their culture's indigenous French music. It's not that the local dance steps are terribly demanding or complex. They're just specific and, for some reason, as incomprehensible to my feet as babble to my ears.

I have learned to live with this condition, however, and I do not permit it to hold me back. Just because I can't dance does not mean I won't dance. In the tight crowd of a Cajun music festival or zydeco club I can just fake it and hope my partner/victim attributes any disjointed movements to the jostling of the pack. But I am always

"Tante Sue" Vasseur, serving the morning crowd at Fred's Lounge in Mamou.

aware that my feet are grossly out of phase with what is supposed to be the easy, natural two-steps and waltzes of the south Louisiana dance floor.

This is why a normal Saturday in Cajun country becomes an around-the-clock indictment of my dancing skills, and that's a lot of bruising for one ego to bear. But the circuit is so much fun, and so sweet, that I keep at it still. The abuse starts early, and stays thick throughout the day.

The convention for live music at small clubs and bars in New Orleans, and every other city in which I've lived, is for bands to begin performing sometime around 10 p.m. On Saturdays in Acadiana, this equation is reversed with a vengeance, and by 9 a.m. a number of lively and quite different music happenings are well under way at Café des Amis in Breaux Bridge, at Savoy Music Center in Eunice, and at Fred's Lounge in Mamou, while a whole second wave of gigs comes along later in the day.

For people in New Orleans, getting a taste of this usually means setting an early Saturday alarm and departing for a morning road trip. After various trials, I have concluded the better option is to get across the Atchafalaya Basin on Friday, stay the night and wake up fresh and already on the scene Saturday morning. For best results, you should consider staying over Saturday night too, since the day can be exhausting, and at the end of it drivers may be left in poor shape for a long run back home. But then that sets up the temptation to stick around for more music on Sunday afternoon and, well, at this rate you may never leave.

I have asked various people during my travels why this Saturday music scene should start so early. I usually get a shrug and a reference to things always being done this way. Others have supposed that it springs from the area's agricultural base, reasoning that farmers who get up early for work may get up early to play too. The most convincing explanation, however, goes back to Fred's Lounge in Mamou and a guy who liked to wake up his neighbors on Saturday mornings with old-fashioned French music.

* * *

One of my very first trips to Cajun country began with an early wake-up call for the drive to Fred's. The town of Mamou is a farming community high up on the Cajun prairie in Evangeline Parish, and Fred's is a small, low, brick bunker of a barroom along a block of drab storefronts on the main drag of Sixth Street. But this externally nondescript bar has a magnetism far out of proportion to its size or appearance, and the fun cooked up here every Saturday morning pulls in an eager crowd mixing international tourists, local farmers, Lafayette college kids, and New Orleans day-trippers.

On this first trip I traveled from New Orleans with my friends Cheryl Gerber and Mark McGrain, who make regular pilgrimages to Fred's and allowed me to tag along. We departed the city at the radically early hour of 7:30 a.m. and arrived in Mamou by 10 a.m. to find the town quiet and the streets rather empty. But the block around Fred's was lined with cars, and the grassy lot behind the place was overflowing with creative parking geometry.

Walking toward the entrance, I could hear drums trebling the windows and the muted sawing of a fiddle inside. I pushed at the bar's metal door but it would only open halfway before it bumped

into someone's back. This seemed uncanny. Fred's was so busy at
10 a.m. that the crowd packed inside already blocked the door's full
swing. We squeezed through to find people crammed into the small
room from one pink-painted wall to the other. They were stacked
up three deep at the bar, cracking cans of Budweiser and stirring
swizzles in plastic cups of bloody Mary cocktails.

Across the room a Cajun band played within a roped-off rectangle
as the crowd danced outside the perimeter. It was one big mass of
dancing people made up of widely diverse parts. A middle-aged man
in a neat golf shirt and with a pager on his belt danced with a woman
in jeans and a windbreaker. A woman in a western shirt festooned
with buckles and feathers was in the bear-hug arms of a red-faced
man who was so huge the side snaps of his overalls were undone
to accommodate his girth. A dark-haired young woman in a pretty
cotton dress leaned against the bar, surveying the room coolly. In a
moment, one of the band's two fiddlers handed off his instrument to
another musician and confidently led this lovely in a waltz through
the tight crowd. The singer started wailing in French, holding the
microphone with both hands, and a group of old women sitting at
the booth against the wall laughed when he winked and teasingly
shook his finger at them.

"Beer?" Mark asked rhetorically, already waving down the lady
behind the bar.

The bartender looked matronly, somewhere in her seventies, with
short white hair and big, round eyeglasses. But she sailed around
the bar with giddy energy, fetching drinks and waving to customers
across the room. As she handed over our beers, I noticed a leather
holster around her waist with a half-pint bottle riding in the pistol
pouch.

"What's the hooch?" I asked her.

"Here!" she yelled. And with no further answer she handed me
the bottle and slid off, as if on skates, to the other side of the bar to
take another order. I took a sip from her open bottle and tasted spicy
cinnamon schnapps.

"Hot Damn!" the lady called over her shoulder, referring, I soon
surmised, to the brand of schnapps in the bottle I was still holding.
"Hot Damn! And we got it for five bucks a half-pint."

"We'll take one," I said.

The woman found a cold bottle in the cooler, uncapped it, held her elbow high and took a dramatic swig directly from its mouth before handing over my purchase. That must have made us even for the sample she gave me, I reasoned.

"Hot Damn!" she yelled again, giggling, and in an instant she was out from behind the bar and moving through the density of dancers, gleefully egging everyone on.

The band finished its song, and the dancers drifted toward the bar and the edges of the room, though there really wasn't much room to move very far. The singer then waved the white-haired lady over to the microphone and introduced her as "Tante Sue de Mamou." Everyone in the crowd cheered. The drummer set the beat, and the band launched into another song with Tante Sue singing in French. She pulled another gulp of schnapps from her holster bottle between verses, and at this move everyone cheered again.

The dancing resumed, and the couples were pressed in so tight they touched whenever they turned or twirled. I was being jostled so much on the edge of all this motion that I felt like I was almost dancing by default, so I decided to give it a shot for real. I had been watching people dance a nearly uniform set of steps and felt confident I could just copy them.

I asked a thin girl in flip-flops to dance, and in a moment, to my astonishment, we were actually dancing. Of course, the crowd was working with me here, basically moving us along in an organic clockwork of shoulders and elbows. I felt like I was getting along okay, so long as no one could see the hokey pokey steps my feet were doing and as long as I kept them off my brave partner's flip-flops. Tante Sue weaved into view, beaming an elfin grin, dancing now with the big guy in the unsnapped overalls.

* * *

Sue Vasseur, or Tante Sue (Aunt Sue), has been the irrepressible persona of Fred's Lounge for a long time now, and Fred's itself played an important role in the early reawakening of popular Cajun culture. Sue was married to Fred Tate, who had taken over a small Mamou saloon just after World War II and renamed it for himself. His older brother was Paul Tate, a local attorney and politician who would help lead the revival of Mamou's Mardi Gras celebration in the 1950s. A lot of the planning and community organizing required to bring the traditions of the rural, Cajun Mardi Gras back to glory took place over the bar and at lounge tables at Fred's.

One of the Mardi Gras boosters from those early days was Revon Reed, who was a Cajun music enthusiast before the traditional sounds had caught on again. A passion for Cajun Mardi Gras and a passion for traditional Cajun music are usually tightly entwined, but Revon went above and beyond. He did his best to stoke interest in the music around the prairie, and he even hosted a radio show spinning Cajun records on a local station during a brief, thirty-minute window allotted for folk music on Saturday mornings.

This was not prime airtime but it was a start, and Revon kept at it, trying to get the old French music back into rotation. In 1962, he approached Fred Tate with the idea of hosting the radio show from his bar. They took a stab at the arrangement, with Revon broadcasting from Fred's during his early morning Saturday slot. Live bands followed, as did the crowds, and Fred's evolved into the big, early party that it is today. As the band plays and the crowd dances and drinks, the Ville Platte radio station KVPI 1050 AM still sets up a live remote to broadcast the Fred's Lounge action over the prairie airwaves. Mamou is surrounded by rice fields and cattle pasture, and on the way to Fred's in the morning, always running a little late, I like to tune in to hear the party in progress while cruising between the roadside ditches.

"We're dancing on the radio!" Tante Sue called from the roped-in band area on my first Fred's visit, stirring up her jubilant crowd and talking to the radio listeners out there too. "How do you like that, everybody? We're dancing on the radio!"

Fred Tate died in 1992. A few years later new owners David and Libby Gillory bought the bar, and Tante Sue stayed on as manager. She is now pushing eighty, but every Saturday she is behind the bar, on the dance floor, and at the microphone, encouraging the crowd and sharing bottles of Hot Damn schnapps, which I've come to regard as some form of Cajun Geritol for its enlivening effects on the vivacious Tante Sue.

Now, the Saturday morning radio tradition makes up nearly the entirety of Fred's operation. With the exception of a few extra days of business during Mardi Gras time, Fred's is open only on Saturdays, and only for a few hours on Saturdays at that. The band begins playing at 9 a.m., and by 2 p.m. it's all over. Bartenders start clearing out the hundreds of empty beer cans that have accumulated on every horizontal surface in the lounge, and they push brooms over the tiny dance floor. Patrons grown accustomed to the darkness of the bar step outside into the dazzling sunlight. Some hit the road. Others, perhaps reenergized by the realization that it's still just a little past lunchtime, move on down to the next stop, either to one of Mamou's rough-edged townie bars or to the nicely renovated Hotel Cazan, where another Cajun band greets the diehards. Meanwhile, down the street, Fred's goes into hibernation until the next Saturday morning.

* * *

From its humble roots as an enthusiast's underpowered AM radio broadcast, Saturday morning at Fred's grew into a popular phenomenon and demonstrated that people would come out early for a good time with good music and rack up some mileage to do it. There is now a whole circuit of morning music stops, each with its own appeal and core following.

While everyone from Cajun bikers to Swedish tourists heads to Fred's for a big raucous party, Saturday mornings at the Savoy Music Center are intimate jam sessions hosted by one of the most influential families in modern Cajun music. That would be the Savoys, and this utterly nondescript music store and instrument shop on the country highway just east of Eunice is their headquarters. The place is set off Highway 190 in a grove of trees, and from the outside it looks about as exciting as a rural dentist office. But on Saturday mornings the line of cars and pickups parked along the highway near its driveway are a dead giveaway that something is going on here.

The Savoy Music Center's weekly jam sessions are open to the public, and they are aimed specifically at musicians interested in sitting in with a random assortment of Cajun fiddlers, guitarists, and accordion players. As dotty as I am with Cajun dance steps, my aptitude with any musical instrument is more embarrassing still. I suspect these conditions may just be related, but at any rate I have never attempted to strum along at these jams. Instead, I content myself with listening from the sidelines and watching the interactions of professional and hobbyist musicians from the region and those who travel a good distance to be part of the morning music here. Since I don't arrive with an instrument, I always bring a small box of hot boudin, which proves to be as effective a conversation piece in this crowd as turning up with an especially pretty guitar. Seated on a collection of padded aluminum chairs, piano benches, and stools, the all-ages group of musicians play together like a rustic string orchestra dressed in denim and boots or muscle shirts and sneakers. They're surrounded by the Savoy retail display cases of guitars and accordions and piles of merchandise boxes, paperwork, and communal sausage trays, while their freewheeling music sounds like the acoustic soundtrack to a household hootenanny.

For visitors, jam sessions like this are a chance to experience Cajun music culture offstage, and for visitors with some musical ability they are opportunities to participate a bit as well. In Breaux Bridge, a downtown café called the Coffee Break hosts its own Pont Breaux Jam on Saturdays in bright rooms filled with local artwork and the aroma of roasted beans. A similar scene of open-play Cajun and bluegrass develops on Sunday afternoons in Arnaudville, a picturesque town at the intersection of bayous Teche and Fuselier, at the instrument repair shop Tom's Fiddle & Bow.

Savoy Music Center, though, also has musical legacy to go along with its musical fellowship. This store is where owner Marc Savoy builds and sells his Acadian-brand accordions when he isn't playing them with his wife, Ann Savoy, the singer, guitarist, and producer. Together, the Savoys are a power couple for the preservation of acoustic Cajun music, recording albums and performing all over the world. Their sons, Joel and Wilson Savoy, were raised in the midst of all this, and now they are highly regarded players among the next generation of Cajun musicians. Wilson is the accordion player and singer in the Pine Leaf Boys, who tour widely. Joel was a founding member of the Red Stick Ramblers, and more recently he helped form Valcour Records. Releases from this Eunice-based label have introduced me to so much interesting new musical talent from the region that I've come to look at it as the Stax of Acadiana. Some of those Valcour-label musicians had their first public experience playing at the Savoy jam sessions, and many of them drop by on random Saturday mornings to catch up with friends and play together, as do the Savoy brothers.

It might seem a bit intimidating for a novice or newcomer to walk in off the country highway and join this kind of musical weight playing on their home turf. But all the interactions I saw from my perch showed friendliness, encouragement, and genuine interest among the aggregation. Certainly, that's the reception I've always experienced here when I arrive with five pounds of boudin all cut up and ready to share.

* * *

The traditional Cajun music and dancing scene carries across a lot of different venues as Saturday stretches on. In Lafayette, restaurants like Prejean's and Randol's have dance floors between the tables and bands on stage, as does D.I.'s out in the Basile countryside and Mulate's in Breaux Bridge, among others. Also in Breaux Bridge, La Poussiere ("the dust") is a straight-up, old-fashioned dancehall, a long, low building that could be confused for a suburban office suite on nondance nights. On Saturday nights, though, and even more so on Sunday afternoons, an intensely local crowd turns up to work the dance floor while traditional Cajun players like Walter Mouton and Jackie Caillier perform.

And in downtown Eunice, a neat, small prairie city and hotbed for Cajun heritage, the Rendezvous des Cajuns strikes up at 6 p.m. each Saturday as a family-oriented, French-language showcase of traditional Cajun music interspersed with folktales, jokes, and community announcements. It's held in the center of town at the Liberty Theater, a restored, vaudeville-vintage performance space where the seating section closest to the stage was removed to provide a dance floor. The show is broadcast on local radio in the area. Barry Jean Ancelet, folklorist and professor at the University of Louisiana at

Lafayette, emcees the weekly show, speaking in French and English and often alternating between the two in midsentence. If the mix of Spanish and English is "Spanglish," this patois must be "Frenglish."

The crowd I joined here leaned heavily toward retirement-age folks, who turned in stately waltzes on the dance floor, munched popcorn from their theater seats, and in some cases had young children in tow. I sat behind one such lady and a boy, who I took to be her grandson, and I eavesdropped keenly as she translated some of the emcee's French narration, which was my only hope of keeping up with the polyglot patter. The whole thing wraps up by 7:30 p.m., in plenty of time for families to get the kids to bed and for the bands to hustle over to perform a night show in Lafayette.

* * *

Saturday is the big night at the zydeco dancehalls too, but this Creole music is also at the heart of one of the three big Saturday morning destinations: Café des Amis. Right in the center of historic Breaux Bridge, a block from the brown, mellow Bayou Teche, Café des Amis hosts an early morning music event nearly as wild as Fred's, though a bit more genteel and with the option of ordering beignets, boudin-stuffed omelets, and crawfish etouffee.

The pretty brick building was originally a general store, and it was being used as an art gallery when local politician Dickie Breaux bought the place in the 1980s. He turned it into a coffee shop, and this eventually evolved into a full-service restaurant serving a solid menu of Cajun dishes. The masterstroke, though, was to create the Saturday morning zydeco breakfast. It's so popular now that people line up outside before the restaurant's 7:30 a.m. opening time to vie for a shot at the first seating.

The tables were thoroughly occupied by the time I arrived at 9 a.m. one Saturday, but I was able to pay a five-dollar cover to hang out at the bar. Joe Hall and the Louisiana Cane Cutters had set up in the bay of one of the old shop windows and they were well into their set. Just as I learned from earlier zydeco dances, the crowd at Café des Amis cleared the floor at the end of each song and returned with new partners once the band's accordion and rubboard got under way again with the next tune. At Café des Amis, however, many of the dancers snuck in a few bites of omelet and swigs of coffee or mimosas before pushing chairs aside and filtering back up past the other diners to reclaim the dance floor.

People were pulling and sliding and whirling around the breakfast tables as they danced with huge smiles on their faces. Couples waiting outside for tables danced on the sidewalk too, just on the other side of the glass. Even the bartenders started dancing with each other, since they would have no customers until the present song ended and the dance floor crowd returned to order more drinks.

Everyone was dancing, and eventually the usual accordion hypnosis and the infectious delight of the crowd took effect to get the better of my dance inhibitions. I found a dance partner and we maneuvered around someone's breakfast to find a patch on the smooth, pine floor. The band was smoking now, with tall Joe Hall singing in thick, stentorian tones and working his chest-sized, pearly-white piano accordion fast. Waitresses dodged the dancers with platters of biscuits and hot coffee held above. The people around us looked great. There were old men and middle-aged women, an easy mix of whites and blacks, young guys in LSU shirts, preppy girls in khakis, and gray-haired women in festival-time tie-dye dresses and sneakers. All the dancers kept an upright posture, held each other in casually tight embraces and followed the fundamental steps of zydeco.

I did my best to mimic the style, but inevitably I broke into off-kilter tapping, awkward lunging, and random rocking motions. Why? Because I simply can't dance. It was like everyone else on the dance floor was making an etouffee, and there I was stirring my usual Irish stew with all its lumpy potatoes. My struggles continue, but at least I've found a lot of good places to practice—morning, noon, or night.

CHAPTER 21

PUTTING MEALS ON THE MAP
Eating Around Acadiana

Pulling in to the nearly empty parking lot outside of Dean's in Henderson on a Sunday night, I had the distinct feeling that a long and wonderful lucky streak of finding great restaurant meals in Cajun country was about to end. In a way, I was almost relieved. Eating around south Louisiana in general—and Acadiana in particular—had proven a glorious journey thus far. At restaurants everywhere, I found generous, inexpensive manifestations of the state's abundant seafood catch, its robust butcher shop traditions and the widespread local faith that a little more butter and pepper never hurt a dish. Still, even the world's great dining cities are also full of convenience eateries and dumpy taverns. I felt it was just a matter of time before I hit such a place out here in Cajun country.

I had been cruising around the Lafayette area all day for a tour of assorted bars and music spots. My barbecue plate lunch from the Breaux Bridge butcher shop Poche's was many miles behind me, and a two-hour nighttime drive back to New Orleans lay ahead. I needed to eat, and Dean's was on the way to the interstate.

I'd never heard of anyone returning from a Cajun country road trip singing the praises of Dean's, and I can't remember any mention of it in the guidebooks or on the Web sites I had been consulting for restaurant tips. It was a squat building with a metal roof overhang and a few beer signs in the windows. It looked like an ordinary roadside café in a small town that happened to be open on Sunday night.

Family lunch at Poche's Market and Restaurant in Breaux Bridge.

If I was fated to have a forgettable meal around these parts, this was as good a time as any.

Anticipating defrosted hamburgers and chicken wings, I entered an all-but-empty dining room that did not do much to lift expectations. I sat on a padded aluminum chair at a table covered by a durable plastic cloth. The dining room shared a wall with the adjacent barroom, where a jukebox was thumping the thin, white paneling and making its songs quite audible at the table. Chintzy light fixtures hung from the ceiling, though the focal point of the room was a twelve-foot-tall Christmas tree, fully illuminated with strings of bulbs and stretching into the pink-painted rafters of the restaurant's exposed ceiling. This was in June.

But my eyes widened with the first scan of the lengthy, laminated menu. I ordered, and shortly the table was occupied by a huge bowl of chocolate-brown gumbo with the curling backs of shrimp tails breaking the surface and crab claws knifing out of the roux, plus a meticulously arranged side plate with scoops of rice and potato salad to add to the bowl. Next came a shrimp combo plate with shrimp boulettes (or little fried dollops of shrimp meat and stuffing), a ladle of shrimp etouffee, a scattering of fried shrimp, a few shrimp stuffed with crabmeat, and a little pile of spicy boiled shrimp in their shells. The jukebox next door started cranking the Guns N' Roses metal ballad "Sweet Child O' Mine," and to me it sounded so much like a celebratory anthem to this unexpectedly impressive meal that I started pumping my fist in the air.

"You need something, baby," the waitress called from the seat she had wearily resumed across the room, misreading my theatrics.

"No, no, sorry," I replied. "I'm just getting a little excited over here."

It was a wonderful dinner. It was inexpensive, fresh, flavorful, tied to local custom and harvest, and prepared with evident care. But it really should not have been such a surprise for me at that point. The words "Louisiana" and "cooking" belong together like "German" and "engineering," and I had experienced many times over just how often this reputation for great food is confirmed within the most unassuming settings. I prejudged Dean's when I pulled up just because it didn't look either fancy or memorably funky, and I really should have known better.

* * *

On my travels, I've learned that no south Louisiana town is too small to support a restaurant worth seeking out, and this knowledge has altered my mental map of the region. For instance, Gibson is a miniscule village along an otherwise deserted stretch of forested highway between Thibodaux and Morgan City, a place accessed by visitors primarily as a departure point for local swamp tours. But thanks to a stop at Chester's Restaurant all I can think about whenever I pass Gibson's lone highway exit is fried chicken. Chester's is a Depression-era roadhouse with dining rooms of vintage wallpaper and faded yellow trim. On the Sunday when Antonia and I visited, this time-warp space was filled with slim, elderly Cajun men with Ronald Reagan haircuts, their cotton-topped wives, and an assortment of folks who looked like they had driven in for afternoon meals with the grandparents. Whenever one of the young waitresses bounced through the slapping doors of the kitchen, everyone craned their necks in inadvertent synchronized fashion to see if she was carrying their meals. Ours arrived on a collection of cardboard trays bearing that memorable, spicy fried chicken, thick onion rings and, for my "New Orleans vegetarian" darling, enormous fried shrimp dusted in red pepper.

I've also learned that south Louisiana restaurants sharing names with common roadkill wildlife need not be feared. For this liberation, I thank Possum's in St. Martinville, which looks like a funeral parlor from the outside but serves the most addictive brown gravy over its broiled steaks and shrimp, and I also credit T-Coons, a lunch counter in Lafayette where the smothered rabbit served on Mondays was good enough to send me scampering back for the short rib fricassee special on Tuesday.

Dowdy and ramshackle structures bode well on the south Louisiana restaurant hunt, as demonstrated at the bayou-style soul food joint Rita Mae's in Morgan City. Everything here seemed homemade, including the list of daily specials that was written on butcher paper and taped to the wall directly above a pair of Bibles, held open on stands. I ordered too much food here after a visit to the nearby Mr. Charlie oil rig museum, but my empathetic, big-boned waitress didn't bat an eye and soon set the cottage's loose floorboards wobbling as she hauled back crunchy fried catfish, ham-speckled white beans over rice, a bowl of okra gumbo, and a super-sized cup of unsweetened tea.

The only sit-down restaurant I could find open after 7 p.m. on a Saturday night in the bayou town of Pierre Part was Landry's, a nondescript storefront most assuredly not related to the corporate restaurant chain of the same name. At this Landry's, I sat under a wall-mounted collection of several hundred vintage beer cans and marveled at another bargain Cajun combination dinner, which this time mounded crawfish stew, crawfish bisque with stuffed crawfish heads, fried crawfish tails, crawfish boulettes, and a crawfish-stuffed potato all on a plastic divider plate, with a cup of gumbo on the side. The crawfish were part of the wild harvest from Belle River a few miles down the road, I was told, and I forked over less for the entire feast than I would have spent on the "honey mustard–glazed chicken breast" at the nearest Chili's franchise.

Another edict of south Louisiana eating maintains that people will travel harrowing distances for the right restaurant, and that such perseverance pays on these trips. Hungry, tired, and seriously doubting my travel directions, I have on several occasions nearly called off the search for restaurants located far between towns on the Cajun prairie. I was nearly snow blind from driving past mile after mile of uninterrupted rice fields at sunset when I finally came upon D.I.'s Restaurant in Basile. The sprawling, metal-topped restaurant is the size of a circus tent, and it seemed like the biggest show around as its dirt parking lot steadily filled with cars, trucks, horse trailers, and even a white stretch limo, which looked as out of place in the rice fields as a yacht at an oyster lugger's wharf. Hundreds of people had trekked out here for dinner. They waited with antsy kids by the entrance, feeding quarters into arcade games until their party could be seated. Then they occupied long rustic tables, where they sorted through platters of barbequed crabs and boiled shrimp and slugged back beers. And later some would waltz across a broad pine dance floor to the fiddle-guitar-accordion music of a traditional Cajun band playing from a dining room stage.

I also nearly missed Bubba Frey's Restaurant on my first pass through Mowata, a town about eight miles outside of Eunice. Actually, calling Mowata a town is a bit of stretch. It's more like the geographic ghost of a one-time rail depot than a modern municipal identity, and as near as I could tell the restaurant and the connected butcher shop/grocery called the Mowata Store made up the entirety of the place. It was night the first time I arrived for dinner, and the illuminated windows for the restaurant threw the only light for miles around.

I had a cup of gumbo with roux the color of café au lait, a plate of fried frog's legs, and a sliced link of the thickest, most peppery boudin it has ever been my pleasure to dispatch. I found my way here on a Saturday night, which is when proprietor Bubba Frey regularly invites a group of musically inclined friends over to play in his dining room, a neat, long hall of cypress siding, bare lightbulbs, and country bric-a-brac. Seated casually on a collection of straight-back chairs, looking like a painting from New Iberia artist George Rodrigue's "oaks and Cajuns" phase, they strummed, sawed, and cranked away for the enjoyment of the big eaters who had joined them at this glowing square in the otherwise lonely rural darkness. Not every Louisiana map bothers even to mark tiny Mowata. But now, in the same way I reflexively correlate swampy Gibson with spicy fried chicken and river town LaPlace with smoky andouille, the prairie pit stop of Mowata to me means burly boudin.

* * *

It takes some pluck to operate an eatery in such isolated areas, but really I think people who open restaurants in any part of Acadiana are brave. After all, they are going toe to toe with Cajun home cooking, which is the source code for most of the restaurant dishes around here anyway. Locals have told me, cruelly, that restaurant cooking only skims the surface of the region's food story, leaving me to envision feasts made from old family recipes and using the yield of the last fishing catch or hunting trip haul.

Thus addled, I have fantasized about staking out St. Martin de Tours Catholic Church and tailing parishioners home after Mass to surprise them in their driveways and somehow negotiate invitations to Sunday suppers. I have even briefly considered posting online ads offering to trade my copywriting skills or yard work services for a place at a Cajun family table. But realistically the best way for unannounced visitors to get an appreciation of home cooking is to attend local festivals that include amateur cooking contests. Family recipes are unleashed, competitive bravura is directed toward the stoves and grills, and samples are usually available in abundance.

The fantastically valuable Huli's Louisiana Festivals and Events Calendar, produced by New Orleanian and Louisiana byways fellow traveler Julie Posner, shows weekend after weekend of various cultural and harvest festivals across the state. Her calendars are hung from home bulletin boards and fridges all over Louisiana, and during my research for this book I kept one in my truck as a monthly crib sheet on things to do on the road. That's how I discovered le Festival de la Viande Boucanee, the Smoked Meat Festival, in Ville Platte.

This event is held in a lot beside the town's civic center one Saturday each June, and it was murderously hot the day my friend Peter Horjus and I found our way there. Cajun bands played on a stage, a metal maintenance barn was pressed into service as a bar, and there was an arts and crafts area, but most everyone kept under the rings of shade thrown by a few oaks on the festival grounds and under runs of large tents that lined the perimeter. The short walk from the truck to the festival gates in this heat was enough to bring sweat through our clothes, but things would get much hotter within the grounds.

Under the tents, cook-off contestants were completing or maintaining their entries. There were about forty-five teams, and each had its own space with smokers gushing hot, meaty plumes and tureens simmering gravies and sauces. Each tent enclosure was crowded with folding tables, camp chairs, pots and pans, and lots of friends and relatives, all of whom were trying to keep cool with the help of big portable fans and ice chests full of beer. The teams were vying for bragging rights and for one of the festival's remarkable trophies, which were miniaturized models of cypress smokehouses faithfully rendered in shrunken detail right down to tiny plastic links of sausage dangling from a smoking rack within.

Smoked meat is a big deal in Ville Platte, and, apart from the annual festival, the Pig Stand on Main Street is the best place to get a taste of its local incarnations. This barbecue restaurant, just a block away from the legendary Cajun/zydeco/swamp pop hub of Floyd's Record Store, was where I had my first encounter with ponce. This is a pig stomach stuffed with sausage, sewn shut, and smoked into a solid, spice-dripping loaf. Ponce makes periodic appearances at a few Cajun butcher shops, where it's sometimes made with a calf's stomach and called chaudin, but never had I seen it in such abundance as at the Smoked Meat Festival, where it turned up at one booth after another. The cook-off judges had an entire awards category for it.

Once dishes were complete and the judges were provisioned, contestants started selling samples to the festival crowd, doling out plates and bowls direct from their crocks and smokers for two or three dollars each. It might have been too hot for many people to brave the dance floor in front of the lonely Cajun band, but Peter and I had plenty of company as we ping-ponged from one tent to another. We were sweating from our hats to our socks the whole time, and whenever we approached a contestant's tent the heat from the grill or smoker only intensified the situation. But the meaty aroma dangling in the air was too appealing to deny. For the next hour, we put away chunks of smoked duck stuffed with jalapeno peppers and cheese, smoked shrimp wrapped with bacon, smoked eggs, smoked quesadillas, marinated rabbit tenderloin wrapped in bacon and smoked, tasso and sausage sauce piquante, smoked boudin, and one ponce sandwich, slathered with a mess of mayonnaise and mustard on white bread. Handing over sweaty bills to tailgate crews of competitive cooks wasn't exactly like eating at a Cajun family table, but it sure blazed new eating trails for me.

I climbed another rung up the learning ladder at that darling of a music festival in Lafayette, the Black Pot Festival & Cookoff. The cook-off part of the schedule got under way on Saturday morning in a small clearing between the vintage homes of the Acadian Village site and the barn pavilion where the bands performed. A tour of the contestants here was a revelation. I already knew that Louisiana recipes tend to accumulate family stories and lore as they are passed down through the generations, but talking with some of the folks here I also learned the same thing happens to their most prized kitchen implements, the black pots that inspired this whole festival and contest. Heavy as diving weights and nearly indestructible, these are the cast-iron pots usually sold at hardware stores and antique shops, pots that turn black from proper use and seasoning, that conduct and retain heat so marvelously well, and that stick around for ages.

Two dozen cooks set up their own outdoor kitchens around the festival grounds. They tended jambalayas deeply imbued with smokehouse flavor, seafood dishes like spicy turtle and alligator sauce piquante and dark gravies that mixed andouille, shrimp and rice. Under one tailgating tent, Tina Vidrine, a home cook from the prairie town of Rayne, was plating an elaborate combination of deer sausage, purple hull peas, and rice, with a rabbit leg balanced over the top of each serving. Across the grounds, Jared Richard of Duson cooked gumbo with hen and smoked turkey necks, a velvety-rich, burgundy-dark concoction that would later prove a cook-off winner.

A lot of good cooking goes into these long-lived black pots, and so does a bit of mythology. One story told on the Cajun prairie holds that when le Grand Dérangement began, the family black pot was the one thing Acadians were sure to take, even packing other belongings inside of it like a travel trunk. The people didn't know where they would end up, the story goes, but if they had their black pots at least they knew they would be able to cook when they got there.

Though that story is apocryphal, the black pots obviously mean a lot to their owners today. Some people describe receiving their own black pot as a rite of passage, and they often become family heirlooms. Marcelle Bienvenu, the St. Martinville–based cookbook author and chronicler of all things edible in Acadiana, told me once that the only items her grandfather bothered writing into his will were his black pots.

"And I was mad when I didn't get just the one I wanted!" she laughed.

While taking a long, slow circuit of the Black Pot cook-off contestants—and while angling for an invitation to try some of the entries—I started talking with Michelle Brown, a friendly, blond-bobbed, middle-aged mom from Eunice. She was cooking a fricassee using venison tenderloin cut from a deer her husband, Greg, had snagged on a recent hunting trip, and she was using a pair of broad, deep cast-iron pots that she said were given to her by her in-laws.

"Their family was no longer as large as they got older, and our family was growing, so we got their black pots," Michelle explained.

"Wow, that's great. I guess your in-laws don't cook much anymore then," I said.

"Oh no, they bought smaller black pots for themselves now that they just cook for two," she said.

Others told me they consider black pots essential gear on camping and hunting trips, where they become focal points around which friends gather. It turns out that when there's good times and good cooking, for many south Louisiana families the black pot is usually nearby.

"There's an expression here that your black pot is like a portable hearth, just like in the home," the Red Stick Ramblers singer Linzay Young told me. "There's one in our family that goes all the way back to my grandmother's great-uncle. He was in a P.O.W. camp in New York after the Civil War, he was a Confederate soldier and got captured. When he came back, all he had was his black pot dangling from his saddle, clanging along. We've had it ever since."

* * *

Backyard smokers, ancestral cookware, family recipes, and freezers full of venison and duck that come with their own personal hunting stories—this is what restaurateurs are up against in Acadiana. Yet the region is thick with restaurants, from far-flung dining halls in the rice fields to homey kitchens perched on the edges of swamps to sophisticated eateries in the cities and larger towns.

I racked up a lot of mileage and studied maps on end in the search for certain crawfish joints and backstreet plate lunch purveyors around the bayous and across the prairie. While I don't regret a bite of it, in the future when I need a concentrated dose of the region's restaurant riches I will just drive straight to Abbeville—eminently edible Abbeville, perhaps the single best eating town in Acadiana.

Located about twenty miles down the Vermilion River from Lafayette, surrounded by sugarcane fields, cattle ranches, and fishing communities, Abbeville is a small town with an outsized culinary personality. It's also one of the prettiest small towns I've visited in south Louisiana.

The Catholic missionary Père Antoine Désiré Mégret established Abbeville in 1843, naming it for his hometown in France and laying out an original town plan modeled after a typical French village. Now, there's the usual modern sprawl of chain restaurants, oil change shops, and discount retailers on the outskirts of town, but the old framework still imbues the historic core with particular charm. Streets wend their way around a pair of complementary town squares, one for the Vermilion Parish courthouse and the other facing St. Mary Magdalen Church and its adjoining cemetery. Vintage commercial buildings line this irregular downtown grid and an old, iron drawbridge crosses the slow-moving Vermilion River in the shadow of the church's steep, towering spire.

I had a serious eating itinerary in hand when I first visited, and even on my preliminary spin around town to get my bearings I kept spotting harbingers of Abbeville's potent food heritage. Just a few blocks from the courthouse, I saw the tall, shining metal silos of the Riviana rice mill, which makes the Water Maid and Mahatma rice brands that were first developed here in the 1920s. As I drew closer to the church and the drawbridge, I noticed a new aroma in the air and soon discovered Steen's Syrup Mill. This factory is the wellspring for the thick-as-honey, saddle-dark cane syrup that is drizzled on biscuits and pancakes and called for by name in so many southern dessert recipes. The century-old C. S. Steen's company still cooks down local cane at this small, downtown mill wedged between the Vermilion's waters and the red brick flank of the big church, and when the sugar harvest rolls in it sends its sweet, roasting scents across town.

One block away, I finally found the first landmark of edible Abbeville I had actually set out to visit—a massive heap of oyster shells, thousands upon thousands of them, mounded up, scattered around and tumbling down a steep bank into the Vermilion like a calcium landslide. I was eager to add a few dozen more to the knoll.

All of these countless shells issued from the back door of Dupuy's Oyster Shop, a small, modern-looking restaurant sheathed in vinyl siding that, despite appearances, claims a history going back nearly to Abbeville's start. Cajun fishermen have long plied Vermilion River and Vermilion Bay twenty miles to the south, and, according to the local story, one of them, Joseph Dupuy, started selling oysters by the riverside in Abbeville on his way back upstream with fresh harvests. He established Dupuy's in 1869 right across the street from St. Mary Magdalen and in doing so laid the seeds for an enduring oyster legacy in the small inland town. Black's Oyster Bar opened directly across the street in 1967, though it was closed at this writing after a slew of ownership changes. In 1995, one of Dupuy's former owners started a new oyster bar called Shucks. It is just across the Vermilion in a bright, contemporary family restaurant space, which even includes a drive-through window for oysters on the go.

While I was outside Dupuy's examining the archeological leavings of oyster feasts past, the bells of St. Mary Magdalen Church began sounding, and soon the downtown streets were a bustle of activity as people poured out of church and headed to their cars parked all around the surrounding blocks. I noticed quite a few couples and families walking straight across the street to Dupuy's front door, however, and I took that as my cue to get in there and beat the after-Mass rush. The restaurant opened at 5 p.m. sharp, just when Saturday services let out across the street. Tables were going fast, but I did get a seat, and soon I settled in for a platter of raw oysters arrayed on a bed of crushed ice and adorned with lemon wedges. It was my first dozen of the day, a second round awaited at Shucks across the river, and I already knew this wouldn't be my last trip to Abbeville.

With all this edible heritage, it seems appropriate that the town's biggest public party is fixated on food. The first weekend in November marks Abbeville's Giant Omelette Celebration, a weekend-long festival that culminates on Sunday with a parade led by local notables and invited guests clad in white chef coats and tall toques. They march through downtown bearing wicker baskets full of some five thousand eggs and lengths of French bread from Poupart's Bakery in Lafayette and proceed to cook a colossal omelet on a twelve-foot-wide skillet set up in the middle of the street, pushing the eggs around with wooden spatulas as long as oars. Sample portions of egg and bread are later divvied up and served to the festival goers.

There was a fun crowd out for the festivities the year I attended. People danced in the blocked-off street by the church, and they cheered the ceremonial procession of chefs and food as enthusiastically as they did when the high-stepping ladies of the Tabasco Girls Dance Team marched past. Festival officials even invite representatives from a number of Abbeville's sister cities overseas to the event, and many of them help cook the giant omelet.

Plenty of people visit Abbeville for this festival each November, but to my mind the window of opportunity for the ultimate Abbeville eating trip is earlier in the year, at some variable annual sweet spot falling between January and April. That's when the shank of the fall-through-spring oyster season will intersect with primetime for the winter-through-early-summer crawfish harvest, and you can get some of the best of both in Abbeville. As famous as Abbeville is for its oyster tradition, it is also a crawfish town in the heartland of what is without a doubt America's crawfish state.

Louisiana produces 90 percent of domestic crawfish, those fresh-water crustaceans that look like minilobsters, turn up in countless Louisiana dishes, and have become mascots of Acadiana. Lots of frozen crawfish meat is shipped in from Asia, but if you're eating whole, in-shell crawfish in America, the type used for boiled craw-fish, it's a safe bet it came from Louisiana. There are some sixteen hundred crawfish farms around the state, most clustered in the Aca-diana region, plus an estimated eight hundred commercial harvest-ers pulling wild crawfish from the Atchafalaya Basin and other areas. Altogether the annual harvest can be anywhere from seventy-five million to more than one hundred million pounds. That's a lot, but given how fast so many locals can peel a crawfish tail, eat the meat, suck the "juice" from the dismembered head and repeat, it's a won-der to me that an ounce of it leaves the state.

Huge caches of the creatures are done-in the old fashioned way at the home crawfish boil, which, like a New England clambake or Hawaiian luau, is more of an event than a mere meal. A boil implies a gathering of family and friends, where bulging sacks of live, agitated crawfish are prepared. An almost tribal methodology ensues, one involving a hierarchy of cooks and cooks' assistants, heavy equip-ment, and open flame, that reliable elixir of manly backyard cooking. To begin, a crawfish or two will be tossed to the lawn to amuse the kids as it skitters away or menaces them with its tiny claws. Then a barrel-sized metal pot will be filled with water and set over a pro-pane burner, which will emit an ominous, hoarse whooshing sound like a minijet engine as it sets the water to boiling. Into the pot go loads of salty, cayenne-red seasoning mix, any conceivable combi-nation of vegetables, links of sausage, and then the crawfish. Once done and drained, it all gets dumped on tables lined with yesterday's newspaper, and the crowd gets to work breaking the crawfish bodies in half and extracting their now-spicy curls of tail meat. Cold beer is administered to cooks, cooks' assistants, and onlookers at each stage in the process.

This is the home-based template for the region's boiled-seafood restaurants, places that can handle truckloads of crawfish per night during the season. They fall broadly into two categories: full-service restaurants with major boiled-seafood operations on premises and the so-called boiling points and seafood patios, which can look as ordinary as plumbing supply outlets in the off-season but are packed with locals when crawfish are on tap.

Some of these restaurants feel impossibly remote, but that just means they're closer to the source. Even the extraordinarily good but notoriously hard-to-find Hawk's, in the old German settlement of Robert's Cove north of Rayne, describes its location as "the middle of nowhere" in its promotional materials. But really, places like this are in the middle of rice country, which doubles as crawfish country. Rice farmers can use the same floodable fields to cultivate crawfish after the summer rice crop has come in, so finding a crawfish specialist surrounded by rice fields is a little like finding a steakhouse surrounded by cattle pasture.

There are also plenty of great in-town crawfish spots. Lafayette has many, from sit-down restaurants like Gator Cove on the Evangeline Throughway to places oriented toward the take-out trade, like Crawfish Time on Moss Road, which even dispenses boiled sacks from a drive-thru window. This opens a great option for the traveler who wants to mimic a backyard boil while on the road: get a take-out sack, collect a six pack, proceed to Girard Park by the University of Louisiana at Lafayette, find a picnic table near a shady oak, and go native.

Little old Abbeville, population twelve thousand or so, not only has two world-class oyster bars but also has two great crawfish spots. These places have convinced me that while Acadiana exports many thousands of tons of its product, the best and biggest don't make it very far from home. At Cajun Claws, a neat, wood-trimmed, tavern-style restaurant on the Abbeville main drag of Charity Street, I ate crawfish so large that their peeled tails were, on average, the size of my thumb. They put the specimens I usually get from New Orleans markets to shame.

It was the same story at Richard's Seafood Patio, which I found across the Vermilion and about a mile from town along an increasingly rural back road. Like Dupuy's, Richard's opens at 5 p.m. sharp, and by the time I arrived just a few minutes later there already was a line stretching out the door and into a dirt parking lot crammed with trucks and bikes. This place is a classic boiling point, housed in the most basic of tin-roofed buildings with a series of boxy additions tacked on over time. Richard's dates back to 1957, giving credence to owner Calvin "Red" Richard's claim that it is the region's oldest boiling point. I stood in line for about twenty minutes with a crowd that included bikers and people who looked fresh from St. Mary Magdalen's Saturday service. We inched forward along a chute lined with windows looking directly into the dining room, where patrons seated before us plowed through platters of steaming crawfish.

"Look at that one, she's peeling those pretty fast," I said to the large, leather-clad man waiting in line behind me.

"Not fast enough," he said. "Where are you from?"

"New Orleans," I replied.

"No, I mean originally, that's no New Orleans accent," he said.

"Oh, well, Rhode Island," I said, wondering how this would go over.

"Rhode Island!" he roared, elbowing the woman behind him. "He's from Rhode Island! Near Maine, right? Lobsters up there, huh?"

"Yup, lots of lobsters," I said.

"We got crawfish here bigger than your lobsters, but I ain't telling you where, Rhode Island, you gonna have to find that on your own," he said, and everyone chuckled a bit.

I laughed too. I'm happy to field Rhode Island jokes for south Louisiana bikers if it helps pass the time in the crawfish line. But if I can force some wisdom from his ribbing it's that the pursuit of good food in south Louisiana should be a lifelong project. Abbeville proved a one-stop, master's level course on the subject, but there are many other towns, many rural spots, many unassuming locales and even a few opportunities to get a taste of competitive cooking on the festival trail. And the biggest lesson, the one I should have known when I pulled up to Dean's with an empty belly and low expectations, is that when it's time to eat in Acadiana even a shot in the dark will likely land pretty well.

CHAPTER 22

CHASING A GOOD TIME

Mardi Gras on the Cajun Prairie

I knew we were on the right track when we arrived at the Saddle Tramp Riders Club in Church Point and found forensic evidence of the party we had just missed. Things were dead quiet as we approached the horse riding club, which looked like a low barn with a screened patio attached. No one was around at all. But hundreds of empty Bud Light cans littered the grassy lot around the club like silver and blue mushrooms, and there was an interlacing minefield of horse droppings. Church Point's courir de Mardi Gras had already departed, but at least we were on their trail.

This was an important trip, and it was vital that we catch up with our quarry. After all, Antonia and I and a few of our New Orleans friends had made a big sacrifice here in the name of exploring Louisiana culture. We had left New Orleans on Mardi Gras weekend, far and away my favorite time of year. We chose to leave the city parade routes, the networks of house parties, and the annual street celebrations so deeply ingrained in our sense of home to instead seek the rural traditions of Mardi Gras in Cajun country, which none of us had experienced. I felt a little like the child who travels to a foreign land on Christmas and anxiously wonders if Santa will still find him.

Finding Mardi Gras celebrations is usually not a problem in areas that do them up. Intricately tied to Catholic heritage, the holiday is celebrated in many different ways but reliably draws the community outside to party as a last, wild run-up before Lent. At the end of the day, the rural Cajun version, le courir de Mardi Gras, is no different.

238

Church Point Mardi Gras revelers race to capture chickens on a farm.

Later, it would seem like the entire town of Church Point (population 4,750) and plenty of their friends were out at the dance and communal gumbo party held downtown.

But the prelude to this, the part we really wanted to experience, is le courir, "the run," which at its most basic involves a group of costumed young men riding from one farmhouse to another on horseback or in wagons and trailers, ritualistically begging for the ingredients for the future gumbo, capturing live chickens by hand, singing and dancing, performing horseback stunts better suited to a pro wrestling ring than a rodeo, and generally painting the countryside with the gaudy, thrilling colors of Mardi Gras abandon. To see this, we'd have to catch up.

* * *

We left New Orleans early for our trip to Church Point, a country crossroads town about twenty miles to the northwest of Lafayette, and we arrived to find the short stretch of single-story main street storefronts buzzing with activity. People had staked out parade watching spots on either side of the street, and they were heating up grills, cracking beers, and walking around to visit friends. A few conflicting directions eventually led us to the Saddle Tramp Riders Club, the traditional starting point for this courir. While contemplating all the dead beer cans and horse pies, we providentially met another latecomer, Ken Dugas, who hails from the area and naturally knew the score much better than we. Easy going, fifty-something, and wearing a gray mustache over his genuine smile, he insisted that we call him Dugas (and that's "du-ga," of course). As is the spirit of Mardi Gras everywhere, we became friends in about fifteen seconds and shortly worked out a plan to find le courir together.

In some areas, the term Mardi Gras—or Fat Tuesday—may interchangeably refer specifically to the day before Ash Wednesday, to the entire Carnival season, to an organized group of Mardi Gras revelers, or even to just an individual in costume. This means you can go to Mardi Gras at the end of Mardi Gras to see the Mardi Gras, and you can even be a Mardi Gras.

So as we drove behind Dugas around a patchwork of large farm spreads and pasture, he would periodically stop, wave us forward and shout out the window that "the Mardi Gras should be right down this way!" The clues were the sheriff's deputies parked in their cruisers at otherwise empty intersections, waiting to stop whatever traffic might come along when le courir passed. After a few turns, we saw a crowd of people up ahead by a string of houses, looking out of place in the otherwise quiet countryside.

"That's where we'll catch the Mardi Gras!" Dugas hollered to us.

The riders had not arrived yet, but we could see them slowly approaching from a mile or so down the long, flat farm road. We joined perhaps two hundred people buzzing with festive anticipation at what was clearly an impending stop on the Mardi Gras route. Families barbecued outside their homes and spectators milled about, sipping beers.

"The Mardi Gras's coming, the Mardi Gras's coming," one young boy started yelling from the side of the road.

The procession was close now, and we ran ahead to inspect its various units as they came upon this small cluster of country homes. Up first was le capitaine, who I later learned was Troy Richard, the captain, leader, and shepherd of this courir. He looked commanding on his mount, dressed in a purple satin cape, white gloves, and a Stetson, which he tipped gallantly to people waving from their front yards. He was a lone sentinel of solemnity, and immediately behind him crested a motley wave of young men, a horde that soon enveloped the area in colorful, loud, moving chaos.

Some of these costumed men trooped by on horseback, many others ran on foot, and still more hung from flatbeds pulled by grinding farm tractors. One pedaled past on a bicycle fitted with a small barbecue grill on its rear, which emitted meaty wafts of smoke as he weaved between the horses and runners. I tried to stay out of the way, but the group came careening and coursing by like a swarm and soon I was entangled in the procession. The young men paid me no mind as they called out for beer, bawled at each other in cowboy voices or blitzed falsetto, and yelled at the rapt kids who watched beside roadside ditches.

They wore colorful costumes, which were individual in design but uniform in concept, with pants and shirts covered in bright patterns and row after row of shredded fringe, like stylized rags. Most wore concealing wire masks with cartoon-like facial features painted over the mesh, and practically all of them were topped with tall cone-shaped hats, the capuchons, which look like festive dunce caps. People who are frightened by clowns would be reduced to quivering shock by this spirited mob. They cruised by with cans of beer and mixed drinks carried in soda bottles, and a few clutched live chickens by the legs, shaking them at the people who cheered from their yards.

I was astounded at the length to which this staggering, boisterous procession stretched. For twenty minutes they continued past me on foot, tractor, or horseback. One tractor towed a bandwagon, where musicians sawed fiddles, hugged accordions, and thumbed electric bass guitars, playing the clopping, clanging Cajun anthem known universally around Acadiana as "the Mardi Gras song." On another trailer, a wire cage held live chickens—the booty collected at earlier stops—while other trailers carried portable toilets and collections of ice chests.

By the time the entire courir arrived, there were hundreds of people roaming around a field by the houses, and they intermingled with the local families and spectators. Dugas was dancing with one of our friends in the grass as the parked bandwagon kept up the tunes. Some riders dismounted and some started doing tricks for the crowd. They stood stock-still with their feet on their horses' backs or they balanced beer cans on their heads as they trotted their horses around. One rose in his saddle and suddenly did a back flip, as if off a turnbuckle, to land squarely on his feet on the grass behind his horse. Another tried the same trick and crashed in a watery ditch, from which he emerged drenched in mud but looking so exuberant I suspected he landed there on purpose.

In a minute, the young men walked purposefully as a group toward a gate leading to the next field, followed by a stout, goateed farmer, the owner of the whole spread, who rode in a golf cart laden with caged chickens. Les Mardi Gras were about to earn more gumbo fixings.

* * *

I had heard about Cajun Mardi Gras frequently, most often while traveling around the Cajun prairie north of Lafayette.

"You're from New Orleans?" someone would say to me. "Oh! You've got to come out here for Mardi Gras. We have the real Mardi Gras."

I've received some slight modification of that claim countless times, all throughout the year, including every time I've visited Mamou, home to a huge and wild Mardi Gras celebration.

I was curious, but the big problem, always, was leaving home at Mardi Gras time. I have friends in New Orleans—people whom I otherwise respect and believe to be interesting, worthwhile people—who have in the past decided to "take a break" from Mardi Gras for a year and travel somewhere else, offering the rationale that Mardi Gras recurs annually and missing one year will only make the next more exciting. To me, that's like saying, "Oh, I just won't eat this week, it'll make the meals next week taste that much more delicious." No thanks. I can't even handle a diet, never mind fasting.

Mardi Gras gets to the heart of the city I call home. It's the defining cultural moment of New Orleans, and taking an active part in the cultural life of New Orleans is as important to me as any other facet of my personal identity. The city isn't just a place where I live and work. Participating in its culture is my hobby and my lifestyle, and participating in Mardi Gras—acting out its deep customs and whimsical, of-the-minute frivolity—is the most important way I connect with the life of my city each year.

I know a lot of other people in Louisiana feel this way too, even if their Mardi Gras experiences are much different from mine, and people do celebrate Mardi Gras in lots of different ways across the state. The traditional New Orleans society-based krewes and the newer, much larger "super krewes" with celebrity guest stars and million-dollar budgets represent one end of the spectrum, while countless small, explosively creative and usually unofficial processions fill the Crescent City's streets with makeshift carnival sidelines. There are boat parades in the river rat country that Rob Arrington showed me on his Jet Ski, like the Krewe of Wrecks (a pun on New Orleans's Rex parade) held on the Tickfaw River, where bass boats, barges, and yachts are elaborately decorated to look like giant alligators, prairie schooners, and galleons as they bear costumed revelers along the riverine party route. In Baton Rouge, people gather in the tiny neighborhood called Spanish Town for a rollicking political satire parade full of send-ups of the elected officials who work in the skyscraper capitol towering directly overhead. In the bayou village of Choupique—near Thibodaux and not far from the swamp tours of Kraemer—it's traditional for masked young men to chase children around town on Mardi Gras morning, then round them up for a public whipping with the acquiescence and encouragement of the kids' parents. Around the state there are dog parades, parades for kids, celebrations in nursing homes and hospital wards, parades of stunning classical beauty and parades made up of hundreds of grunting, spewing semis pulling crudely decorated flatbed floats through city streets.

And in Acadiana, even something that seems as traditional as le courir de Mardi Gras can differ remarkably from one prairie community to another. Mamou has the most famous bash of the lot. As in other towns, riders meet at a central point, depart early in the morning, complete their route collecting gumbo ingredients, and then promenade back into town. Here, though, they return to find as many as twenty thousand people jamming the short stretch of Sixth Street. The riders come thundering in like a fantastical scene from some medieval western or debauched Roman triumph. By then they are fully drunk and their rag and cone hat costumes are covered in mud and dust. They hoot and shriek hoarsely and still they perform tricks and stunts. Some stand on their saddles as the horses saunter down the street, wavering like uneasy surfers and flailing their captive chickens by the feet like the heads of defeated foes. The wassail goes on all day, with people dancing and eating and drinking in the streets.

Les courir are traditionally segregated by gender, and typically they remain segregated by race as well, with whites and blacks organizing their own runs and little intermingling between them. For instance, Andrew Cezar, proprietor of the Metro Soileau Downs track, holds a black Creole courir each year. Some communities organize les courir specifically for women and others for children. Still, it remains largely a rite of passage for young men, who are directed and chaperoned by older, experienced veterans, les capitianes of each courir and their assistants.

One thing that makes the Church Point courir unique—and of special interest to visitors to the region trying to do a little of New Orleans Mardi Gras and a little of Cajun Mardi Gras—is that it always occurs on the Sunday before Mardi Gras, rather than on Tuesday, the ne plus ultra of Carnival season. This was appealing to me, because it meant I could get my first taste of le courir de Mardi Gras without missing the biggest annual day in the life of my city. I could do it all. But I had one lingering reservation about this plan. Can one properly celebrate Fat Tuesday on a Sunday? Well, it worked out pretty well for us in Church Point, and I learned that there was a good story behind the Sunday schedule.

Though most traditional les courir had died out by World War II, interest in Cajun Mardi Gras was growing again in the late 1950s as some communities began reviving them. Those early meetings at Fred's Lounge in Mamou were starting to bear fruit. In order to keep the momentum going, two local boosters, Elton Richard of Church Point and state senator Paul Tate of Mamou (brother of

Fred Tate of Fred's Lounge), concluded that if their respective runs were held on different days, more people could participate in each. But Tuesday is clearly the most desirable day for any run, it being Mardi Gras day and all. So in 1968, as the story goes, the two men simply flipped a coin to determine which town would hold the run on Tuesday. Mamou won the toss and Church Point has held a Sunday run ever since.

Eunice hosts a huge courir too, which is open to both men and women and has drawn more than two thousand riders on horseback or in trailers in recent years. Not everyone feels that bigger is better when it comes to Mardi Gras, however, and some alternative off-shoots have emerged. One is the Faquetigue courir, which is held near Eunice (Faquetigue was an earlier name for the town of Eunice) and is composed of many of the musicians from today's most exciting Cajun bands, like the Red Stick Ramblers, Pine Leaf Boys, and Lost Bayou Ramblers. But large or small, on Tuesday or Sunday, on horseback or on trailers, les courir all over Cajun country are united by their roots to a place and time very far away: medieval France.

* * *

My first visit to Church Point made it clear why so many people I met around Acadiana wanted me to see their Mardi Gras—"the real Mardi Gras," as they so provocatively called it. Le courir is as important to them as the street traditions in New Orleans are to me, yet to most of the world the picture of Mardi Gras in Louisiana is a television image of huge parades, tons of plastic beads, and French Quarter debauchery. Le courir de Mardi Gras isn't some Cajun version of the New Orleans standard or a rural interpretation of the city ways. Rather, it's an ancient tradition the original Acadian settlers carried with them when they first left seventeenth-century France. It has evolved throughout the four centuries of their culture's New World experience, but today it still has echoes of the old feudal order. All this, and it's a rip-roaring good time full of drunken revelry.

"It's the Mardi Gras of peasants, while New Orleans has the Mardi Gras of royalty. The traditions came over at different times and in different ships," said Larry Miller, a retired accordion maker from the Cajun rice town of Iota.

Larry, who was seventy-three when we spoke, has been involved with the deeply traditional Tee Mamou–Iota courir de Mardi Gras in his hometown since he was a teenager in the early 1950s. His father participated in the tradition before him, and his children and grandchildren run with it today. His wife, Jackie, is a leading courir costume maker, crafting the masks, the tall hats, and the full rag suits for many riders each year.

Larry describes himself as "a shade tree folklorist," but his telling of the origins of le courir match up pretty well with the description LSU professor and folklorist Carolyn Ware shared with me. While there is no written history documenting the earliest phases of the tradition, Carolyn said, it fits with a common pattern of medieval European traditions that include roving house visits, ritualized begging, and costume disguises.

To tell his story of le courir, Larry picked up the thread with annual pre-Lenten, end-of-winter celebrations in France. His theory is that bands of peasants would move from one well-to-do house to the next in their villages, dressed in cursory, homemade costumes to stage little performances and beg for food. Miller believes most would have been too poor to own horses, so they ran to cover more ground on the big day, hence today's term "courir," or run. The begging ritual now plays out in the house-to-house gathering of chickens, sausage, rice, and onions for the Mardi Gras gumbo, while the backflips, mud baths, and horse tricks may hark back to the peasants' antics put on for the gentry.

Many Acadian communities held les courir through the early twentieth century, but most were discontinued once America entered World War II and the young men who traditionally participate in these runs left home for military service. However, many rice farmers were exempted from the draft because their easy-to-ship, easy-to-store crop was deemed a strategic commodity for the war effort.

"Because of that, there were still a lot of young men around for the Mardi Gras in those years in some areas, and they continued the Tee Mamou–Iota run even when the others stopped," Larry said.

While a few of these traditions carried on in Acadiana's rice belt, most others would not resume until the 1960s when they were revived as part of the resurgence of Cajun culture overall. The ones that continued without interruption had to do so by new means, however, after a mosquito-borne epidemic decimated the local horse population in the 1940s. As a result, Larry said, the riders started using trucks and tractors, which today help this courir make the rounds of modern farms that are now widely spread out along the Tee Mamou and Iota rice fields.

So the oldest continually held courir de Mardi Gras proceeds on trucks and tractors, while others use horses, neither of which were likely part of the original "runs" in feudal France. And they didn't have Bud Light back then, either, which is now in such abundant supply along les courir routes. But that's how it goes in communities that embrace living traditions rather than stage historical reenactments.

Still, Larry and other Tee Mamou–Iota boosters hold up their run as the region's most faithful courir preservation effort because of organizers' strict adherence to surviving customs. In order to ride on Mardi Gras day, young men must wear the traditional rag suit, mesh mask, and capuchon costume, and they must attend a series of meetings earlier in the year to learn and rehearse the rituals.

The tradition throughout Acadiana holds that once the Mardi Gras approaches a farm, le capitaine waves a flag to signal the property owner and secure permission to proceed. The masked men then dismount from horses or trailers and begin the ritualized begging. They grovel on their hands and knees and put on a big show of it. This is where the horse tricks come in at some of the runs.

Long retired from the run, Larry is a lead organizer of the Iota Mardi Gras Festival Association, which is separate from le courir itself but closely coordinates its own Mardi Gras activities to the run schedule. Like the other les courir, this one concludes back in town where the festival association stages a big public party for locals and visitors. The costumed riders eat their gumbo, then many crash for a while, exhausted by the day, before heading to D.I.'s Restaurant in Basile for a nighttime party full of singing, dancing, eating, climbing on rafters, and general end-of-Mardi Gras revelry.

* * *

For visitors, the surest way to see le courir is to attend the downtown parties in the late afternoon. You just park, hang out, dance to the bands that most towns have performing on street stages, and wait with the gathered community for the run to return. That's the climax of the day, though, and I had gotten a tip about how to reach the heart of the action from Donald Lejeune, a longtime courir participant and drummer for the Cajun band the Lafayette Rhythm Devils.

"The right way to do the Mardi Gras is to meet up with the riders in the morning, then follow them and watch the day evolve," Donald told me. "It might start slow but, like orchestra music, the tempo goes up as the day goes on, once guys start getting into the beer. The Mardi Gras guys interact with each other and the families they're visiting much differently out on the road and at the farms than they do when they get to town and they're managing in a big crowd. You have to understand, the people whose houses we show up at, we've known these people all our lives. You know what you can get away with and what they won't take, and it's always right on that edge, which is what makes it really fun. Mardi Gras is all about balancing on that line of what's too much."

That's the advice that brought Antonia and me and our small group of friends to a field on the outskirts of Church Point on a Sunday morning for our first taste of le courir, surrounded by horses, tractors, giddy locals, fiddle music, and hundreds of buzzed young men in costume. Dugas was still dancing with the ladies near the bandwagon, and I was trailing a costumed crew of a few dozen riders and the farmer's golf cart to the rear field.

Hours later, the whole group of horses, wagons, and trailers would parade through town, just like at Mamou and other communities, hoisting beers, kissing and hugging women on the sidelines, doing horse tricks, and clowning it up to tease and gently scare young kids along the downtown route. And they would wave their live or recently expired chickens with the triumphant glee of successful sport fishermen showing off a wet trophy catch. Those birds come from cages and coops like the ones the farmer was bringing out to his field in his golf cart that morning, and they also provide one of the central games of the day: the chicken chase.

Back in the field, le capitaine had all the costumed young men spread out in a line as the farmer handled his birds. The men looked intense and eager as they stood in the empty pasture, stretched into a starting line like William Wallace's army waiting to charge before a *Braveheart* battle scene. The farmer gave some last-minute instructions while cradling the doomed chicken gently, almost protectively, in the crook of his arm. Then he paced off to a set distance, and the Mardi Gras men began to lean forward in anticipation. Some assumed the sprinter's starting stance.

The farmer tossed the chicken into the air and in an instant the chase was on. The men bounded forward in their red and yellow and blue and green rag suits, pushing each other out of the way as the startled bird landed and leapt off again ahead of them. The fastest runners crashed down on the chicken like football players going after a fumble, but still it managed to escape and the chase continued a few seconds more until waves of diving men in their rag costumes entered the melee. Finally, a young man came up with the outraged chicken in his grasp and a look of surprise and delight on his face. A round of cheers and happy hoots went up among the other men, and there was more shouting and clapping from a crowd that had gathered to watch from the periphery.

This same contest was repeated a few more times with new chickens until the farmer was through donating livestock. Then le capitaine gave the word, and the group started back toward the horses and the wagons, toward the band and the ice chests and the adulation of their families waiting by the road to see them off again. They would proceed on to more farms, stage more chicken chases, and eventually return to the party in town.

Those who had won the chickens held them in their arms as they strode off through the grass, and everyone wore big, beaming smiles. The sun was shining down, friends were bringing them fresh beers, and they were ribbing each other and laughing loudly out in this trampled field. They had been at this run since the haze of early morning, and they had many more adventures ahead. They seemed like the happiest men on earth, and I recognized the look immediately. They looked just the way I feel when I walk around the streets of New Orleans, in my element and doing my thing on Mardi Gras day. It's always a very real feeling, and to them I'm certain le courir is the real Mardi Gras.

CHAPTER 23

EDGE OF THE GULF, END OF THE ROAD
Cameron Parish and Louisiana's Outback

My big, detailed state highway atlas proved an invaluable tool as I ventured out of New Orleans for weekends on the road. But any map that focuses on highways and the tight grids of population centers can only show you so much of Louisiana.

For all the time I spent plotting road trips, I learned to appreciate this region in a new way once I left the road behind entirely and shoved off from marinas and boat launches. Roads that look like dead ends on maps often become gateways to wild Louisiana, with all its beauty and staggering natural productivity. Learning to see the region from the waterline, I discovered the vast realms of wetlands and lakes and the branching webs of rivers and bayous that shape and define so many communities here and run through the hearts of so many Louisianians. I learned that this is as inseparable from the south Louisiana identity as French heritage and turbulent history. This would be obvious to locals raised on the water, but it had barely registered in the urban perspective I originally developed about my adopted home from within New Orleans.

Traveling along the Creole Nature Trail far out at the southwestern corner of the state, I felt like I needed to find yet another perspective. To get the most out of a very long drive through south Louisiana's least populated area, I decided I would try to imagine what it looked like to a bird flying above. Winged creatures vastly outnumber people in the area covered by this drive anyway, and they

Holly Beach, along the Gulf in the southwest corner of Louisiana.

are a big reason why something called the Creole Nature Trail exists in the first place.

The trail is the tourism marketing designation for a 180-mile scenic drive that descends south from the city of Lake Charles, skirts a sandy stretch of the Gulf Coast around Holly Beach, and makes its way back up toward Lake Charles in a great U shape. In 2002, the trail was named an All-American Road by the U.S. Department of Transportation, a title intended to point out highway runs around the country with such unique features that drives through them qualify as tourist attractions all on their own. In an inspired bit of branding, the remote region around the Creole Nature Trail in Cameron and lower Calcasieu parishes is called "Louisiana's Outback." The masterminds behind the original Old Spanish Trail marketing scheme would have approved, I think. Certainly, the campaign worked on me. If Louisiana had an outback, I wanted to see it.

Lake Charles presents a heavily industrialized landscape of petrochemical plants and casinos. But from this gritty starting point the trail quickly leads to prairie and pasture, then salt marsh and wetlands on down to the Gulf beaches. Just a few miles outside the city's refinery ring, the view through my truck's windshield shifted to cattle ranches and open plain. Soon it changed again to spans of olive- and umber-colored grasses interspersed with wet moats, dark kettle ponds, and sudden broad, straight channels. It was pretty but it seemed forbidding too. Roadside sights of houses and ranches grew farther apart, and I couldn't help but wonder what it would be like to have engine trouble out here. The two-lane road was the lone trail through long stretches of otherwise impassable terrain.

But, again, I was thinking about the trip too much from the driver's seat. While coastal Louisiana may lack obvious soaring vistas, there is always that deep, pulsing fecundity of fresh water, salt water, land, and the half-land of the marshes. To birds winging in from above, this particular area has to look like feathered heaven.

Like Grand Isle far to the east, the Creole Nature Trail sits along a migratory flyway, one of those aerial routes that birds follow from north to south and back again on their seasonal journeys. What I saw as trackless and remote landscapes the birds would know instinctually to be prime habitat, and they flock to Cameron Parish in stunning numbers and diversity. As many as three hundred different species of birds visit Louisiana's Outback throughout the year, and four hundred thousand ducks alone splash down in this welcoming mosaic of reed and water every winter.

For this reason, the Creole Nature Trail is marketed to bird watchers, who can cruise the long stretches of road here while filling in a birding checklist longer than a spoiled child's petition to Santa. But when people from south Louisiana have their eyes on birds, it usually means trouble for the birds. The area has long been popular with hunters, who annually greet the ducks, geese, quail, and other future contributors to the Cajun smoker and black pot with more artillery than ever burst over Fort Sumter.

* * *

This unbroken bird habitat and the gun and rod territory continued on until I came to Hackberry, the first town I encountered since the outskirts of Lake Charles. This isn't a very big town, but I was relieved to discover that it at least contained a gas station, the first

I'd seen since leaving Lake Charles. When I noticed a sign for West Main Street, I decided to veer off the Creole Nature Trail for a bit and see if there was some kind of village center in Hackberry. I spotted a church, a cemetery, and a high school in quick succession, but then West Main got real rural real fast. Before long the road forked, and both options led me to the gates of private property. I doubled back and explored a few more turns, but every side street I tried led to watery dead ends or entrances to homestead ranches.

On one of these country roads, though, after a few lefts and rights, I noticed a large, curious clearing. The area was lined with wire fences, and I saw what looked like a network of pipes running close to the ground and leading in the direction of a few small buildings and minor storage tanks. I had noticed some oil field infrastructure just outside Hackberry proper, where a few pump jacks nodded away over oil wells by the edge of the road. I assumed this little complex must be related. It turned out I was right, but only in a barest tip-of-the-iceberg sort of way.

I would later learn that the little clearing I had stumbled upon on my aimless tour off the Creole Nature Trail was the surface support area for the West Hackberry National Strategic Petroleum Reserve, one of just five sites where the federal government keeps its emergency oil stash. This reserve is a fuel stockpile that was created in 1975 after the shock of the Arab oil embargo. The Department of Energy describes it as "an emergency response tool the President can use should the United States be confronted with an economically-threatening disruption in oil supplies."

The five sites together hold 725 million barrels of oil, which is about equal to what America was going through every thirty-five days at the time of this writing. It's a lode the government says is worth about $17 billion, and the West Hackberry facility can hold almost a third of it all on its own. Yet I was able to drive right past this ocean of amassed oil without an inkling of its immense scope, because all of it is stored neatly underground in hollowed-out salt deposits, relatives of the same salt dome islands that prove such enduring tourists attractions over in Iberia Parish.

Unlike Avery Island and Jefferson Island, though, these massive salt formations in Cameron Parish have no domes and are contained entirely below the surface. The Department of Energy decided they would make perfect sites for the long-term storage of the nation's oil hoard. Engineers pumped in fresh water to dissolve some of the salt and create a series of giant caverns within the deposits. Some plunge two thousand feet deep, which is enough room to swallow Chicago's Sears Tower (antenna and all) or, more to the point, millions upon millions of barrels of oil. The ancient salt formations provided rock-solid chambers that the government says are much more secure and cheaper than anything it could build on the surface. Thanks to the simple and widely understood proposition that oil floats on water, the storage site managers can extract the oil simply by pumping water into the cavern, which displaces the oil and brings it to the top for collection in pipelines.

The Strategic Petroleum Reserve tends to come up in news reports whenever international oil prices seem beyond control and pundits and policy advisors debate the merits of injecting some of the stock-pile into the marketplace. The physical supply itself, however, keeps a very low profile.

I became intrigued by the West Hackberry site once I learned I had so obliviously driven past such a massive piece of the American energy equation. So I started reading about it and checked it out using the Google Earth mapping program. There it all appeared on my computer screen back home—the town of Hackberry, West Main Street, the turns I had wandered, and finally the tidy, modest-seeming reserve site. From this aerial perspective, it looked like nothing more than a collection of paved rectangles flush to the ground, like small parking lots or building slabs wiped clean. And, I thought, to migrating birds choosing between marsh and lake, it must look like the least promising patch of the Louisiana Outback for miles and miles around.

* * *

I departed Hackberry, and the next phase of the Creole Nature Trail carried me farther south and through an area where the grasslands fell away and coastal marsh took over. The shimmering road before me now looked like a land bridge lined with slim banks of white gravel. Water came right up to the edge on either side. Eventually there was a sign for the Sabine National Wildlife Refuge, where a dirt parking lot was full of cars and pickups. I saw a few people heading down a boardwalk that zigzagged across the marsh, though most people were fishing from small boats in the adjacent channels and casting nets from the side of a small bridge, coming up with bundles of crabs. Many of the continent's ducks and geese migrating along the Mississippi flyway congregate at this sanctuary in the winter, as if it's their own private Florida.

The scenery here was captivating, even without conjuring my imaginary bird's-eye view. The boardwalk took me about a mile into the refuge, and at its end I looked over a sprawling vista of brassy, smoky-green marsh reeds blooming up in bursts and clusters. In the distance, I could see a few of this region's distinctive cheniers, or sandy ridges topped with oaks, their French namesakes. They looked like frozen dark waves across the flat marsh, and I could see birds circling in great numbers around some of the nearer cheniers like halos of gulls over inbound shrimp boats. The view was a vivid lesson in how engrossing the Louisiana landscape can be, even without majestic mountains and canyons to anchor the scenery.

The Sabine refuge is one of four huge, protected sites along the Creole Nature Trail, and it's the largest coastal marsh sanctuary on the entire Gulf, encompassing 124,500 acres. These days, however, much more of that refuge acreage has been rendered open water. The U.S. Fish and Wildlife Service says the refuge has lost about 40,000 acres of habitat, or nearly a third of its total area, to coastal erosion. The blame falls to the usual fatal mix of oil field canals that cut up the landscape, levees that block natural replenishment from sediment-laden river waters, and hurricanes that periodically roar in to carry off large swaths of weakened marsh.

Even out here in Louisiana's Outback, there's no escaping Louisiana's existential peril, and no one knows it better than the people who live along the Creole Nature Trail in Cameron Parish. This is one of the largest of Louisiana's sixty-four parishes, and also its least populated, with fewer than ten thousand residents. The parish covers about five thousand square miles and has just one stoplight. The towns here have never been very big, but the ceaseless creep of erosion and the impact of hurricanes have taken a very heavy toll.

The modern saga of destruction started with Hurricane Audrey in 1957. Few people evacuated before the storm, and the result for these tiny, utterly flat seaside communities was horrific. More than five hundred people were killed, mostly in Cameron Parish and adjacent Vermilion Parish. Some bodies were found twenty-five miles away from where these people had been seen alive last. The precise death toll was unknown, however, because the bodies of close to two hundred people reported missing were never recovered. Presumably they were swept into the Gulf or lost in the expansive wetlands and alligator marshes.

What I saw driving through coastal Cameron Parish was the result of much more recent calamity. Coverage of Hurricane Rita in late September 2005 was largely overshadowed by the destruction wrought just four weeks earlier by Hurricane Katrina. But Rita was a cataclysm for the isolated communities of Cameron Parish, and it also savaged Lake Charles, more than thirty very flat miles inland. All of Cameron Parish was flooded, and most structures here were destroyed or badly damaged. Three years later Cameron was pummeled again by Hurricane Ike, which wrecked much of what had been rebuilt since Rita.

There were only a few reported deaths in the whole region from Rita and Ike, thanks to massive evacuation efforts that didn't exist back in the 1950s when Audrey struck. But one major casualty of the 2005 and 2008 storms was Holly Beach, a budget beachfront getaway right on the Gulf and a key link on the Creole Nature Trail.

I was still eager to check it out. I had heard stories about Holly Beach all over Acadiana from people who invariably referred to it as "the Cajun Riveria." While I was not expecting Saint-Tropez I had come to trust that when real live Cajuns describe something as "Cajun" it usually turns out to be delicious, hilarious, or really fun.

Before the most recent storms, Holly Beach was composed of a few hundred camps and cabins, some sandy motels, and a couple of bars, all banded together in a small, densely settled cluster by the water. People always described it as having a take-it-or-leave-it aesthetic that wasn't lux by any stretch but was very affordable. Most lots here were a uniform 1,250 square feet and, before Rita hit, thirty thousand dollars would get you a decent Holly Beach camp—a place to bring the family to fish and crab and cook and a place to party on weekends.

But when Rita devastated the entire parish it smashed and swept away just about everything in Holly Beach besides the town's resilient iron water tower. Poststorm construction codes now require twenty-foot elevations and much larger lots, and that has made it impossible for much of the old Holly Beach crowd to rebuild here.

As I drove around the community's old street grid of about twenty-five long, rectangular blocks, I counted at least ten blank slabs for every modern, colorful camp built anew on towering pilings. Some people had parked RVs on their old sites and decorated all around them with rippling flags and windsocks, though for blocks on end there was nothing but cleared foundation slabs and the broken concrete steps that once led to cabin doors. It was a Sunday in late August when I visited, high summer, yet this battered beach town seemed nearly empty. When I passed one site and spotted a few festive-looking retirees lounging in the sun outside their RV, we simultaneously waved to each other as eagerly as if hailing a parade float. I was happy to spot someone around here, and they looked excited too.

The actual beach at Holly Beach was much like the one I found at Grand Isle. It was broad, hard-packed, and lacked much in the way of visual features beyond the oil platforms standing in clear view offshore. There were a few people driving their trucks across the sand and people surf-casting at the water's edge or splashing around in the low waves. I had a quick swim in the warm, sandy water, collected a few ashtray-sized seashells, and headed back onto the Creole Natural Trail.

* * *

Later, I hopped an auto ferry over the Cameron shipping canal and drove through the area's largest town. I passed its many storm-blown buildings, the resilient, gray, 1930s-era Cameron Parish courthouse, and the omnipresent signs of the town's busy fishing and offshore oil support industries. I continued along the Creole Nature Trail past many more cheniers and took a long spur to visit the coastal Rockefeller Wildlife Refuge, a prolific alligator nesting area and a state research site focused on the resurgent reptiles. I passed through the miniscule but evocatively named town of Creole and drove over a swooping, graceful bridge spanning the Gulf Intracoastal Canal, which provided a brief view over the marsh that was finally up there with the bird's-eye perspective I'd spent the day imagining.

Yet I couldn't stop thinking about something I had seen from the road just outside Holly Beach, and it stayed with me for the long drive all the way back home to New Orleans. A few miles past the last of the beach community camp slabs, on a stretch of the Creole Nature Trail straddling marsh and open Gulf, I noticed a pair of large, red, maritime channel markers leaning toward the road and looking as though they'd been washed against the shore.

Maybe they were supposed to be there. Maybe they were marking the beachhead for a pipeline trucking ashore from the Gulf rigs. After learning about West Hackberry's gigantic underground oil storage site and the eighty-three thousand miles of pipeline veining the state I make no assumptions about where Louisiana's energy infrastructure might appear. Still, these big, red, listing markers seemed alien and misplaced sitting there in the sand as small waves broke around their partially exposed, barnacled bases. I stopped the truck and got out to take a look around.

The Creole Nature Trail had brought me to the very rim of the region I had been exploring so ardently, the region that had given me so much in return for the effort. Ten years earlier, when I first arrived in New Orleans, I could not have imagined the things I would experience on these trips—the diversity of the places I would discover, the people I would meet and the fun I would have simply by setting off to see what I could find in south Louisiana. Now I stood by a beach at the ragged edge of my range, an area far off in the corner of the state, the last gasp of Acadiana before everything turns into Texas.

The old river towns and bayou villages of my earlier travels sat all the way across the state, and the Cajun and Creole communities through rice country and horse country and down into sugar country seemed distant too. I stood outside the truck at the edge of the Gulf and at the end of the road. I stared at these strange channel markers, which looked like rooks from a chessboard titling toward shore or like derelict, falling lighthouses. The boxy, mechanical hulks of oil platforms staked the Gulf horizon, silent and distant. There was not a soul around.

I turned around and gazed over the marsh on the other side of the road. To the birds, it probably still looked pretty good. But as I stood there on the road, on the slim barrier between Gulf and marsh, I thought about the forces at work in south Louisiana. I thought about the erosion and the shackled rivers, the creeping water and the passing time and the infuriating politics that keep it all ticking down. I thought about the people and the history and the places that bind south Louisiana together and make it such a compelling, satisfying, addicting place to live even as the bottom falls out.

The open immensity of the Gulf was behind me while the protecting marsh beyond the road seemed so forlorn, a brittle and salted patchwork that stretched on until all features dissolved in the blank haze ahead. I felt very alone, and a sense of desolation crept into my heart. The scene before me looked like the very end of the earth, but of course I knew it wasn't anything so important as that. It was just the end of Louisiana.

APPENDIX: RAMBLE ON
Notes on Trips and Travel Resources

Much of the generic advice given to travelers applies to trips around south Louisiana. Bring sunscreen and bug spray in the hot months (roughly March through October), call to confirm hours of operation or event dates before departing, watch for weather warnings, etc. But the three specific imperatives I learned about travel in this unique and incredibly rewarding pocket of America were to keep the radio tuned to local stations while driving, to use secondary roads and scenic byways as much as possible, and to do whatever is necessary to get out on the water during some point in your travels.

The dashboard radio has a lot of competition in this age of digital entertainment, but it added enormously to these trips. The commentary and accents of local radio hosts, the event listings and community announcements, even the commercials for local businesses—they all filled my travels with more regional flavor between destinations, and also gave me ideas for different places to explore. For those traveling east of the Atchafalaya, I recommend the Larose-based KLRZ 100.3 FM (www.klrzfm.com) for swamp pop and Cajun music; and of course the indomitable and far-reaching New Orleans stations WWOZ 90.7 FM (www.wwoz.org), a nonprofit roots music station, and WWNO 89.9 FM, a National Public Radio (NPR) affiliate. West of the Atchafalaya, I tune in to KBON 101.1 FM (www.kbon.com), broadcasting a diverse mix of Louisiana music from downtown Eunice; the Lafayette-based NPR affiliate KRVS 88.7 FM (www.krvs.org); and the Opelousas zydeco and soul channel KFXZ 105.9 FM (www.z1059.com).

My driving soundtrack switched from iPod mixes to local radio around the same time that I began bypassing the interstate in favor of secondary roads whenever the opportunity arose. This means slower going between destinations, but I gladly put in the time once I realized how these older, pokier routes led me through the south Louisiana I had set out to experience in the first place.

The Louisiana interstates can tell their own tales as they cut across swamp and marsh and bridge the monumental Mississippi and Atchafalaya rivers, and in some areas they are the only roads available. But eventually, I came to view interstate miles like time spent above the clouds in air travel, while the smaller routes reveal the greater detail and interlocking context of towns, cultivated land, wild areas, and water.

Sunset over Lake Verret in Assumption Parish.

My epic roads included Highway 1, which shadows Bayou Lafourche all the way to Grand Isle where it ends abruptly and appropriately at a marina; and Highway 182, which starts in the swampland southwest of New Orleans, parallels Bayou Teche for a leg of the Old Spanish Trail, cuts through Lafayette and continues on up into prairie country. The main prairie highway itself, Highway 190, links Baton Rouge with Opelousas and Eunice and includes so many great boudin stops and music destinations along the way. And of course there's the meandering River Road on either side of the Mississippi, with its alternating industrial and agricultural landscapes.

There is no missing the importance of waterways in this region. Travelers are forever crossing bridges and hopping on ferries, driving alongside bayous and rivers as they meander through town centers, and catching glimpses of the wild, marshy immensity of America's largest wetlands region at the side of the road or the end of the line. These natural and manmade waterways define the geography, influence the culture, and shape the future of south Louisiana to such a huge extent that I now believe one can only glean the edges of the south Louisiana experience from dry land. Fortunately, small boat and canoe rentals, charters, and guided tours abound, making the bayous, swamps, lakes, and offshore areas readily accessible to visitors.

I must note, however, that at this writing the impacts of the 2010 BP oil disaster off Louisiana's coast are unknown. The following travel notes are provided with optimism that the coastal areas they describe will be accessible and ready for visitors when you read this.

There are many routes, waterways, towns, festivals, and destinations, and there are many ways to explore and enjoy the spectacular natural and cultural wealth of south Louisiana. What follows below are chapter-by-chapter notes about specific trips and topics covered by this book, provided as a starting point for those who undertake their own Louisiana rambles. I hope I see you out there.

PART I: EAST OF THE ATCHAFALAYA

Chapter 1. Manchac by Moonlight:
Paddling New Orleans's Wild Border by Day and Night

From the urban hub of New Orleans, scenes of otherworldly wildness are just a quick drive away. Within twenty minutes, travelers can find themselves in deepest swamp—mesmerizing, fecund landscapes teeming with animals, enmeshed in vigorously abundant vegetation, and intricately laced by quiet water.

Visitors can get an easy view of this at the National Park Service's Barataria Preserve (6588 Barataria Blvd., Marrero, 504-689-3690, ext. 10; www.nps.gov/jela), a twenty-thousand-acre site with boardwalks, dirt trails, and canoe launches. The preserve offers free, ranger-led trail walks daily and a monthly evening version under the full moon (reservations required).

Visitors can rent canoes or join guided canoe trips into the Barataria Preserve from Bayou Barn (7145 Barataria Blvd., Crown Point, 800-862-2968; www.bayoubarn.net), which runs a restaurant and a party venue on Bayou des Familles.

Byron Almquist and his guides with Canoe & Trail Adventures (www.canoeandtrail.com) host outdoor outings in the swamps and bayous near New Orleans. Moonlight paddles like the one described in this chapter usually are scheduled on Saturdays closest to the monthly full moon.

Chapter 2. Alight Christmas:
River Levee Bonfires and Papa Noel

By tradition, levee-top bonfires along the River Road (Highway 44) in the St. James Parish towns of Gramercy, Lutcher, and Paulina are lit on December 24 at 7 p.m. Crowds congregate around the levee long beforehand. Local restaurants and bars are open for those not attending the many nearby house parties, but I found the best-equipped visitors had packed their own refreshments for the evening.

St. James Parish also hosts its Festival of the Bonfires during an earlier December weekend, featuring carnival rides, crafts, live music, and the lighting of a solitary levee bonfire each festival night as a tiny prelude to the full conflagration to come on Christmas Eve. See www.festivalofthebonfires.org or call 225-869-1717.

At this writing, the riverboat bonfire tour I took was discontinued, but tour operators including Gray Line New Orleans (800-535-7786; www.graylinenewor leans.com) offer bus excursions from New Orleans to the bonfire area.

Chapter 3. Airboats and Alligators:
Swamp Tours and Louisiana's Favorite Dinosaur

Alligators are feeding and on the move during warm weather, so spring, summer, and early fall is gator-spotting time in south Louisiana. These cold-blooded reptiles lay low in muddy burrows during winter months.

Many small companies across southeast Louisiana offer narrated swamp and bayou tours by airboat or pontoon barge, and plenty depart from launches within an hour's drive of New Orleans. Alligators will be part of any warm-weather tour, and that's when I recommend booking a trip. But these ecosystems offer plenty for visitors to experience at any time of year. Migratory birds are prevalent in fall and spring, and swamp plants bloom in different stages through the seasons. Always call to confirm tour availability, since large group bookings, local weather, or water levels can alter operators' schedules from day to day. The swamp tour operators mentioned in this chapter are:

Airboat Tours by Arthur
4262 Hwy. 90, Des Allemands, 800-975-9345; www.airboattours.com

A Cajun Man's Swamp Cruise
3109 Southdown Mandalay Rd., Houma, 985-868-4625; www.cajunman.com

Honey Island Swamp Tours
41490 Crawford Landing Rd., Slidell, 985-641-1769; www.honeyislandswamp.com

Zam's Bayou Swamp Tours
136 Kraemer Bayou Rd., Kraemer, 985-633-7881

In addition, a few good places for up-close alligator encounters include:

Insta-Gator Ranch—a commercial alligator ranch offering a detailed and interactive tour.
23440 Lowe Davis Rd., Covington, 985-892-3669; www.insta-gatorranch.com.

Cypress Island Preserve (Lake Martin)—managed by the Nature Conservancy, a ninety-five-hundred-acre property centered on Lake Martin and sitting between Lafayette and Breaux Bridge. It's an important rookery for wading birds and is home to many alligators, which can readily be seen from walking paths or a driving trail. Located off Highway 31. See www.nature.org/louisiana.

Rockefeller Wildlife Refuge—an enormous, seventy-six-thousand-acre protected property in the southwest corner of the state, along a spur of the Creole Nature Trail (see chapter 23). The alligator population here is so robust the state uses the site for its research programs on the animal's recovery and ongoing management. See www.creolenaturetrail.org.

Chapter 4. River Road Revisited:
Plantation Tours and the Slavery Legacy

Slave-based plantations thrived all across Louisiana, and the surviving examples help tell different chapters of regional history. The stretch of River Road between New Orleans and Baton Rouge—the focus of this chapter—has an especially dense and diverse cluster of these historic properties that are open to the public.

A little primer on terminology and geography can go a long way for newcomers trying to navigate in this part of Louisiana. First, it's important to know that the term "River Road" is applied to two separate roadways, each of which follows the path of the Mississippi on opposite banks. Also remember that all sense of direction in this area is based on the river, and its many twists and turns mean conventional compass points are of little use to travelers seeking directions here. While the Mississippi runs generally north to south, it turns to follow a west-to-east course through much of River Road plantation country. Yet destinations geographically to the north of the river are still said to be on the east bank, while those to the south are part of the west bank. Travelers must imagine the winding river ironed into a straight north-to-south line for the local coordinates to make sense. Muddling things further, state highway numbers change as the River Road routes make their way upstream, though Highway 44 on the east bank and Highway 18 on the west bank carry travelers through most of the River Road area described in this chapter.

No matter where you go in River Road plantation country, you will see sugarcane fields, the modern heirs to the state's antebellum agricultural legacy. Some of the surviving plantations that open their historic manor houses to the public for tours continue to bring in commercial cane harvests, including St. Joseph Plantation and Evergreen Plantation.

The list below includes River Road properties mentioned in this chapter, plus the small but instructive River Road African American Museum. Listings are arranged by their approximate distance from New Orleans. Tour operators offer bus excursions and package deals so that several properties can be visited in one trip, and solo travelers can easily hit three in a day and have the flexibility to add side trips to their itinerary.

Some of the plantations have restaurants or snack bars, but for day-trippers in search of lunch I recommend stopping at restaurants off-property for a more diverse experience in the area. For instance, on the west bank in Vacherie, about halfway between the Laura and Oak Alley plantations, you can count on good lunches from a pair of homey, authentic Cajun restaurants. Spuddy's Cajun Foods (2644 Hwy. 20, Vacherie, 225-265-4013) smokes its own andouille for gumbo, po-boys, and even sausage salads (or to load into a cooler to bring home), while B&C Seafood Market & Cajun Restaurant (2155 Hwy. 18, Vacherie, 225-265-8356) is more about grilled and fried local seafood. On the east bank, Hymel's Restaurant (8740 Hwy. 44, Convent, 225-562-9910) is a great place for fried or boiled seafood and cold draft beers en route to Houmas House or Bocage plantations or the Sunshine Bridge leading to Donaldsonville. In the same vicinity, there's also the Cabin Restaurant (5405 Hwy. 44, Gonzales, www.thecabinrestaurant. com), which is housed in a collection of historic outbuildings rescued from now-demolished plantations and renovated as dining rooms.

Properties within forty miles of downtown New Orleans:

Destrehan Plantation
13034 River Rd., Destrehan, 985-764-9315; www.destrehanplantation.org

San Francisco Plantation
2646 Hwy. 44, Garyville, 888-322-1756; www.sanfranciscoplantation.org

Properties within sixty miles of New Orleans:

Evergreen Plantation
4677 Hwy. 18, Edgard, 985-497-3837; www.evergreenplantation.org

Laura Plantation
2247 Hwy. 18, Vacherie, 888-799-7690; www.lauraplantation.com

St. Joseph Plantation
3535 Hwy. 18, Vacherie, 225-265-4078; www.stjosephplantation.com

Oak Alley Plantation
3645 Hwy. 18, Vacherie, 1-800-442-5539; www.oakalleyplantation.com

Houmas House Plantation & Gardens
40136 Hwy. 942, Darrow, 225-473-9380; www.houmashouse.com

Bocage Plantation
39050 Hwy. 942, Darrow, 225-588-8000; www.bocageplantation.com

Properties farther than sixty miles from New Orleans:

River Road African American Museum
406 Charles St., Donaldsonville, 225-474-5553; www.africanamericanmuseum.org

Nottoway Plantation
31025 Hwy. 1, White Castle, 866-527-6884; www.nottoway.com

Chapter 5. Angola's Incarcerated Cowboys:
A Culture That Persists Behind Bars

The Angola Prison Rodeo is held during four consecutive Saturdays in October and on one weekend in April. Gates open in the morning, and most visitors spend a few hours perusing the food booths and a sprawling market of bargain-priced, inmate-made crafts. Inmates and prison employees staff these booths and craft tables themselves. Inmate bands perform gospel, country, and rock throughout the day. Rodeo action commences in a covered arena in the early afternoon. Tickets usually sell out, so be sure to order in advance.

There is a festival atmosphere here, but visitors should never forget they are on the grounds of a maximum-security prison. All vehicles and visitors may be searched, and ice chests, alcohol, weapons, or anything else considered contraband is forbidden. Also, cell phones and cameras are not allowed inside the rodeo grounds. For specific rules, dates, and details, contact the prison at 225-655-2133 or see www.angolarodeo.com.

The Angola Museum and its unusual gift shop are located just outside the prison's main gates and are open year-round. See www.angolamuseum.org. Angola's Prison View Golf Course is open to the public year-round, though a background check is required to use the facility. See www.prisonviewgolf.com.

The road to Angola, Highway 61, passes St. Francisville, a historic town that in geography, history, and culture stands apart from the Cajun and Creole heartland areas explored in this book but which is well worth its own visit. St. Francisville sits high on ridges over the Mississippi River and in the heart of "English Louisiana." It's the second-oldest incorporated town in the state, though its enduring identity developed after waves of British loyalists settled here following the American Revolution. They created a community of gothic churches with oak-shaded graveyards, a densely settled downtown that is now home to more than 140 historic homes, and a cluster of grand plantations in the surrounding countryside, many of which are open to the public today.

During the third weekend in March, the West Feliciana Historical Society holds its Audubon Pilgrimage (see www.audubonpilgrimage.info), a community-wide festival with tours of homes, formal gardens, and churches led by costumed characters, plus social events in the evening. The festival celebrates the time that artist-naturalist John James Audubon spent in the area, working as a tutor for a wealthy family and developing his famous bird folios on the side. The historic plantation where he stayed, Oakley House (1788 Hwy. 965, St. Francisville, 888-677-2838; www.crt.state.la.us/Parks/iaudubon.aspx), is open year-round as a state museum.

Other historic homes in and around St. Francisville have been converted into B and Bs (see www.stfrancisville.us for listings), including the Myrtles Plantation (7747 Hwy. 61., St. Francisville, 225-635-6277; www.myrtlesplantation.com), which eagerly burnishes a reputation for ghosts.

Also along the route between Baton Rouge and Angola is the Port Hudson State Historic Site (236 Hwy. 61, Jackson, 888-677-3400; www.crt.state.la.us/parks/ipthudson.aspx), which commemorates a decisive Civil War battle for control of the Mississippi. Visitors today can tour a military history museum devoted to the epic clash, and sure-footed hikers can explore miles of trails that swoop and dive through steep, wooded ravines.

Chapter 6. Petroleum Pipe Dreams: Oil, Oil Everywhere and the Future of the Coast

Anyone who loved Tonka trucks or Erector Sets as a kid will probably find the burly bustle of south Louisiana's oil and gas ports and the retrofuturistic skylines of the state's vast refineries fascinating. Major facilities are closed to the public, but they are so massive that travelers can get a good glimpse of things from the road without trespassing. For instance, make a small detour off Highway 1 on the way to the fishing docks and boat launches of Grand Isle (see chapter 9), and the short offshoot of Highway 3090 will lead to Port Fourchon, a nexus of the Gulf's offshore energy industry.

By far the most extensive and accessible attraction for people interested in the industrial history of the oil business is the International Petroleum Museum & Exposition (111 First St., Morgan City, 985-384-3744; www.rigmuseum.com) in Morgan City. Its principal attraction, the pioneering oil rig named Mr. Charlie, is open for tours that take in nearly every inch of the vintage platform, which is still used by drilling companies as a hands-on training facility. Visitors can also poke around a collection of small submersible vehicles, escape pods, and assorted other retired offshore equipment displayed around a riverfront yard adjacent to the rig.

Morgan City's Shrimp and Petroleum Festival, held each Labor Day weekend, is the town's biggest annual draw. Bands perform in the pretty, oak-lined town square while food booths and a craft fair sit in the shade of the highway overpass. For visitors, the most interesting parts of the day occur along the riverfront, past the city's twenty-foot-high concrete floodwall. That's where the blessing of the fleet ceremony takes place, with a boat parade of local watercraft decorated for the day. The climax comes when two large workboats nudge up so close to each other that the festival's king and queen riding at the bow of each vessel may reach out and clink glasses in a champagne toast. See www.shrimp-petrofest.org for schedules.

Chapter 7. Andouille Ever:
Sausage Road Trips and a Kitchen Divided

There are people who might spend a weekend driving around Napa Valley sleuthing out tiny wineries, those fabled, practically secret boutique operations that make just a few barrels a year and sell only through the cellar door. For the porcine passionate, the same thrill of the hunt and joy of discovery can be found on the sausage trail around south Louisiana. Always bring a cooler, and never be shy about asking locals at any shop, restaurant, or gas station for their personal favorite butcher shops. A great one might be very close by. The specific sausage types discussed in this chapter are the most prominent: andouille and boudin.

Andouille
Once I discovered the unique and compelling andouille sausage produced in LaPlace, this river town in St. John the Baptist Parish became one of my very first Louisiana road trip destinations.

Airline Highway (a.k.a. Highway 61), the preinterstate route connecting New Orleans with Baton Rouge, is the main drag in LaPlace. Amid dense suburban clutter, Bailey's World Famous Andouille (513 W. Airline Hwy., LaPlace, 985-652-9090; www.baileysandouille.com) and Jacob's World Famous Andouille (505 W. Airline Hwy., LaPlace, 985-652-9080; www.cajunsausage.com) do business just a few doors from each other on the same block. Wayne Jacob's Smokehouse (769 W. Fifth St., LaPlace, 985-652-9990) has a somewhat more rural setting along West Fifth Street, closer to the river.

Wayne Jacob's is my personal favorite of the LaPlace field. This place has had a succession of owners since Nolan "Nat" Jacob first opened the shop in 1950. The current owner and chief sausage maker is thirty-something LaPlace native David Rauch. His brother John runs WJ's Smokehouse Restaurant under the same roof, and naturally he uses many of David's products on his menu.

While local demand for andouille spikes during the cool weather months, it is produced and available year-round. Of the three shops listed above, only Jacob's World Famous Andouille is approved by the USDA to ship its product. The others sell through their shops exclusively.

LaPlace also hosts its annual, three-day Andouille Festival in October. See www.andouillefestival.com.

The neighboring town of Reserve shares the same robust andouille tradition, and any extensive tour of the River Parish sausage options should include stops at Cox's Meat Market (1162 Hwy. 44, Reserve, 985-536-2491), a small butcher shop in the shadow of the river levee, and Don's Country Store (318 Central Ave., Reserve, 985-536-2316), a larger operation where you can get cast-iron pots, hardware, and a full load of groceries.

Boudin

An andouille road trip is essentially a foraging run for cooking ingredients. But boudin, the rice and pork sausage that has inspired so many Acadian road trips in its own right, is generally eaten out of hand. It is served at butcher shops and gas stations (and butcher shops that double as gas stations), so the opportunity to try a link of boudin arises every few miles around Cajun country. The three Breaux Bridge boudin purveyors mentioned in this chapter are:

Bayou Boudin & Cracklin's (100 W. Mills Ave., Breaux Bridge, 337-332-6158; www.bayoucabins.com), which doubles as a bed and breakfast with cute, vintage cabins right on Bayou Teche.

Charlie T's Specialty Meats (530 Berard St., Breaux Bridge, 337-332-2426), a squat brick grocery store serving plate lunches to go.

Poche's Market (3015 Main Hwy., Breaux Bridge, 337-332-2108; www .pochesmarket.com), a busy butcher shop far out on the edge of town with a well-stocked hot lunch line and a large, clean dining room.

There are many, many others, and even travelers just passing through the region needn't venture far from the interstate to get a taste. See www.boudin link.com for obsessively detailed reviews and rankings of nearly one hundred boudin shops across Acadiana, plus a few in cities around the country.

Chapter 8. Have Cooler, Will Float:
Tubing Your Time Away on the Amite River

South Louisiana tubing operations generally operate between April and early September. The last big blowout for the season is typically Labor Day weekend. Most tubing operators follow the same rules: don't bring glass containers (think of the foot wounds) or Styrofoam coolers, but do bring sunscreen, a sun hat, ice chests, bottled water, and lunch. I recommend bringing a pair of old sneakers or water shoes to wear in the river and a change of clothes for the end of the day. Draw straws to pick a designated driver.

Of the three operators listed below, Tiki Tubing is closest to Baton Rouge, while the other two are marginally closer to New Orleans, located near the Mississippi state line.

Tiki Tubing (on the Amite River)
33203 Hwy. 1019, Denham Springs, 225-223-1156; www.tikitubing.com

Bogue Chitto Canoeing and Tubing Center (on the Bogue Chitto River)
10237 Choctaw Rd., Bogalusa, 985-735-1173; www.tubingboguechitto.com

Wayne's World Canoeing and Tubing (on the Bogue Chitto River)
51439 Camp Circle Rd., Franklinton, 985-795-2004; www.canoelariver.com

Chapter 9. The Search for Sand:
Casting Off from Grand Isle

Less than sixty miles separates New Orleans from Grand Isle, as the crow flies. But it takes those of us stuck on land more than two hours to drive the distance, thanks to a circuitous route that must wend through three different parishes to get around large bodies of open water and expanses of impassable marsh.

The trip brings travelers through a succession of small towns lining Bayou Lafourche along Highway 1 (see chapter 13), including the notorious speed trap zones between the fishing villages of Larose and Golden Meadow. The journey includes a drive over the Leeville Bridge, a soaring, swooping, modern highway bridge that crosses Bayou Lafourche. This is a toll bridge, yet there are no tollbooths where travelers can simply pay with cash. Rather, in a puzzling and inconvenient arrangement for tourists, tolls are maintained with cameras and scanners and must be paid in advance at a series of kiosks at designated gas stations or online. For information, see www.geauxpass.com.

Fishing is the main travel draw for Grand Isle. A good starting point for information on charters, marinas, bait shops, and fishing piers on the island itself is Grand Isle's tourism department (985-787-2997; www.grand-isle.com). Also, Grand Isle State Park (888-787-2559, www.crt.state.la.us/parks/igrdisle.aspx), located on the southeast corner of the island, has a large beach and campsites.

Summer is the busiest season on Grand Isle, though travelers who visit in the fall and spring will find the fishing just as good, the Gulf sunsets just as lovely, and the atmosphere more serene with far fewer people buzzing around on four-wheelers and golf carts. In April, the conservation-minded Grand Isle Migratory Bird Festival (800-259-0869; www.btnep.org) invites nature enthusiasts to visit while the island teems with birds resting after their epic, seasonal Gulf crossings.

The search for sand along the muddy, dissolving Louisiana coast can be frustrating, though the manmade beach at Cypremort Point State Park in St. Mary Parish was a refreshing surprise. See www.crt.state.la.us/parks/icyprempt.aspx.

Holly Beach (see chapter 23) is another option for getting into the Gulf, this time in the far southwestern corner of the state. But the best public swimming spot I found in south Louisiana was the manmade beach at Lake End Park, a campground run by Morgan City on the shore of Lake Palourde. The water was clear and relatively cool, and you can swim around stands of cypress that grow right in the water itself. See www.lakeendpark.net.

Chapter 10. Capitol Ideas:
Stalking the Halls of Power in Baton Rouge

The Louisiana State Capitol is the centerpiece of a large campus of architecturally impressive government buildings, formal gardens, and historic sites along the Baton Rouge riverfront known as Capitol Park (702 N. River Rd., Baton Rouge, 225-219-1200; www.crt.state.la.us). There's a welcome center on the grounds where visitors can pick up maps for self-guided walking tours. Highlights include the Louisiana State Museum, completed in 2006, with its many history and cultural exhibits; the beautiful State Library of Louisiana; the Pentagon Barracks, a complex of former military housing built in the 1820s; the tomb of Huey P. Long; the Old Arsenal, an army installation built in 1835 that now houses a Civil War exhibit; and an Indian mound that overlooks Capitol Lake.

The towering capitol building is open to the public daily, and in addition to its decorous halls there is an open-air observation deck on the twenty-seventh floor offering a panorama of the Mississippi River and all of Baton Rouge (plus the massive petrochemical complex just upriver). I think the most interesting time for a visit is when the building is in use and you can see the gears of representative government grinding away. The annual legislative session usually runs from late March to late June, and the governor may also call special sessions at other times of the year as well. For information about legislative sessions, see www .legis.state.la.us.

The retired Old State Capitol, which houses Louisiana's Museum of Political History, is located about a mile away from the modern capitol and is open for self-guided tours. See www.sos.louisiana.gov/osc.

Chapter 11. The River Rats:
Riverine Pub Crawls Around Livingston Parish

Though they look like obscure trickles on the map, the rivers and bayous of Livingston Parish between Lake Maurepas and Baton Rouge are honeycombed with waterfront communities, and these waterways also comprise the framework for a robust collection of bars, restaurants, and marinas serving the boating crowd.

Naturally, the best way to experience the "river rat" culture of this area is from the water. Rob Arrington (a.k.a. River Rat Rob) periodically organizes outings for people with their own Jet Skis and small boats on the Amite River, Lake Maurepas, and other waterways. His Web site, www.riverratrob.com, provides event details, information on other river doings throughout the year, river maps, and listings for the many bars and marinas in the area.

For people who don't have access to watercraft, or who would rather have someone else "drive," the Tickfaw Water Taxi (877-263-9750; www.bayouriver boatadventures.com) offers group tours and boat taxi service to some of the bars in this area reachable only by water.

Chapter 12. Gone Fishin':
Chasing Bounty Inland and Offshore

As the shoreline and piers of Grand Isle so fruitfully demonstrate, it isn't necessary to have a boat to enjoy great fishing in south Louisiana. You might find someone fishing, cast-netting, or crabbing anywhere water meets land in the region, whether that's from a dock or just by the edge of the road.

But getting out on the water is the goal that sends countless anglers off to south Louisiana's end-of-the-road launches and marinas on any given weekend. Those who don't have their own boat trailers rattling behind their trucks usually have reservations with charter fishing captains in hand.

There are many local charter captains specializing in freshwater (a.k.a. "inside water") areas, brackish marsh areas, or offshore fishing in the Gulf. The Louisiana Charter Boat Association provides a directory of charter captains operating across south Louisiana. See www.fishlcba.com. The Coastal Conservation Association of Louisiana also has a directory of fishing guides. See www.ccalouisiana.com.

Offshore charters are generally the most expensive, and their launch points sit the farthest away from the cities. For offshore fishing from Venice, I shipped out with Capt. James Peters of Osprey Charters (www.ospreycharters.net).

State catch limits always apply, and anglers also need a state fishing license, whether they fish every weekend or just tag along on a charter with some buddies. For information and online license applications, see www.wlf.louisiana .gov/fishing.

Chapter 13. Lafourche the Long Way:
The World's "Longest Village Street" and Houma Headquarters

Bayou Lafourche stretches from the dam at its historic headwaters in Donaldsonville through three parishes before emptying into the Gulf of Mexico near Port Fourchon. Roads parallel its course, including Highway 1 on its western bank. It makes for a very long drive, but it's an interesting trip that threads through a string of small towns and through the heart of downtown Thibodaux. The Wetlands Acadian Cultural Center (314 Saint Mary St., Thibodaux, 985-448-1375; www.nps.gov/jela/), a program of the National Park Service, is a recommended stop along the way in downtown Thibodaux, with exhibits explaining Acadian history and culture in the area and regular music events.

The Barataria-Terrebonne National Estuary Program (800-259-0869; www.btnep.org), a local environmental group, hosts the annual Paddle Bayou Lafourche event early each spring. Those who complete the entire journey travel more than fifty miles over the course of four days in canoes or kayaks, though others may choose to participate in shorter legs of the trip.

The United Houma Nation, which hosts a dinner for Paddle Bayou Lafourche participants, holds other public events throughout the year, including autumn powwows and Elder Fest, which celebrates the tribe's oldest members. See www.unitedhoumanation.org.

PART II: WEST OF THE ATCHAFALAYA

Chapter 14. Cast-Iron Cajun Culture: Acadian Journeys and Jam Sessions

Visitors can explore the roots and history of the Cajun people at a number of cultural sites and museums, though attending one of the area's great festivals is a chance to experience the contemporary culture firsthand and participate in the celebration. Three important annual festivals all held in Lafayette are listed here.

Festival International de Louisiane. The largest music festival in Lafayette, this late April event features artists from around the globe and has a special emphasis on performers from the Francophone world—from France to Canada to Africa to New Orleans. Naturally, many local Cajun and zydeco bands anchor the schedule each year. The festival is held on a series of outdoor stages across downtown Lafayette and takes over the city center for the weekend. For festival updates, see www.festivalinternational.com.

Festivals Acadiens et Creoles. In the 1970s, three different organizations hosting annual celebrations of resurgent Cajun culture in Lafayette began coordinating their events, forming the basis for today's Festivals Acadiens et Creoles. More organizations and attractions joined the action over the years, creating today's weekend-long itinerary of music, food, and crafts (and its curious, pluralized name). The event is held early in October, with most Saturday and Sunday programming taking place at Girard Park (500 Girard Park Dr., Lafayette), on the campus of the University of Louisiana at Lafayette, while a Friday night music event is held in downtown Lafayette. See www.festivalsacadiens.com.

South Louisiana Black Pot Festival & Cookoff. First held in 2006, this sweet-heart of a festival takes place during one October weekend at the Acadian Village (200 Greenleaf Dr., Lafayette, 337-981-2364; www.acadianvillage.org), a folk life museum modeled after an early bayou settlement. Festival goers are welcome to camp and join after-hours acoustic jam sessions on Friday and Saturday nights around the grounds. An outdoor cooking contest featuring cast-iron "black pots" is held on Saturday afternoon. See www.blackpotfestival.com.

Travelers looking for more historical perspective and conventional cultural education will find much to explore around the region. In particular, the town of St. Martinville (www.stmartinville.org) has a small but pretty downtown centered on Bayou Teche with a cluster of Acadian cultural sites. The Acadian Memorial (121 New Market St., St. Martinville, 337-394-2258; www.acadianme morial.org) is a powerfully evocative tribute to the Acadian exile and the reunion in colonial Louisiana, offering a humanized glimpse of historic tumult through recorded personal narratives and an interactive mural. In addition, the St. Martinville Cultural Heritage Center, located adjacent to the Acadian Memorial, houses two small museums under one roof: the African American Museum and the Museum of the Acadian Memorial, which relates the stories of two very different diasporas. The famous Evangeline Oak grows in a tiny bayou-side park next to the center. Just outside downtown St. Martinville, the Evangeline-Longfellow State Historic Site (1200 N. Main Street, St. Martinville, 888-677-2900; www.crt.state.la.us/parks/ilongfell.aspx) features a reproduction Cajun farmstead and education center.

In Lafayette, two major Acadian cultural centers sit next to each other on the banks of the Vermilion River. The National Park Service's Acadian Cultural Center (501 Fisher Rd., Lafayette, 337-232-0789; www.nps.gov/jela) features daily talks on local history and, in the spring and fall, ranger-led boat tours on the Vermilion. Just steps away, Vermilionville (300 Fisher Rd., Lafayette, 866-992-2968; www.vermilionville.org) is a re-created Cajun village with many different kinds of buildings, plus costumed craft demonstrators, a restaurant, and a music hall where Cajun and zydeco bands regularly perform.

Chapter 15. Horsing Around Acadiana:
Of Jockeys, Knights, and Racetracks in the Rough

Though it features costumed men on horseback brandishing lances, the Louisiana Tournoi is more akin to a rural tailgating party than a renaissance fair. The event is held in a field in the Ville Platte Industrial Park, behind the National Guard Armory (just off Tate Cove Road, less than a mile from downtown Ville Platte). Visitors pay a small admission at the gate, drive their vehicles over the rutted field, and park practically on the horse ring. Local concessionaires sell hot food and cold drinks, though many people bring ice chests and grills to have their own cookouts during the races. Tournoi contenders also gather for a qualification round in Ville Platte a few weeks before the championship, and another party crops up around this contest.

The championship is held on an October Sunday coinciding with the Louisiana Cotton Festival in downtown Ville Platte in the early afternoon. The races are followed by Le Tournoi Ball at Ville Platte's Northside Civic Center (704 N. Soileau St., 337-363-3167) in town. See www.louisianatournoi.com.

A few tracks in south Louisiana offer more conventional horseracing throughout the year. Both Delta Downs (2717 Delta Downs Dr., Vinton, 800-589-7441; www.deltadowns.com) and Evangeline Downs (2235 Cresswell Lane, Opelousas, 866-472-2466; www.evangelinedowns.com) are known as "racinos," or thoroughbred racetracks attached to casinos with slot machines and video poker but no table games. By contrast, trottingbred races at Metro Soileau Downs (off Hwy. 104 in Allen Parish, seven miles east of Oberlin; see www.allenparish.com/soileaudowns.htm) remain casual in the extreme. The racing season at Evangeline Downs is April through Labor Day, and the season at Delta Downs is October through March, while Metro Soileau Downs holds races every other Saturday from April through October.

Chapter 16. Zydeco's Tight Squeeze:
Creole Music's Dancehalls and Dynasties

Zydeco's cradle in central Acadiana remains its hotbed. Various clubs across the area host zydeco dances, usually on the weekends, while big stars of the regional zydeco circuit perform at trail rides on most Sunday afternoons (see chapter 18).

My favorite resource for listings on zydeco and other south Louisiana music events is compiled online by Louisiana roots music aficionado Patsy Hebert. Her Web listings are extensive, highly detailed, and reliably up to date. They include links to venues and local weather forecasts (important for outdoor events), travel directions, and even tips on the type of dance floor to expect and whether or not a venue permits smoking. See www.thepatsyreport.arnb.org.

Another good resource specifically for zydeco events is www.zydeconline.com, which includes community announcements and news stories related to what its editors call "the zydeco nation."

These listings calendars get particularly busy around zydeco festival weekends, including the Zydeco Extravaganza (www.zydecoextra.com), held at the Evangeline Downs race course and casino in Opelousas (see chapter 15) each Memorial Day weekend, and the Southwest Louisiana Zydeco Music Festival (www.zydeco.org), held outside Opelousas in the tiny farming community of Plaisance in a melon field each Labor Day weekend.

Zydeco is also a major component of the music lineups at many other Louisiana festivals, including the Festivals Acadiens et Creoles, Festival International de Louisiane, and the South Louisiana Black Pot Festival & Cookoff (see chapter 14).

The three dancehalls mentioned in this chapter are listed below. They are generally open only for dances on the weekends but their schedules are unpredictable, so call or check listings before a trip.

El Sid O's Zydeco & Blues Club
1523 Martin Luther King Dr., Lafayette, 318-235-0647

Slim's Y-Ki-Ki
8410 Hwy. 182, Opelousas, 337-942-6242; www.slimsykiki.com

Zydeco Hall of Fame (formerly Richard's)
11154 Hwy. 190, Lawtell, 337-349-8827; www.thezydecohalloffame.com

Chapter 17. "Island" Hopping in Iberia Parish:
Exploring the Salt Domes and the Old Spanish Trail Through Teche Country

Iberia Parish is salt dome territory in south Louisiana. Avery Island and its lesser-known but fascinating sibling Jefferson Island (5505 Rip Van Winkle Road, New Iberia, 337-359-8525; www.ripvanwinklegardens.com) are about a dozen miles apart, and travelers can hit both destinations in the same day with plenty of time left to explore downtown New Iberia.

The Tabasco hot sauce factory tour (Avery Island Road, 337-365-8173, www.tabasco.com) is the marquee draw for Avery Island, though the island's lush, rambling Jungle Gardens (Avery Island Road, 337-369-6243; www.junglegardens.org) are much more captivating. The gardens' variegated plantings have something different to offer throughout the year, though the mild weather of spring and fall are the best times to get out and explore the property on foot. To get the optimal experience from the island, bring bicycles to pedal around the rolling roads that trace the grounds and a lunch to eat at its verdant picnic areas.

If gazing at the inner workings of the Tabasco plant induces cravings for spicy food, you're certainly in the right area. The route between New Orleans and Avery Island is peppered with some fantastic boiled-seafood joints (see chapter 21). Try Guiding Star (4404 Hwy. 90, New Iberia, 337-365-9113) or the Boiling Point (7413 Hwy. 90, New Iberia, 337-365-7596), which are each spare-looking, roadhouse-style restaurants serving excellent boiled crawfish in the winter-through-spring season and boiled shrimp and crabs other times. Guiding Star even uses Tabasco pepper mash leftover from the hot sauce production process to season its seafood. This area is thick with other great places to eat, like the hole-in-the-wall sandwich shop and plate lunch joint Bon Creole (1409 East Saint Peter St., New Iberia, 337-367-6181) in downtown New Iberia, the seafood restaurant Yellow

Bowl (19466 Hwy. 182, Jeanerette, 337-276-5512) in the countryside between Franklin and Jeanerette and, for a snack, historic LeJeune's Bakery (1510 Main St., Jeanerette, 337-276-5690; www.lejeunesbakery.com).

The Iberia Parish Welcome Center (2513 Hwy. 14, New Iberia, 888-942-3742; www.iberiatravel.com), just off the highway outside of New Iberia, has exceptionally friendly staffers and is crammed to bursting with flyers and various maps, including a number that detail self-guided walking tours of the town's historic center. One, dubbed "Dave's Domain," leads visitors on a tour of highlights from the Dave Robicheaux series of detective novels written by New Iberia resident James Lee Burke.

Like Franklin (www.franklin-la.com), another town along Bayou Teche, New Iberia is indeed a walkable town with a lot of historic architecture and shady oaks to make those walks pleasant and interesting.

Two of New Iberia's most heavily promoted tourist attractions are each tied to the area's agricultural heritage, and each offers its own charm from opposite ends of the opulence spectrum. Most prominent is the beautiful, historic plantation home Shadows On the Teche (317 East Main St., New Iberia, 337-369-6446; www.shadowsontheteche.org), found on the bayou and in the center of town. It was once the hub of a slave-based sugar plantation and the tour of the house and gardens is enriched by reams of family documents that were found in its attic. Less than a mile away, and across the railroad tracks that bisect New Iberia, the town's other big attraction is the homely but still interesting factory tour of the historic Conrad Rice Mill (307 Ann St., New Iberia, 800-551-3245; www.conrad ricemill.com), the oldest operating rice mill in the nation, which demonstrates how the region's rice harvest is brought to market.

During the hot months, a trek down to the small beach at Cypremort Point State Park (see chapter 9) can make a nice side trip to a New Iberia visit.

Chapter 18. Saddle Sounds:
Dusty Dance Floors and Creole Trail Rides

Zydeco music and western horse culture commingle for a dusty good time in Louisiana's black Creole rendition of the trail ride. These are usually weekend-long events, and riders and their families and friends sometimes camp on the party grounds for the duration. The climax comes on Sunday with an itinerary that includes a long ride around the countryside followed by a zydeco dance back at the ranch or rural club hosting the event. Visitors should expect to pay a cover at the gate, and they should bring cash for the food and drinks sold around the grounds.

I stumbled upon my first few trail rides, which seem to be promoted primarily by handbills, flyers, and local radio announcements. Once I started looking for them, however, I found help yet again from the invaluable Patsy Report at www.thepatsyreport.arnb.org and also from the listings calendar at www.zyde coonline.com.

Chapter 19. Henderson's Wild Side:
Over the Top in an Atchafalaya Levee Town

Henderson is a tiny town that earned a big place in my heart during the travels for this book. Marinas and swamp tour operations along the Atchafalaya Basin levee are jumping-off points for exploring the edges of North America's largest swamp. Back on (usually) dry land, the bars, restaurants, and dancehalls that have grown up around the marina operations are at least as popular with locals as they are with visitors. These are the types of places you might imagine are secluded deep in backwoods settings only the locals can find. Yet in Henderson all of this is accessible just a few minutes from Interstate 10, not far from Lafay- ette. Take exit 115.

Houseboat rentals provide a uniquely intimate way to experience the swamp. Some are berthed at the marina dockside, and these can be used as floating motel rooms for people exploring the area by day. Others can be pushed out to quiet swamp coves for total seclusion for a weekend or for longer stints.

The establishments below are listed in the order in which travelers come upon them heading south from the interstate along the levee road.

Pat's Fisherman's Wharf (1008 Henderson Levee Rd., Henderson, 337-228-7512; www.patsfishermanswharf.com)—a huge dancehall on Bayou Amy, with a res- taurant and motel.

McGee's Landing (1337 Henderson Levee Rd., Henderson, 337-228-2384; www .mcgeeslanding.com)—swamp tours, houseboat rentals, restaurant, and bar with live music.

Angelle's Whiskey River Landing (1365 Henderson Levee Rd., Henderson, 337- 228-2277; www.whiskeyriverlanding.net)—a dancehall with Sunday afternoon zydeco shows and a view of the swamp.

Atchafalaya Basin Landing & Marina (1377 Henderson Levee Rd., Henderson, 337-228-7880; www.basinlanding.com)—swamp tours, houseboat rentals, and the attached Turtles Bar.

In addition, visitors can get a quick tutorial on the basin's history and heri- tage by visiting the state-run Atchafalaya Welcome Center (337-228-1094; www .dnr.louisiana.gov/sec/atchafalaya), which includes a small museum and a multimedia presentation featuring animatronic models of swamp creatures. Take exit 121 off Interstate 10, just east of Henderson.

Chapter 20. A Cajun Wake-Up Call:
Music on a Louisiana Saturday Morning

Saturday morning in central Acadiana can be a surprisingly rewarding time for fans of Cajun and zydeco music. The "big three" music events scheduled that morning are the zydeco breakfast at Café des Amis in Breaux Bridge, the acoustic jam session at Savoy Music Center in Eunice, and the Cajun music show and radio broadcast at Fred's Lounge in Mamou. All three are in progress by 9 a.m.

It's possible to hit them all, but such an itinerary requires a very early start and strict time discipline at each stop due to the distances between each town. It's a forty-five-mile drive from Breaux Bridge to Eunice and another twelve miles from Eunice to Mamou. One needn't rush around to cram them all in, though. Each is quite distinct, and for fans of south Louisiana music each is certainly a worthwhile travel destination all on its own.

Café des Amis (140 East Bridge St., Breaux Bridge, 337-332-5273; www.cafedesamis.com). Zydeco breakfast is held Saturdays, 8:30 a.m. to 11:30 a.m. Doors open at 7:30 a.m., and no reservations are taken, so expect a wait to get a table. Visitors may also pay a modest cover to simply hang out at the bar and dance.

Savoy Music Center (4413 Hwy. 190, Eunice, 337-457-9563; www.savoymusiccenter.com). The open, acoustic jam session is held Saturdays from 9 a.m. to noon.

Fred's Lounge (420 6th St., Mamou, 337-468-5411). With the exception of the weekend before Mardi Gras (see chapter 22), Fred's is open only on Saturdays, with regular hours from 8 a.m. to 2 p.m. Music begins at 9 a.m.

Other regular music destinations mentioned in this chapter are listed below.

The Coffee Break (109 North Main St., Breaux Bridge, 337-442-6607). Once the zydeco breakfast begins to break up at Café des Amis, the open, acoustic jam session at this coffee shop just around the corner picks up. It's held Saturdays from 11 a.m. to 2 p.m.

D.I.'s Cajun Restaurant (6561 Evangeline Hwy., a.k.a. Hwy. 97, Basile, 337-432-5141; www.discajunrestaurant.biz). This is a big destination for Cajun Mardi Gras groups, but bands perform year-round from the dining room stage. Call for music nights and times.

Hotel Cazan (401 Sixth St., Mamou, 337-468-5100; www.hotelcazan.com). Die-hards seeking more music after Fred's Lounge in Mamou closes on Saturday afternoons migrate down the block to the bar of this tiny, nicely renovated hotel.

La Poussiere (1215 Grand Pointe Ave., Breaux Bridge, 337-332-1721; www.lapous siere.com). Nondescript from the outside and easy to bypass, this old-fashioned dancehall is the real deal and features traditional Cajun bands on Saturday nights and Sunday afternoons.

Liberty Theater (200 West Park Ave., Eunice, 337-457-7389; www.eunice-la.com/ libertyschedule.html). The *Rendezvous des Cajuns* radio show is held in the 1920s vintage movie theater in the center of downtown Eunice on Saturdays, begin-ning at 6 p.m. Tickets are required. The featured performers each week par-ticipate in additional music programming beginning at 3 p.m. at the adjacent Prairie Acadian Cultural Center, a unit of the National Park Service (250 West Park Ave., Eunice 337-457-8499; www.nps.gov/jela). *Rendezvous des Cajuns* is broadcast live on Eunice radio station KEUN 105.5 FM/1490 AM and Lafayette-based NPR affiliate KRVS 88.7 FM.

Mulate's (325 West Mills Ave., Breaux Bridge, 337-332-4648). A decent Cajun res-taurant, a much better Cajun dance hall, this is another long, low building on the road between Breaux Bridge and Lafayette that doesn't look like much from outside but has a nice country ambiance inside with a large bar, wood-plank ceiling, and lots of dancing space between the dinner tables. Call for perfor-mance times.

Prejean's Restaurant (3480 Interstate 49, Lafayette, 337-896-3247; www.pre-jeans.com). Take Interstate 49 leading north from Lafayette a little farther than you might think necessary and you'll find this huge compound of a restaurant looming up on the adjacent highway access road. Primarily a restaurant—and a very good, midrange one with a creative touch on Cajun fare—it also hosts Cajun bands nightly during dinnertime and during the breakfast/brunch shift on Saturdays and Sundays.

Randol's (2320 Kaliste Saloom Road, Lafayette, 337-981-7080; www.randols. com). Another big restaurant, this one is closer to downtown Lafayette, with average food but a large dance floor and a solid lineup of Cajun bands nightly, with an occasional dash of zydeco.

Tom's Fiddle & Bow (204 Fuselier St., Arnaudville, 337-754-5528; www.toms fiddleandbow.com.). This instrument repair shop and music store in the pretty

bayou town of Arnaudville hosts its JAMbalaya acoustic jam on Sundays from
1 p.m. to 3 p.m.

Chapter 21. Putting Meals on the Map:
Eating Around Acadiana

I was pretty pleased with myself when—tired and hungry at the end of a long
day—I stumbled upon Dean's Restaurant & Bar (1288 Henderson Hwy., Henderson, 337-228-1441) where the Cajun cooking so exceeded my expectations.
But really the odds are on your side when you want to find a great meal in south
Louisiana. After all, rather than rolling the dice on Dean's, I might just as well
have pulled into Robin's (1409 Henderson Hwy., Henderson, 337-228-7594; www
.robincajunfood.com), an equally unaffected-looking restaurant located a few
blocks down the same quiet road. On a later trip through Henderson I did eat at
Robin's, where I learned its name is pronounced "row-ban's" and that its crawfish
dishes, gumbos, and Tabasco ice cream are worth a detour off the nearby interstate no matter what your final destination may be.

It's like this all over south Louisiana. For all the research you can put into
planning meals on the road, just trusting serendipity and the luck of the draw
usually delivers satisfying results in this region.

Yes, there are many national chain restaurants and fast food joints that may
look like safer bets to the wary traveler. And yes, upscale, fine-dining options
are thin to nonexistent outside of the cities. But the flavor and food heritage of
Acadiana is deliciously communicated at casual, family-oriented, usually family-
owned eateries, and these turn up in even the smallest communities. They are
generally inexpensive (entrees under ten dollars) or moderately priced (entrees
under fifteen dollars), and while they often do not look like much from the street
you can count on memorable meals. Get people in the restaurant talking about
their other favorite places to eat (an incredibly easy undertaking in south Louisiana) and you'll soon have a list of destinations down the road.

Here are details on the mere sampling of restaurants mentioned in this chapter, arranged by travel regions (see appendix listings for chapter 20 for more restaurants with live music and appendix listings for chapter 7 for butcher shops).

Abbeville
Dupuy's Oyster Shop (108 S. Main St., Abbeville, 337-893-2336; www.dupuysoyster
shop.com) doesn't look like much of a landmark from the street, but this cozy,
well-run oyster house traces its start to 1869.

Cajun Claws (1928 Charity St., Abbeville, 337-893-9437; www.cajunclawscrawfish
.com) is a crawfish specialist with a tavern feel, just outside Abbeville's downtown center.

Richard's Seafood Patio (1516 S. Henry St., Abbeville, 337-893-1146) is across the Vermilion River from the town center and down a winding road. It's a vintage boiling point with a large menu and a devoted regular following.

Shucks (701 W. Port St., Abbeville, 337-898-3311; www.shucksrestaurant.com) is a spacious and modern restaurant, where oysters are shucked in their own glassed-in prep room.

Also in Abbeville, watch for a possible return of Black's Oyster Bar, founded in the 1960s just around the corner from Dupuy's. It was out of business at this writing, but different owners have periodically reopened the place in recent years.

Morgan City Area
Chester's Cypress Inn (1995 Hwy. 20, Donner, 985-446-6821) is en route to a cluster of swamp tour operators, and is a vintage roadhouse with superlative fried chicken, chicken livers, and frog legs.

Landry's Seafood Restaurant (3612 Hwy. 70, Pierre Part, 985-252-6909) has sprawling combination platters stocked with seafood from the nearby Atchafalaya Basin.

Rita Mae's (711 Federal Ave., Morgan City, 985-384-3550) serves soul food in a homey setting; look for the daily specials menu taped to the wall above the Bible display.

Lafayette Area
Crawfish Time Inc. (3401 Moss St., Lafayette, 337-236-6129) is a boiled-seafood specialist that is beyond spare but has a convenient drive-up window, and most people get sacks of crawfish to go.

Gator Cove (2601 S.E. Evangeline Thruway, Lafayette, 337-264-1373; www.gatorcove.com) is a full-service restaurant with a varied menu and a massive boiled-crawfish operation.

Possum's Restaurant (1007 Little Oak Dr., St. Martinville, 337-394-3233), just outside historic downtown St. Martinville, is a large, family restaurant with succulent, gravy-drenched meat and seafood platters.

T-Coon's Restaurant (1900 W. Pinhook Rd., Lafayette, 337-233-0422; www.tcoons.com) is a breakfast and lunch joint, nestled in a strip mall, with excellent smothered meat specials.

Cajun Prairie Area

Bubba Frey's (29017 Crowley Eunice Hwy., a.k.a. Hwy. 13, Eunice, 337-550-1992), well outside downtown Eunice, is connected to the Mowata Store butcher shop; don't miss the exceptional boudin and the casual Cajun music sessions early on Saturday nights. Just get a link of boudin at the market if it's daytime and you're in a hurry.

D. I.'s Restaurant (6561 Evangeline Hwy., a.k.a. Hwy. 97, Basile, 337-432-5141; www.discajunrestaurant.biz) is a huge restaurant surrounded for miles by rice fields, specializing in boiled crawfish, shrimp, and crabs seasonally; it has live Cajun music and dancing on weekends.

Hawk's (Hawk's Road, off Hwy. 98, Roberts Cove, 337-788-3266; www.hawk scrawfish.com) is a purist among crawfish-boiling points, with exceptionally large, clean-tasting creatures. It's notoriously difficult to find; see Web site for a map.

Food-Focused Festivals

Festivals come in all shapes and sizes in south Louisiana, and many of them revolve around food, from important local crops to seafood catches to specific dishes. Spring and fall are the busy seasons for festivals, though they pop up year-round in various communities. New Orleans–based festival enthusiast Julie Posner produces an indispensable resource with her Huli's Louisiana Festivals and Events Calendar, a wall calendar with listings, festival profiles, and travel tips. See details at www.louisiana-festivals.com.

Three festivals are mentioned in this chapter.

Le Festival de la Viande Boucanee (the Smoked Meat Festival) is held on the last full weekend in June in Ville Platte at the North Side Civic Center, 704 N. Soileau St., Ville Platte; www.smokedmeatfestival.com.

South Louisiana Black Pot Festival & Cookoff is in the appendix listing for chapter 14.

Giant Omelette Celebration is held the first full weekend in November in downtown Abbeville. See www.giantomelette.org.

Chapter 22. Chasing a Good Time:
Mardi Gras on the Cajun Prairie

The Catholic calendar determines the Mardi Gras schedule each year. So it goes in Mamou and Church Point, so it goes in New Orleans, Port-au-Prince, Rio de Janeiro, Venice, and everywhere else that observes this pre-Lenten period of revelry and abandon.

Mardi Gras—French for "Fat Tuesday"—is always the day before Ash Wednesday, which begins the Lenten season leading to Easter. Since Easter falls on a different date from year to year, so too does Mardi Gras.

Communities across Louisiana celebrate Mardi Gras, and they do it up in different ways. Many cities have parades modeled after the processions in New Orleans, with floats packed with masked riders freely throwing plastic beads and other novelties to crowds lining their routes. See www.mardigraslafayette.net for information about Lafayette-area parades and events, and see www.swlamar digras.com for events in the Lake Charles area.

The rural traditions of courir de Mardi Gras described in this chapter are something else altogether, and they present quite a different experience for visitors. Traveling by horseback and on wagons and trailers, riders in these Mardi Gras celebrations depart early in the morning, typically around 7 a.m., and range around the countryside, stopping at private homes and farms predetermined by each group's leader, or le capitaine. While the public cannot simply jump in with these riders, people can certainly follow them along their routes, provided they don't interfere with the groups' activities.

While I highly recommend trying to catch at least part of a run in progress, another strategy for visitors is to join the large public parties held in each host town, where crowds dance to live music and party with plenty of food and drink as they await the arrival of le courir in the afternoon, usually around 3 p.m.

Towns where le courir de Mardi Gras has grown especially popular also host street parties and related events during the days leading up to Fat Tuesday (except in Church Point, where Sunday is the traditional day for the run). The general itinerary in Mamou typically begins the Saturday before Mardi Gras with bands playing on Sixth Street in the heart of the community's small downtown area. The riders traditionally depart Tuesday morning from the American Legion Post on Main Street, then return to Sixth Street in the afternoon as the outdoor party continues.

Check the sites below for updates on other runs as Mardi Gras draws near each year.

Church Point, www.churchpointmardigras.com
Eunice, www.eunice-la.com
Tee Mamou-Iota, www.iotamardigras.com

Chapter 23. Edge of the Gulf, End of the Road: Cameron Parish and Louisiana's Outback

The Creole Nature Trail is the name for a long scenic highway running through the very southwestern corner of Louisiana. It forms a giant loop around Calcasieu Lake, beginning and ending just off Interstate 10 on either side of the city of Lake Charles. It continues south to the Gulf Coast, to the beach community of Holly Beach and the port town of Cameron. Optional spurs to the east and the west along the coast will bring the total length of the trail to 180 miles, though any way you cut it this is a day-long expedition once you build in time to stop and explore on foot.

The route is home to four National Wildlife Refuge sites, including the enormous Sabine Wildlife Refuge. The whole area exudes rugged beauty, and it is a wonderland for fishing, hunting, and birding, though there are very few amenities for the casual traveler. I recommend departing for the Creole Nature Trail with a full tank of gas and a picnic lunch.

Details, maps, and planning resources are available at www.creolenaturetrail .org.

Index